GEORGE B. McCLELLAN

George B. McClellan

THE MAN WHO SAVED THE UNION

By

H. J. ECKENRODE

Historian of the Virginia Conservation Commission

and

BRYAN CONRAD

Assistant Historian of the Virginia Conservation Commission
Colonel, the United States Army

CHAPEL HILL

THE UNIVERSITY OF NORTH CAROLINA PRESS

1941

COPYRIGHT, 1941, BY
THE UNIVERSITY OF NORTH CAROLINA PRESS

TO
N. CLARENCE SMITH
CHAIRMAN OF THE
VIRGINIA CONSERVATION COMMISSION

FOREWORD

THIS BOOK ORIGINATED in studies made by the historians of the Conservation Commission in the Richmond battlefield area, which is comprised in the Richmond Battlefield Park, a charge of the commission. These battlefields are the best preserved and least studied (because long inaccessible) in the country. A detailed examination of the terrain convinced the historians, both of them Southerners, that McClellan was a great general and that he has been underestimated by historians. Their opinion was confirmed by a study of the records. They came to the conclusion that it was McClellan who prevented the defeat of the North in 1861-62 when the Confederacy was relatively stronger than it was at a later time.

Since there seemed to be no military reasons for the animadversions cast on McClellan, the historians of the commission were persuaded that the hostile feeling toward him is political, springing mainly from his candidacy against Lincoln in the election of 1864. Believing that politics should not be permitted to influence military judgments, they have written this book, partly for the purpose of doing justice to a great man who has suffered at the hands of history. It is based on the ground itself and the original sources, and is believed to be a contribution to American and Virginia history.

CONTENTS

	Foreword	vii
I.	Youth, Education, Adventure	1
II.	Development	10
III.	Small Beginning of a Notable Career	18
IV.	He Saves the Union for the First Time	26
V.	Embarkation on a Great Adventure	44
VI.	The First Great Battle	60
VII.	Beginning of the Infernal Week Known as the Seven Days' Battles	72
VIII.	Gaines's Mill, June 27	89
IX.	Glendale, June 30	100
X.	Malvern Hill, July 1	112
XI.	The Plot Matures, But Providence (Or, From the Other Point of View, Satan) Frustrates It	122
XII.	He Saves the Union in Spite of Itself	153
XIII.	Sharpsburg, Or, If You Prefer It, Antietam Creek	182
XIV.	Comedy After Tragedy, But Comedy With a Bad Ending	211
XV.	Exchange of Presidential Courtesies	237
XVI.	He Seeks Vindication	262
XVII.	The Placid Years and Peace	275
	Index	285

MAPS

The Peninsula	53
Battle of Fair Oaks	69
Battle of Mechanicsville	85
Battle of Gaines's Mill	95
Battle of Savage's Station	103
Battle of Frayser's Farm, or Glendale	109
Battle of Malvern Hill	115
Battle of Crampton's Gap	185
Battle of South Mountain	187
Battle of Sharpsburg (Antietam)	191

GEORGE B. McCLELLAN

CHAPTER ONE

YOUTH, EDUCATION, ADVENTURE

A GENERATION AGO historians condemned Thucydides for declaring that war is the chief theme of history; they fancied that it was the bickering of political parties. However, the events of the past quarter century have so borne out the observation of the ancient Greek that few people are now inclined to disagree with him.

In this connection it is to be noted that the United States has made important contributions to the art of war, for in our conflict of 1861-65 the ironclad, the submarine, the railway gun, the military telegraph, and the torpedo had their real origins, while the use of earthworks in maneuver and the open order of infantry advance were essentially American improvements. We have done our share in the realm of Mars. Moreover the American Civil War should no longer be studied as an isolated phenomenon but as a significant event, and one of tremendous consequences, in the overthrow of the old agricultural order by industrialism. As much as any other nation, we are a part of world history.

The portrayer of men of action necessarily writes biography from a very different angle from biographers of artists, especially writers. The interest in men of action lies in the action itself; all else is merely corroborative and supplementary. But narratives of artists are literary history or criticism rather than biography unless they deal extensively with private life. From this point of view love is an incident in the career of Washington or Grant or Lee but all-important in the lives of Shelley and

Byron. To be particular, the business and military career of George B. McClellan is the important matter. That he was successful in love and enjoyed a happy family life is gratifying, but what counts with him was what he did in his wonderful, German-like organization of the Army of the Potomac, in the terrible withdrawal to James River, and amidst the flames and detonations of Sharpsburg.

Pennsylvania, the great mother that has poured out so many sons and daughters, north, south, west, was the birthplace of the first commander of the Union armies in the War between the States. It might be recollected that Jefferson Davis's grandfather was from Philadelphia, where George B. McClellan was born on December 3, 1826.

He came into a home of culture, something that colored his life all the way through; if he could have sometimes forgotten that he was a gentleman it might have been better for him. McClellan's father, George McClellan, graduated from Yale in 1816 and from the medical school of the University of Pennsylvania in 1819, thus enjoying the best education the America of that day could afford. He soon rose to eminence, becoming one of the founders of the Jefferson Medical College in 1825.

His wife was Elizabeth S. Brinton, a woman of character, to whom her son, the future general, was devoted. She made the pleasant home in which George B. McClellan passed the happy years of his boyhood. After a good preparatory education, he entered the University of Pennsylvania in 1840, remaining there two years. Then fate stepped in and he received an appointment to the United States Military Academy at West Point in 1842. This change in his education was probably due to economic pressure, for Dr. McClellan, though distinguished, was far from well-to-do.

McClellan's precocity is shown by the fact that he was less than sixteen years old when he entered West Point; his ability and fine physique must have caused a suspension of regulations in his case. Although rather short of stature—"Little Mac" to his admiring soldiers—five feet, eight inches tall, he was well developed, with a large chest expansion. Handsome in face, graceful in carriage, he was one of the most attractive boys of his class, especially as he was endowed with a rare magnetism of manner. It was evident from the outset that he was cut out for something beyond the ordinary career.

Acutely homesick at first, McClellan soon grew to like West Point and did well in his studies. His chief friends were among the Southern boys, and Dr. William Starr Myers remarks, rather acidly, "It is evident that the culture, refinement and airs of the gallant, so characteristic of the Southern 'aristocrat,' were exceedingly attractive to McClellan and struck a responsive chord in his consciously 'gentle' nature."[1] The fact is that most of the Southern youths at West Point came of cultured families while the Northerners and Westerners were often plain farm boys. In time great generals developed from both strains.

McClellan's chief friend at the academy seems to have been Gustavus W. Smith, who once happened to catch him and prevent his falling when he slipped on the stairs. McClellan remarked, "Well, that settles it! We shall be firm friends after this." Smith, two years ahead of McClellan in class, became an instructor in the latter's last years at school. A tragic quirk of fate made these two comrades commanders of opposing armies for one day.

McClellan was always an excellent student, being especially accomplished in mathematics. Still he found time for the lighter side of life, becoming a seasoned and pleasing society man. All his life he was fond of society and mixed much in the "best circles" of New York and other cities. General Dabney H. Maury, C.S.A., thus describes McClellan, in whose class he was at West Point:

"I remember that it was about the middle of June, 1842, when we first met in the section room at West Point. The class was at first arranged according to alphabetical order, and our initial letters placed us for a brief space side by side. For a very brief space it was, for he pushed at once to the head, while I plodded along in the middle through all the long four years of my cadetship.... After the Mexican War, while we were both at West

[1] *General George Brinton McClellan* (New York, D. Appleton-Century Co., 1934), p. 12. Extracts used by special permission of the publishers. In many respects this is the best biography.

Point as instructors, we were, of course, daily associated together for several years, and a happy association it was. A brighter, kindlier, more genial gentleman did not live than he. Sharing freely in all the convivial hospitality of the mess, he was a constant student of his profession. Having been instructed in the Classics and French before he came to the Academy, he learned Spanish and German there, and before he was sent to Europe to study and report upon the cavalry service of the great military powers, he had acquired sufficient knowledge of the Russian language to enable him to make a satisfactory and valuable report. ... He was an excellent horseman, and one of our most athletic and best swordsmen."

It was almost inevitable that McClellan should choose the engineers as his arm of the service, for that was the tiptop branch and his mathematical faculty was strong; he was essentially a military engineer and a great one. No other American general has ever possessed the topographical sense in the same proportion.

McClellan finished his course at West Point just as the dogs of war were being unloosed. "Hip! Hip! Hurrah!" was his reaction to the news from Mexico. He was determined to go to the war, either in the engineers or the dragoons. He graduated second in his class on June 30, 1846, beyond doubt the most scientific mind of the lot. George E. Pickett, who finished last, and Stonewall Jackson were classmates. The one man who beat McClellan out, rather technically and by a few points, was never heard from in the great war of fifteen years later. McClellan found himself a second lieutenant at something less than twenty years of age.

His assignment was to a company of engineers at West Point training for the front. The company left on September 24, 1846, arriving after an uneventful voyage at Brazos de Santiago. Thence it proceeded to Matamoros, where McClellan was taken sick, remaining in a hospital for two weeks. At Camargo he had a relapse and was hospitalized again. In December, 1846, he was for a time at the mouth of the Rio Grande, with Gideon J. Pillow, Patterson, and other officers. McClellan's letters are filled with caustic criticism of the volunteers, who were generally a

YOUTH, EDUCATION, ADVENTURE 5

rough lot and sometimes ill-treated the natives.[2] Beyond a doubt, he here learned the need of discipline and training to turn recruits into reliable soldiers; always in his later career he stressed training.

McClellan was in the march overland to Tampico, which took about a month; his command reached the place late in January, 1847. His letters are filled with satire of Robert Patterson, a general whose inefficiency was not brought out by the Mexicans, but was revealed by Joseph E. Johnston in 1861. At Victoria, on January 4, 1847, McClellan came into contact with troops commanded by John A. Quitman; General Zachary Taylor, head of an army, was also there. After ten days at Victoria, his command went on to Tampico, arriving on January 23. There was no fighting but a rough march through desert country. At Tampico, McClellan spent a rather enjoyable month which included many "champagne suppers."

Tired of doing nothing, he was happy when he sailed from Tampico to the island of Lobos, where Winfield Scott's forces, gathered for the march on Mexico City, were encamped. The army presently sailed to a small island near Vera Cruz. Swift, captain of McClellan's engineer company, was taken ill and went to New Orleans, where he died. He was succeeded by McClellan's crony, Gustavus Smith.

Up to this time McClellan's service had been nominal, but with the army's approach to Vera Cruz he was called on to perform the duties of a military engineer. At that time the American army had exceedingly few engineer officers; every one counted. McClellan in this work came into close contact with Totten, chief of engineers and a competent officer. From all the evidence, he carried out his duties with courage and skill and, beyond doubt, he increased in self-confidence. Young as he was, he knew that he was abler than most of the men around him. Vera Cruz surrendered near the end of March, 1847, furnishing Scott his base of supplies for the march across the mountains to Mexico City.

[2] McClellan saw the volunteers at a disadvantage from every angle. He wrote in his diary: "I have seen more suffering since I came here than I could have imagined to exist—it is really awful—I allude to the sufferings of the volunteers. They literally die like dogs."

McClellan had a not unimportant share in Scott's operations, partly because the engineer organization of the army was so small and so essential in that unknown country of tropical vegetation and towering mountains. The engineer company had as officers G. W. Smith and McClellan, ten sergeants, ten corporals, thirty-nine artificers, thirty-nine privates and two musicians. Later McClellan was assigned to the general staff of the army, which included R. E. Lee, P. G. T. Beauregard, G. W. Smith, and Benjamin Huger, all of them of note (on the Southern side) in the war of 1861.

The American army was strangely intermixed. It included regulars of the first quality and volunteer regiments from several states, untrained and lacking in discipline but brave and accustomed to the use of firearms. Few armies have ever had such an array of talent among the younger officers and such a lack of it among the commanders, with the exception of Scott, on whose ability and courage the fate of the expedition depended. Twiggs, Pillow, Patterson were all incapable, and the two latter were destined for disgrace in later wars.

Scott advanced along the great highway from Vera Cruz to Mexico, known as the National Road and built on the line followed by Cortez in the conquest. It passed through some of the most entrancing regions of the world, mounting from gorgeous tropical scenes to magnificent peaks. The approach to the capital of Mexico is probably unequaled by anything else on the globe.

It was a glorious experience for such a boy as McClellan, just of the age to appreciate adventure in foreign lands and the excitement of war amidst exotic scenes. His vivid impressions were jotted down in his diary, which remains as one of our principal sources of information on Scott's expedition to Mexico City.

Along the cement highway the American army moved comfortably, enjoying the glorious country spread out before them. These adventurers from northern climes had never seen anything to compare with the tropical luxuriance of flowers that surrounded them. "Matted tangles of leafage spattered with gold, big tulipans gleaming in the shadows like a red rose..., blossoms like scarlet hornets... and blooms like red-hot hair brushes... were balanced with big, close masses of white throats and purple mouths and with banks of the greenish-white cuatismilla, discharging invisible clouds of a fragrance that seemed to be locust blended with lily of the valley." [3]

In these tropic lowlands there were no enemies, no fighting to be done. The march was a romance—romance made more romantic by the Spanish names. But at Cerro Gordo the National Road upgrades abruptly, and here in a mighty gorge alongside a river bed the Mexicans had made preparations to receive the visitors from the North. There the invaders saw two towering hills before them, La Atalaya and El Telegrafo, the keys of the Mexican position. It is all very far away now but it even yet sends a glow of patriotic pride through American veins to read how Scott's troops, clambering up goat paths and through cactus bushes, took these hills at the bayonet's point and drove the defenders away in rout.

Cerro Gordo discouraged Santa Anna, the Mexican commander, who made no further resistance for some time. The American army continued to follow the National Road, which led ever upward through a country covered with cactus and mesquite and, then, through gorgeous groves of every sort of tree, upward until the army stood a mile above sea level and still marched upward. Now superb mountain landscapes spread out on every side—views of miles and miles of field and forest with haciendas and silver streams in the distance. To the boy McClellan it was enchanted ground, a fairyland inhabited by ogres in green and red who were the Mexican soldiers.

Scott at length reached Puebla, the heart of Mexico, set in its circle of tremendous peaks. Here the Mexicans might have made a stand and did attempt a surprise that failed. McClellan was in the thick of the fighting. Here Scott had to remain for several months, as most of his volunteers went home because their short terms of enlistment had expired. He waited until Franklin Pierce, destined to be a president of the United States, arrived with reinforcements, enabling him to continue his advance.

Still upward toward Mexico City the army climbed, not op-

[3] Justin H. Smith, *The War with Mexico* (New York, 1919), Vol. II, p. 46.

posed by Mexicans. Santa Anna had concentrated troops and munitions in the vicinity of his capital, where he hoped to make a victorious stand. He had reason to hope for success, for he was fighting behind fortifications and was in much superior force.

The fighting in the vicinity of the capital city was fierce and the American losses were considerable. Mexico lies in a bowl of lakes and marshes two miles above sea level and surrounded by giant mountains, among them Popocatepetl, one of the great volcanoes of earth. The rim of the basin afforded many defensive positions, of which the Mexicans sought to take advantage though handicapped by the several lines of approach from which Scott might choose.

Now the engineer officers were of moment. The generals on a far flank decided to attack the Mexicans at one point but had to secure Scott's consent to their plan of action. Then it was that R. E. Lee crossed on foot at night the famous Pedregal, which was a vast lava field on a mountain top, a plain of fire frozen into rock. Scott gave his consent and the battle of Contreras followed, in which McClellan played a considerable part. He, with Lee, put in position the guns of John B. Magruder's battery, which had much to do with driving the Mexicans from their position. McClellan was slightly wounded in this operation. As the three men toiled about the guns, Fate did not withdraw the curtain of the future to show both Magruder and Lee as the commanders of armies destined to oppose McClellan. Fate was kind, for these three young men were joined in ardent comradeship in a dangerous and glorious adventure.

After Contreras came the actions of Churubusco, Molino del Rey and Chapultepec, in two of which McClellan bore a part. For Contreras and Churubusco he received the brevet of first lieutenant and for Chapultepec, that of captain. He declined a brevet for Molino del Rey because he was not actually present in that engagement, an honorable stand for an officer to take. The army entered Mexico on September 14, 1847, McClellan with it. Colonel Joseph E. Totten issued an order thanking the engineer officers for their service. It is interesting to note that R. E. Lee, P. G. T. Beauregard, G. W. Smith, and G. B. McClellan were included, all four of them destined to high rank in the great war that was to follow a decade and a half later.

It was in this campaign that McClellan received word of his father's death and, later, of the involved condition of the estate. This gave him great trouble, for he wished to settle his father's debts and secure a support for his mother and her smaller children. He and his brother John appear to have assumed the burden, which troubled them both for ten years.

After a long and enjoyable stay in Mexico City, McClellan returned to the United States in June, 1848. He had made a name for himself, though he was only twenty-one years old. In fact, no other young officer had come out of the war with a more brilliant reputation. The Fates smiled on him.

CHAPTER TWO

DEVELOPMENT

The next three years McClellan was at West Point with his company of engineers. He was not happy. According to the awkward organization that then obtained in the United States army, the engineers there were not a part of the academy although under the superintendent. This made for misunderstanding and heartburnings. Dr. Myers says of him at this time, "McClellan was showing evidences of those traits which were to be a handicap throughout his military life. He was sensitive, a little jealous and even conceited, not to mention extremely critical of his superiors. These same traits made him, as already stated, one of the most difficult subordinates with whom any commander at the time had to deal."[1]

This is a harsh judgment. The fact is that McClellan felt his anomalous position under the superintendent of the academy and, much more, was bored by the routine nature of his duties. Army life in peacetime has often been found to be insupportably dull to men of mental vigor and nervous power, and McClellan was a human dynamo, robustly healthy and eager to find some outlet for his abounding energies. In consequence he had many tilts with Captain Henry Brewerton, the superintendent. Time after time Colonel Totten was called on to decide some point at issue between the two men.

Weary of the dreary round, McClellan wished to go to Oregon or California but had to remain at West Point. To his application Totten replied that a trained engineer officer was

[1] *Op. cit.*, p. 55.

needed at the academy. Continued pleas brought no better luck, and in January, 1849, he wrote his brother John that he had given up the hope of going to California. Forced to confine himself to routine duty, McClellan entered on an extensive course of reading that resulted in making him, perhaps, the best educated officer in the army. Not only history interested him; he made a profound study of the United States Constitution, a study that had an important bearing on his future. From being more or less a Whig, his reading converted him to states' rights; he became and remained until the end of his life an ardent member of the Democratic party.

Dissatisfied with his situation, determined to make some change, McClellan was among the applicants for the professorship of artillery tactics and natural philosophy in the Virginia Military Institute at Lexington. This military school, even then, was second only to West Point; the record of its graduates has been most honorable. Besides McClellan, Jesse L. Reno, W. S. Rosecrans, Gustavus W. Smith, and Thomas Jonathan Jackson entered the competition. Jackson was chosen. Although he was a failure as a teacher, Jackson's years in Lexington devoted to the study of his profession resulted in bringing to fruition military talents second to none in American history. Probably McClellan would not have stayed at V.M.I. long; for if West Point irked him, the little mountain village would have bored him beyond endurance. As it was, he continued to peg along at West Point, indulging in continual disputes which Dr. Myers thinks were indicative of his egotistic temperament, but which may be considered more fairly as outbursts of youthful self-assertion against official suppression. McClellan was very young, very strong and healthy, every inch a high-spirited American boy.

He for a time was in command of the engineer company at West Point, acquitting himself well so far as the work went. In June, 1851, he was sent as an assistant engineer to Fort Delaware on the river of that name. He was not there long, being summoned in January, 1852, on special duty with the commander in chief. Much to his delight, he was detailed to accompany Captain Randolph B. Marcy in an expedition to explore the sources of the Red River of Arkansas. Incredible as it may seem, less than a century ago much of the country west of the Mississippi River was as little known as Central Africa. McClellan was engineer officer, quartermaster, and commissary to the expedition, all of which duties he performed admirably.

The expedition left Fort Belknap, Texas, on the Brazos River, on May 1, 1852. Shortly thereafter the wanderers vanished into the unknown, from which came disturbing rumors that all of them had been massacred by Comanche Indians. Fortunately, the report proved to be untrue; indeed, the expedition met with few difficulties. McClellan enjoyed it thoroughly; painted Indians were there and vast herds of buffalo and unfenced prairies gorgeous with flowers of every color, a paradise into which the serpent of civilization had not yet entered. The explorers went on to Fort Arbuckle and thence returned to Napoleon and finally to Memphis.

This journey had a most important bearing on McClellan's life, for it was then that he met the woman who was destined to become his wife. She was Ellen Marcy, the elder of the two daughters of his commander. Described as beautiful and charming, she must have been all that, for she had the young officers in the army at her feet. But there was no love affair with McClellan at this time. The two became friends and remained so for a number of years until circumstances favored McClellan's suit. Handsome as he was, he did not take her by storm.

Going from Memphis to New Orleans, McClellan joined General Percifer Smith, his new commanding officer. But he was with Smith only a short time, transferring to Corpus Christi, Texas, to labor on harbor improvements. His work there was considered notably good by his superiors.

His next assignment was one that would have delighted the heart of any adventurous young man—to make surveys to determine the best route of the transcontinental railroad from the Mississippi River to the Pacific Coast. This was a scheme that was to enter into politics and have much to do in determining the history of America. Jefferson Davis, then Secretary of War, desired a southern route to the Pacific, while Stephen A. Douglas was determined that the new city of Chicago should be the eastern terminus. This conflict of views had something to do with the repeal of the Missouri Compromise and the events that led up to the War between the States.

While engaged in the work McClellan came into friendly relations with Captain Beauregard, destined to fame as a Confederate commander. Gustavus W. Smith, another Confederate, had long been his close friend. Joseph E. Johnston was a third. Indeed, McClellan's intimates in the army were nearly all from the South, his opponents in the years to come.

He was not destined to survey southern routes. Instead, he was sent by Davis to make explorations for a military road across the Sierra Nevada to Puget's Sound. He spent three months of 1853 in exploring the Cascade Range from the Columbia River to the Canada line but without discovering the main gaps, later used by railways. He passed the winter of 1853-54 in Washington Territory, returning thence to Washington city. Jefferson Davis seems to have been impressed by his ability, for he sent him on a secret mission to San Domingo to determine the value of the harbor of Samana. McClellan reported favorably on it.

McClellan now prepared to enter another branch of the service, for in 1855 he was promoted to captain and assigned to duty in the First Cavalry Regiment, commanded by Colonel E. V. Sumner, destined to be one of his corps generals in 1862. However, he did not serve in the cavalry. An exceedingly important assignment sent him off to another continent.

The Crimean War was illustrating with blood and tears the carelessness in organization long characteristic of Britain. The armies of Britain and France were striving and starving before the walls of Sebastopol; the United States government decided to send American officers as observers. Three were chosen: Major Richard Delafield, Major Alfred Mordecai, and Captain George B. McClellan. The two first are unknown to fame, both much older than McClellan and of no particular competence. This chance to observe European armies and European military methods at close range gave a definite advantage to McClellan over his future opponent, Lee; for when Lee was called to leadership in the War between the States, he had never seen a larger force than Scott's ten thousand men in Mexico.

The three military commissioners encountered all sorts of difficulties. James Buchanan, Minister to England, gave them no assistance whatever. They received a discouraging notice from the French government that they would not be permitted to inspect the French army in the Crimea if they expected to continue on to Russia. But in Paris McClellan was consoled by a near view of the French emperor and empress. He did not consider Eugenie beautiful.

The commission went on to Berlin and from there to Warsaw and St. Petersburg. Staying a week at Warsaw, the officers were well entertained; indeed, they found the Russians most kind and considerate—so much so that McClellan came to sympathize with Russia in a war in which, as a matter of fact, Russia was in the right. Arriving at St. Petersburg, the commission was again well received but was refused permission to visit Sebastopol. The officers continued as far as Moscow and then went back to St. Petersburg, where they spent some time inspecting fortifications.

Returning by way of Prussia, the commission saw the fortifications at Koenigsburg and visited the cavalry school. Leaving Berlin in September, they passed through Vienna to Trieste, where they took a steamer for Constantinople. The last stage of that journey carried them to Sebastopol. Cordially entertained by British officers, McClellan and his companions made a detailed study of the Russian fortifications and the Allied counterworks. They even visited the trenches, viewing war on a larger scale than had ever been witnessed in America.

At Vienna the commissioners were entertained at a diplomatic dinner which gave McClellan an insight into the most polished society of that period. Experience had rounded him out; he no longer felt embarrassment or restraint in any company; he had become a finished man of the world. Italy, France, and Germany were covered in order. McClellan, crossing to England, completed the round by a trip to Scotland. The commission sailed for home in April, 1856, having been abroad for a year and having studied European armies and military methods under what were, on the whole, advantageous conditions. When George B. McClellan returned to the United States, he was by far the best trained officer the United States army had ever had. His observation of European methods was to have an important influence on his subsequent career, especially in determining him to discard the haphazard organization and training then in vogue in the United States. When McClellan was called on to organize an army it was, as far as possible, on the European model. It was a real army, not a collection of commands.

McClellan's report was published in 1857. His model of the Hungarian saddle used by the Prussian cavalry resulted in the "McClellan saddle," by far the best equipment of that sort seen in the United States up to that time. The French uniform, brought into the American army by him, remained in use for many years. His notebooks show sketches made by him of European uniforms, and many such pictures were published. Dr. Myers remarks, "We now can see a strengthening of his personal belief that organization must be of a perfection almost unattainable, and that this inevitably made him slow and hesitant."[2] But to just this thing, intensive preparation, the amazing victories won by the German army have been due. If McClellan had been left alone to organize, equip, and train the Union army in 1861-62, it is probable that the War between the States would have been shortened by two years. So much for preparation.

McClellan had determined to leave the service. All American officers in those days decided to leave the army or agonized over it, Lee among them. Some went into civil life and bettered themselves; the most did not. Army life is not a good training for civil pursuits. The field in which many officers seem to have done best was the ministry; quite a number of them turned preacher, and Leonidas Polk became bishop of Louisiana.

A man of an intensely practical turn of mind, McClellan was bent on gaining a larger reward for his talents than the meager army pay. When, therefore, an offer was made him to become chief engineer of the Illinois Central Railroad at a beginning salary of $3,000, with the promise of a raise to $5,000, he gladly accepted it. This was far better than half-starving for twenty years on a captain's pay and probably retiring without ever having reached the grade of major. It took Lee years and years to pass from captain to lieutenant colonel; he almost broke his

[2] *Op. cit.*, p. 102.

heart over it. McClellan was an excellent business man and prospered with the railroad, although he was perhaps somewhat tempted by hazardous schemes broached by army friends, such as accompanying William Walker on his desperate adventures. But McClellan was too canny to give up the certain for a rainbow.

His first home was in Chicago, but in September, 1860, he became president of the eastern division of the Ohio and Mississippi Railroad, with headquarters at Cincinnati. With a high official position and a salary of $10,000 (large in that day), McClellan had attained a most gratifying degree of success. And his happiness was now crowned by love.

McClellan had courted "Nellie" Marcy for some years in a delicate and eminently gentlemanly way. The cave man was not in style in that exceedingly polite age. The Marcy family favored him, especially after he became a railroad official at a satisfactory salary. Captain Marcy had gone through so much as an army officer that he did not wish his daughters to marry in the service. McClellan, too, was an eligible suitor in every way in the eyes of the somewhat aristocratic Marcy family. He was good-looking and well-bred and highly educated. A man of excellent habits, he had the makings of a model husband.

Nellie liked him but did not love him—at least, at first. She was engaged for a time to Ambrose Powell Hill, later one of Lee's lieutenants and a promising army officer. She seems to have loved him, and he undoubtedly loved her. All accounts of her describe her beauty; but it must be confessed that the photographs, depicting her in the frightful gowns and still more frightful headdressing of the mid-century, fail to bear this out. But only a beauty of the first water could look well in the most unbecoming clothes the female sex has worn in the last six thousand years.

Nellie Marcy was a flirt, but she was a Christian flirt; that is, she left few incurable wounds. In fact, she was a girl of principle and definitely religious. Her influence in this respect deepened McClellan's religious convictions, not prominent in early life.

At length she yielded to his suit, urged as she was by her

family. The marriage took place in Calvary Episcopal Church, New York, on May 22, 1860. McClellan's cup was full; life beckoned to him. Young, healthy, successful, he was now the husband of a girl not only charming but sweet and good. His happiness was, however, too much like that of a dream. Less than a year later the storm of war broke over the United States, carrying McClellan away from wife and work, taking him into the midst of titanic toils and great dangers, leaving him in the end a disillusioned and unhappy man. But soldiers probably have no right to happiness. They are trained for calamity, and must be ready to give all when calamity comes.

CHAPTER THREE

SMALL BEGINNING OF A NOTABLE CAREER

GEORGE B. MCCLELLAN had no hesitation as to his course in 1861, for he believed in the Constitution and that the Constitution had established an unbreakable Union. But he also believed that the Constitution fully guarantees states' rights; and it became more and more difficult as events progressed to reconcile the indissoluble Union with the powers possessed by the states. However, McClellan remained unshaken in his convictions until the end of his life, despite the embarrassment occasioned by them.

Being a staunch Unionist, and a prominent railroad executive, McClellan was prepared to take part in the war at its very opening, accepting an appointment as major general commanding the Ohio volunteers, on April 23, 1861. This office was entirely a state affair, having no relation to the federal government. It is interesting to note that McClellan declares in his book that the Union was saved in the West by the action of the state governments, that the Washington government did nothing at all for some time following the opening of hostilities.[1] He gave up a salary of $10,000 for the scant pay of a militia general, a sacrifice cheerfully made.

McClellan immediately attempted to get in touch with Winfield Scott, commander in chief of the American army, sending him several messages in which he suggested that the states between the Alleghenies and the Mississippi be organized as a

[1] *McClellan's Own Story* (New York, Charles L. Webster and Co., 1887), p. 43.

military department under a head. On May 13, 1861, he received an order (dated May 3) appointing him to the command of the Department of the Ohio, consisting of Indiana, Ohio, and Illinois, with later additions of western Pennsylvania and western Virginia.

It was at this time that the antagonism between McClellan and Winfield Scott, so unfortunate later, had its origin. McClellan began the organization of the troops of his department with all the enthusiasm and skill of a young and able executive; he had to do with a worn-out veteran accustomed to the delays of red tape. McClellan states that Scott emphatically refused to give him artillery and cavalry for his department, but the governors of his states mustered in some cavalry companies that afterwards entered the United States service. At an early date McClellan wished to make contact with General Patterson commanding Union forces on the upper Potomac, but received word that "the region beyond Piedmont is not within General McClellan's command. When his opinion is desired about matters there it will be asked for." One cannot wonder that McClellan conceived a dislike for the crotchety old head of the United States army. The matter was not without importance, too. Patterson had become rattled, facing Joseph E. Johnston, and he called on McClellan for help. This the latter could have furnished to some extent; he might even have taken command in person. Patterson's supineness enabled Johnston to slip out of the Shenandoah Valley and join Beauregard for the battle of Manassas (Bull Run). If McClellan had been with Patterson, the campaign would perhaps have had a different ending.

It was about this time that U. S. Grant, down-and-out ex-tanner, visited McClellan's headquarters, hat in hand, requesting a job on his staff or in some capacity. McClellan was not there but somebody promised the humble supplicant a place when the general returned. However, McClellan relates that a good fairy secured Grant the offer of a colonelcy of an Illinois regiment, thereby saving him from the ill fate of being associated with McClellan. Grant did not come back.

It was evident from the first that McClellan's military operations would take place in western Virginia contiguous to Ohio.

At that time this section was the wildest country east of the Rocky Mountains. A wilderness of tumbled mountains running in all directions, crowned by magnificent forests and watered by crystal rivers, its principal inhabitants were bears and deer. A hunter's paradise, a succession of breath-taking mountain views, it had no superior then in the wide boundaries of the United States. Oil wells and coal mines have done nothing to improve its scenic beauty.

The people of this section presented two strongly antagonistic types. Some of them had ventured over the mountains from eastern Virginia, bringing with them the traditions and prejudices of that country; nowhere were there stouter Southerners than in the Virginia mountains. Opposed to them in appearance, culture, and views of life were the immigrants from Pennsylvania and Ohio who had come into western Virginia in numbers. The latter people did not hunt and ride horseback and enjoy life leisurely; instead, they toiled and saved and went to church regularly, when there were churches. It was something of the old rivalry of Cavalier and Puritan that made the cleavage between Confederates and Unionists peculiarly sharp and bitter in western Virginia.

In this part of Virginia the Unionists enjoyed advantages. Not only were a majority of the people (though not so large a majority as is generally supposed) Union in sentiment, but they were favored by geographical conditions. Eastern Virginia is separated from this region by mountain ranges hard to cross in that time of few and bad roads. Consequently, it was difficult for the Confederates to penetrate western Virginia, while easy for the Unionists because Ohio lay just across a river from it. The Confederates made a fight to retain western Virginia in the summer and autumn of 1861, but conditions were too much for them. However, they might have accomplished something if it had not been for McClellan. To him more than to any other man was due the Union victory in the Virginia mountains.

He pushed the organization of the Middle-West volunteers with skill and speed. Recognizing as no other American officer did the supreme importance of a staff, McClellan did the best he could to find competent assistants. His father-in-law, R. B.

Marcy, made a satisfactory chief of staff, remaining with McClellan through his military career. Seth Williams, a good officer, became adjutant general. McClellan attempted to secure the services of a former rival in love, the able Gordon Granger, but the government would not let him have Granger. Day after day went on the weary but essential work of drilling men as ignorant of military routine as the "straw-foot, t'other foot" raw recruits of the Revolutionary army; of organizing the units and finding competent or partially competent officers to command them; of securing clothing and supplies and arms and ammunition and medical stores—all this McClellan attended to with little professional assistance. In an amazingly short time he turned the crude boys from the Middle West into soldiers capable of rendering service.

In this work McClellan bombarded Washington with demands, thereby making himself unpopular. At first really nothing but a militia general, he began to sign himself, "Major General, United States Army." The order appointing him to that rank was actually not issued until August 22, 1861, though it was dated back to May 14. The consequence was that he became the ranking officer of the United States army after Winfield Scott. This rapid rise was, perhaps, not for his best interests. He might have lasted longer if he had grown more slowly.

Nevertheless, almost alone among Union commanders, McClellan had definite plans for the subjugation of the South. His idea was to occupy eastern Tennessee in force and penetrate into Alabama, taking the Confederates in the East in flank. From the very beginning he realized, as the authorities in Washington did not, that the defeat of the main Confederate army in Virginia and the capture of Richmond would have to be accomplished to end the war. But his suggestions, sometimes rather tactlessly made, irritated old Winfield Scott, gouty and disinclined to listen to the views of young officers who did not know their place. On May 21, 1861, Scott wrote in an injured way, in reply to McClellan's suggestion that he join hands with Patterson and clear the Shenandoah Valley of Confederate forces, bidding McClellan mind his own business.[2]

[2] Myers, *op. cit.*, p. 175.

McClellan was wide in his outlook, taking in all the theatres of the war. He was determined to keep Kentucky out of Confederate hands, even though that state was not in his department. In this connection he had a somewhat unsatisfactory experience with Simon Bolivar Buckner, at that early period a Kentucky militia general. Buckner told McClellan of his wish to keep Kentucky neutral in the war between the sections. McClellan answered that he would not permit Confederate troops to occupy the state. Buckner took this answer to mean that McClellan consented to Kentucky's neutrality, though the latter stated that he had no authority to guarantee it. Unfortunately for McClellan, he did not express himself forcibly enough; Buckner declared he had consented to neutrality, much to McClellan's injury.[3] It gave Republicans ammunition to fire at him. One has to admit that McClellan was somewhat indefinite in this matter. Nevertheless, the Washington government was favorably impressed by his energy and success in organizing recruits and enlarged his department by adding to it Missouri.

McClellan, however, was not destined to campaign in Missouri; he was being inevitably drawn to western Virginia, where the Union men were organizing a state government in opposition to that at Richmond. Though styled the "Restored Government of Virginia," it was a mere forerunner for a secession movement from Virginia and the formation of a new state.

The Richmond government, not willing to relinquish a part of the state, sent a handful of troops to the western mountains, commanded by Colonel G. A. Porterfield. These troops were entirely untrained and distant from their base of supplies. All the same, Porterfield cut the Baltimore and Ohio Railroad near Grafton, thus breaking communications between Washington and the West.

McClellan was not prepared to endure this. He sent to Grafton a force that surprised and routed Porterfield's recruits. The engagement became known as the "Philippi races," the same name as the great battle that decided the fate of Rome after the murder of Julius Caesar.

[3] Arndt M. Stickles, *Simon Bolivar Buckner, Borderland Knight* (Chapel Hill, The University of North Carolina Press, 1940), p. 59.

The Confederate government now took a hand in the game, dispatching several thousand troops under General Robert S. Garnett to the village of Beverly, whither the defeated Porterfield had made his way. This aroused McClellan to personal action. Postponing his organization of troops, he moved with his volunteers into western Virginia. His men were only half-trained but were far better drilled, equipped, and supplied than the Confederates and were in much larger force. The Southerners, at a great distance from their base, were in need of everything and suffered from the uncongenial mountain climate. The summer of 1861 was a very rainy season. As he marched, McClellan issued a rhetorical proclamation which began, "Soldiers—You are ordered to cross the frontier and enter upon the soil of Virginia. Your mission is to restore peace and confidence, to protect the majesty of the law, and to rescue our brethren from the grasp of armed traitors." Generals burst forth in such fashion in those days. It should be noted that McClellan entered on his invasion of Virginia entirely on his own responsibility, without orders of any sort from Washington.

In the little campaign that followed he was brilliantly successful. A general is not to be judged by the size of the campaign, but by his adjustment of means to end. Jackson conducted his famous Valley Campaign with a small force, but his accomplishments were out of all proportion to his numbers. Likewise, McClellan's West Virginia Campaign, while confined to a few small actions, was of importance in the long run. Virginia was deprived of its whole western section and the Confederate flank was opened to attack. When Sheridan, in 1864, conquered the Shenandoah Valley, all of Virginia west of the Blue Ridge was lost to the South. If the Confederates could have maintained themselves in western Virginia, Union movements in the Shenandoah Valley would have been imperiled. Furthermore, the Baltimore and Ohio Railroad, which was the main communication between Washington and the West, would have been permanently cut.

The campaign in western Virginia in 1861 was like nothing in a civilized country—more like army movements in the Himalayas, such as, for instance, Colonel Younghusband's expedition to Lhasa. In some cases there were no human habitations for many miles; the roads were mainly trails through wild mountains whose gloomy gorges were alight with rhododendron and laurel; the troops forded, often at peril, clear brooks and rushing torrents. Often they were hungry and always—or it seemed always—the rain was descending in drizzle or downpour. The Confederates, usually half-fed and lacking every comfort, were in worse case than the Unionists, and they were also much outnumbered. Yet it is possible to see that McClellan won the campaign less by reason of numbers than by logistics, by better fed and better equipped troops who were, moreover, better trained. This is no reflection on the Confederates in western Virginia, who showed a courage and endurance beyond all praise. But the gods fought against them.[4]

Confederates coming from eastern Virginia passed one mountain range after another until they sometimes thought those ridges ran to infinity. On one such towering series of slopes, called Rich Mountain, General John Pegram held position with a small body of troops, protecting Garnett at Beverly. McClellan, making a turning movement by night, surprised and captured most of this force, which was not supported by Garnett. Then he turned against the latter, who was compelled to make a precipitate retreat. The bluecoats followed fast and followed faster on the retiring gray-backs, catching them at a crossing of Cheat River known as Carrick's Ford. Garnett, lingering behind the rearguard, was killed; his force was badly defeated. The Confederates lost all their guns and equipment and a considerable number of men. McClellan's losses were nominal. It was a brilliant success, one that meant everything for the future. And the conquest was permanent. When Robert E. Lee came in the late summer to retrieve the cause, he found the Unionists so firmly planted in the Virginia mountains that he could do nothing.

McClellan was elated. On July 16, he issued to his soldiers another flamboyant proclamation in the style of Napoleon. "I am more than satisfied with you. You have annihilated two armies commanded by educated and experienced soldiers en-

[4] *Southern Historical Society Papers*, Vol. XXVII, pp. 38-41.

trenched in mountain fastnesses prepared at their leisure." [5]

The imitation of Napoleon may have been something more than unconscious, for at that time McClellan was being dubbed "The Young Napoleon" by the newspapers. It was an unfortunate comparison; Napoleon was supposed to strike with the speed of a cobra, while McClellan, when he came into command of the Union army, spent months in training troops to win the war. The Americans of that period thought that military training was superfluous; they had the old militia idea that citizens fighting for hearth and home were invincible against anybody. But when the other side is fighting just as hard for hearth and home—what then? That was the nut McClellan had to crack.

He had little time to speculate. Only a few days after Carrick's Ford came the news of the rout of the main Union army near Washington. The government, which had paid little attention to McClellan up to this time, suddenly remembered that he had won victories in western Virginia. Victories! That was needed, that the Union must have—a general who could win victories. The day after the battle of Bull Run the message that spelled supreme opportunity went forth to McClellan.

[5] Myers, *op. cit.*, p. 189.

CHAPTER FOUR

HE SAVES THE UNION FOR THE FIRST TIME

ON THE DAY AFTER THE ROUT of the First Manassas (Bull Run) the badly scared Washington government summoned McClellan to the capital to take command of a situation rapidly getting out of hand. Recovered from the illusion that the secession movement would collapse after one battle, enabling the government to restore its authority in the Southern states, the chiefs now found Washington in danger. Indeed, if the Confederates had not been so disorganized by their unexpected victory they would have pushed on to the Potomac. The message to McClellan said, "Circumstances make your presence here necessary. Charge Rosecrantz or some other general with your present department and come here without delay. Lorenzo Thomas, Adj. Gen."

McClellan arrived in Washington on July 26 and visited Winfield Scott, head of the army, and Lorenzo Thomas, Adjutant General. Calling on Lincoln, McClellan was informed that he was in command of Washington and the troops there. The President requested him to return to the White House later to attend a cabinet session. However, when McClellan informed Scott that Lincoln had asked him to a cabinet meeting, the commander in chief became highly indignant that such an invitation had been extended to a subordinate without including the head of the army; he detained McClellan until it was too late for him to attend the meeting. He then sent McClellan around Washington to order stragglers back to their commands. This reveals the demoralization of the period; Washington was filled with soldiers who had left the army in the rout of the First Manassas and had failed to return to duty. McClellan, going again to the White House, explained to the President the cause of his absence from the conference, which seems to have amused the humorous Lincoln.

Assuming command of the "Division of the Potomac," the next day, July 27, he found everything in a state of utmost confusion and disorganization. There were about 50,000 infantry and 1,000 cavalry, with a few batteries. The dispositions for the protection of the city were utterly inadequate. "The camps were located without regard to purposes of defense or instruction, the roads were not picketed, and there was no attempt at organization into brigades.... There was nothing to prevent the enemy shelling the city from heights within easy range, which could be occupied by a hostile column almost without resistance. Many soldiers had deserted, and the streets of Washington were crowded with straggling officers and men, absent from their stations without authority, whose behavior indicated the general want of discipline and organization."[1]

Without delay McClellan began to cleanse the Augean Stable. In the first place he organized a staff, for, almost alone among American officers, he understood the duties of a staff. Lee did not, and Lee's inadequate staff was a handicap to him throughout the war.

The Army of the Potomac, as the Union host now came to be called (the name, by the way, was first used by the Confederates), was an armed mob with only the most elementary organization; some of the troops did not even know the drill. McClellan established brigades of four regiments each and, later, when this simple system was understood, formed divisions of three brigades each. This was as far as he wished to go in organization at that time, and he was quite right, as there were no officers in the army capable of properly commanding more than three brigades. However, the government insisted on piling the divisions into corps. McClellan opposed it; this was one

---

[1] *The War of the Rebellion: A Compilation of the Official Records of the Union and Confederate Armies* (Washington, Government Printing Office, 1880-1901), Ser. I, Vol. V, p. 11. Hereafter cited as *O. R.*

of the first causes of disagreement between general and government.

In the next few months McClellan completed the organization of a modern army out of the chaos existing when he reached Washington. In the first place, he had to get rid of political appointees holding important military offices; in doing so, he made many enemies and probably laid the foundation for his subsequent troubles. His dismissal of an officer named Hamilton, with strong political support, brought McClellan into conflict with Lincoln himself. Fitz John Porter, a personal friend and one of the most competent officers of the army, was first appointed to the command of the brigades and was succeeded by Ambrose E. Burnside and Silas Casey.

McClellan then grappled with the enormous task of establishing an army on the European model. The artillery was reorganized and modern artillery provided. The engineering corps received his attention, especially the topographical engineers. Owing to this department, McClellan in his campaign in Virginia had far better maps and far fuller knowledge of the terrain than the Confederate commanders fighting near their own capital. The medical and quartermaster departments were given much attention. McClellan was always careful to have, as far as was possible, competent medical treatment for his troops, even when, as in his insistence on hospital tents, it meant delay, one of the causes of his dismissal. The subsistence department was carefully organized, with the result that rations were generally available for the troops at all times and seasons. A signal corps was established; telegraphic communications received McClellan's especial care. Officers were instructed, troops drilled.

McClellan's theory of war was precisely that of the German army of modern times. It was that, in order to succeed, all necessary preparations should be made in advance, that nothing should be left to chance. Not only weapons and ammunition, but clothing, food, shoes, tents, blankets, medical supplies—everything—received detailed attention. As a result of McClellan's activities, when the Union army next took the field it was not only better organized and trained than the opposing army but incomparably better armed, better fed, better clothed, better equipped in every way. The resources of the Union made this possible, it is true; but if no great administrator such as McClellan had taken advantage of them, it is probable that the Army of the Potomac would have been nearly as wretchedly clothed and equipped as the Army of Northern Virginia. Up to that time war in the United States had been conducted on haphazard methods, "muddling through." And indeed, it took the Washington government so long to learn the necessity of proper clothing and outfit that McClellan fell into disfavor for his refusal to undertake a campaign in Virginia, in October, 1862, with an army that had lost its equipment under Pope and required re-equipment before it could be made effective.

In his vast work McClellan had the support of Secretary of State Seward and Secretary of War Simon Cameron. Chase seems also to have favored him at first but to have turned against him, probably because of his friendship for Cameron, Chase's enemy. His relations with Scott, his commander in chief, were not so fortunate.

Beyond doubt Scott viewed him with the dislike that a failing leader feels for his destined successor; that is human and natural. But the successor can smooth matters by tact; here McClellan was at fault. Indeed, one can see that tactlessness had much to do with denying him the success he would otherwise have won. On August 4, McClellan sent the President a general summary of his views on the conduct of the war. It showed a high degree of intelligence but seems to have been prepared without consultation with the commanding general. Perhaps its most striking feature is McClellan's early recognition of the importance of railroads in war. "It cannot be ignored that the construction of railroads has introduced a new and very important element into war, by the great facilities thus given for concentrating at particular positions large masses of troops from remote sections, and by creating new strategic points and lines of operations."[2]

McClellan, on August 6, had a long talk with Seward in regard to Scott, who he felt was obstructing reorganization. Seward seems to have restrained McClellan, for the latter burst

[2] O.R., Ser. I, Vol. V, p. 7.

out, "How does he think that I can save the country when clogged by General Scott?" He went on to say, most petulantly, "I don't know whether Scott is a dotard or a traitor! I can't tell which." In a letter of August 9, McClellan complains bitterly that Scott could not understand the danger of an attack by Beauregard, which he considered imminent. That this was no idle fear we know from Confederate information. At that very time Beauregard was considering an invasion of Maryland before McClellan could complete his reorganization of the Union army, about which the Confederates knew everything. In September, Beauregard and Johnston attempted to induce Davis to reinforce them for the projected advance, but the cautious Southern executive refused; McClellan was permitted to complete his reorganization without interference.

At this time things were still so critical in Washington that the Maryland legislature was on the verge of passing an ordinance of secession. McClellan nipped this danger in the bud by arresting, in September, 1861, the legislature. This act brought on him the fury of the extreme states' rights men and is seldom mentioned by historians. If the Confederates had invaded Maryland at this moment, the attitude of the legislature would have been serious.

McClellan was more than tactless in his treatment of Scott; he rather lost his head under the strain to which he was subjected; probably no other American military officer ever worked with such terrific energy. In the late summer and autumn of 1861 he slept little; he had no privacy; he was called on to decide a hundred matters. That he was able to accomplish what he did was due to his remarkable influence over his subordinates. His personality was magnetic; men who came into contact with him almost always retained for him an admiration that grew into affection.

McClellan, however, did not always rise above the prejudices of the age. Those prejudices led him to undervalue Lincoln, as in fact did nearly all the people about the great president. Stanton was outspoken in his contempt for his chief.

The reasons for this lay in the ideal of the statesman then held by the American people, an ideal that had come down from the be-wigged politicians of the past. The politicians in 1861 no longer wore wigs but they were as impressive with their black stocks and their top hats and their highly important manner. Daniel Webster was the best example of the type, Webster with his tremendous presence and his voice that rumbled like an organ in a cathedral. These statesmen, with their ponderous and humorless eloquence, inspired mirth in Lincoln; and McClellan, like others, failed to understand that an official who put on no weighty air and illustrated his remarks with funny stories—always very apt—might be a man of powerful intelligence and original views. It was not until the end of his career that Lincoln was at all appreciated.

McClellan frankly considered Lincoln incompetent as the head of a government in a great crisis. He did not know what was going to happen but he felt that there would be some kind of change. He wrote his wife: "I receive letter after letter—have conversation after conversation calling on me to save the nation—alluding to the Presidency, Dictatorship, etc. As I hope one day to be united with you forever in heaven, I have no aspiration—I will never accept the Presidency—I would cheerfully take the Dictatorship and agree to lay down my life when the country is saved. I am not spoiled by my unexpected and new position—I feel sure that God will give me the strength and wisdom to preserve this great nation—but I tell you, who share all my thoughts, that I have no selfish feeling in the matter. I feel that God has placed a great work in my hands—I have not sought it—I know how weak I am—but I know that I mean to do right and I believe that God will help me and give me the wisdom I do not possess." [3]

It should be remembered that McClellan at this time was a young man—a very young man for such tremendous responsibilities—and that he was pouring out to his wife his secret thoughts, his feeling that Lincoln was inadequate and would possibly be superseded by somebody. To McClellan the preservation of the Union was the single important matter. If the Union could be preserved under Lincoln, so well and good; but if Lincoln could not do the work, then he should be put aside

[3] Myers, *op. cit.*, p. 215.

for somebody who could. Such a letter should not be written to anybody, not even a wife.

McClellan thought just what hundreds of others thought, but the others were not indiscreet enough to put their meditations on paper. Discretion was not one of McClellan's virtues. If it had been, his career would probably have been happier. It is not impossible that the shrewd and observant Lincoln saw something of what was passing in his mind and did not like it. At all events, McClellan, from being high in the President's favor, began slowly but surely to decline.

McClellan was young and worked with the physical recklessness that characterizes the young. He did not become tired until he was exhausted and cross; it was partly the peevishness arising from fatigue that colored his manner and talk at times —unfortunately for himself. In this early period he lived in a house in Jackson Square near the White House and took his meals at restaurants. Sometimes he did not get dinner until ten o'clock at night. This disregard for his health was to have important consequences.

McClellan was troubled by the difficulty of getting adequate officers. Americans, then even more than now, were unmilitary; it was hard to take men out of the store and off the farm and transform them into competent officers in weeks or months; West Point graduates were few and were generally reserved for high command. In September, McClellan was gratified by having his staff reinforced by three French princes, the Prince de Joinville and his nephews. One of them, the Comte de Paris, wrote a history of the war. McClellan, like Americans of all times, was rather tickled at having royalty in close contact with him; here royalty was subordinate to him. All three of the princes conceived an admiration for him and remained friends for life. As they were men of the world, acquainted with the notables of Europe, their feeling for McClellan is a testimonial to his unusual personality and to the magnetism he rarely failed to exert on all about him.

Late in October there came an event that had a bearing on McClellan's subsequent career. On August 20, he had assumed command of the Army of the Potomac without losing his control of the troops in the vicinity of Washington. On October 21, Colonel Edward D. Baker, a political soldier, crossed the Potomac River at Ball's Bluff near Leesburg to reconnoiter. Attacked by a Confederate force, he was killed and his brigade was demolished. Baker, a former senator and a friend of Lincoln, was the first important man to fall on the Union side, and his death created something of a commotion. McClellan was blamed for the defeat, which, coming only a few months after Bull Run, was bitterly felt; a year later it would hardly have been noticed. It is difficult to see how McClellan could have been responsible for the affair, as he could not keep personally in touch with the troops guarding the river for miles. Yet when he attempted to prevent other like disasters, he was blamed for not destroying Confederate batteries on the Potomac some miles below Washington. To have landed troops to attack these batteries would have been to imperil the landing force, but all the same McClellan was censured for not doing what he properly claimed was a matter for the navy. In other words, McClellan was damned if he did or didn't. If a Union force crossed the river and was defeated he was blamed, and he was blamed if Union troops did not cross the river.

The Ball's Bluff affair had something to do with Stanton's growing antagonism to McClellan. On February 9, 1862, General Charles P. Stone, commanding the division along the Potomac to which Baker had belonged, was arrested and confined for months without charges being made against him. In fact, no charges were ever preferred against him. The order of arrest was issued by Stanton, who claimed that he did so at the instance of a congressional committee. McClellan sustained Stone and, by so doing, incurred the further hostility of the radicals in Congress.

The whole matter was political. Stone had (according to orders) restored two runaway slaves to their owners. This action was condemned by Governor Andrew of Massachusetts in a rather heated correspondence. The result was that the radicals in Congress seized the occasion of the Ball's Bluff disaster to ruin Stone, an officer of ability and patriotism. Even at that early date they were trying to advance the emancipation issue (in spite of Lincoln's conservative attitude) and were enraged by Stone's return of slaves, even though done in obedience to orders. Ridiculous accusations were made of Stone's correspondence with the Confederates. McClellan suffered from the aspersions cast on his subordinate, whom he was too loyal and generous to throw to the lions. He tried to have Stone put on his staff.

Pressure was now being put on him to take the offensive against the Confederate army under Johnston at Manassas; he was condemned then and has been condemned since for not doing so. Of all his decisions the one not to take the offensive in the autumn and winter of 1861-62 was the wisest.

It was true that the army was vastly improved but it was still only half trained. As late as the end of October there were only about 80,000 men ready for field duty; some of the batteries were unfit for service. In other words, the Army of the Potomac at that time was not prepared to take the offensive against a gallant foe on the foe's own terms.

The presence of the Confederates so close to Washington as Manassas was annoying to the authorities. Civilians soon forget the lessons of military disaster; the officials who were shaking in their shoes in August, 1861, were all for another advance in October. They wanted McClellan to move forward and end the war by winning a great victory over Johnston at Manassas. This was easy to say but very difficult to do, as McClellan fully realized.

In the first place the Confederate fieldworks at Manassas were extensive and formidable. They were held by the best defensive general in America and manned by an army that looked on itself as definitely superior to the bluecoated opponents. The best men of the South were here—little trained, it is true, but brave and determined. Johnston would have asked nothing better than to be assaulted in his carefully selected and strongly fortified position.

McClellan saw all this, but the authorities did not. They could not visualize the peril of hurling a half-trained volunteer army against strong fieldworks held by a valiant enemy.

That McClellan planned to take the field is possible, but only if the chances favored success. He was no gambler, and it was not needful for the stronger Union to gamble. The Confederacy was the power that had to gamble or lose. By McClellan's plan, the advance would not be postponed beyond November 25. However, the impracticability of campaigning in Virginia in wintertime was really the deciding factor. To advance against the Manassas fortifications in cold weather, over bottomless roads with a still raw army, was not in the nature of the feasible. McClellan came to understand this but he had to be ready to take the offensive if forced to do so. Political considerations moved the government, which wished to win an advantage in Virginia before winter stopped army movements.

Meanwhile McClellan's relations with Scott grew worse. Perhaps the greatest blot on his military career was his inconsiderate treatment of the latter. "Old Fuss and Feathers" had become a military monument, but he had served the United States well and had remained on the Union side, although a Virginian by birth. He should have been eased out of his office with courtesy, not with beratings. Unquestionably McClellan's slighting remarks came to the old general's ears and influenced him. Beyond doubt he retaliated by reflections on McClellan's abilities, and such observations had considerable weight with the authorities.

Scott gave his side of the trouble in a letter to Cameron of October 4, 1861. He complained that McClellan paid no attention whatever to his orders, adding, "Has then a senior no corrective power over a junior officer in case of such persistent neglect and disobedience? The remedy by arrest and trial before a court martial would probably soon cure the evil.... I shall try to hold out till the arrival of Maj. Genl. Halleck, as his presence will give increased confidence to the safety of the Union —and, being, as I am, unable to ride in the saddle, or to walk, by reason of dropsy in my feet and legs and paralysis in the small of my back, I shall definitely retire from the army." [4]

This is an important letter because it reveals the fact that the scheme to supersede McClellan began even before his formal appointment to command and was inaugurated by Scott, not by

[4] Myers, *op. cit.*, p. 222.

Stanton; Stanton simply took up where Scott left off. The idea stamped by Scott on the authorities was that McClellan was not competent for command of all the armies but that Halleck was. He impressed this on Lincoln when, later, the President visited him in his retirement and asked his advice. Thus, McClellan's inconsiderate treatment of Scott was visited with vengeance on his head. The fact that Halleck's incompetence endangered the Union did not alter the fact that he was brought East to replace McClellan on Scott's initiative.

McClellan brought all this on himself by his hostility to Scott, whose physical infirmities would soon have forced his retirement if left alone. Unable to get Scott dismissed immediately, McClellan began to intrigue. On October 26, he conferred at the home of Postmaster General Montgomery Blair with Senators Wade, Trumbull and Chandler. Wade and Chandler, both radicals, were not of McClellan's political school at all, but they agreed "to make a desperate effort tomorrow to have General Scott retired at once.... He is ever in my way and I am sure does not desire effective action." [5] Chase was a party to the retirement of Scott. This senatorial action was successful; Scott went before he could summon Halleck from the West.

On November 1, McClellan received the following note: "Lieut. Gen. Scott having been, upon his own application, placed on the list of retired officers, with the advice, and the concurrence of the entire cabinet, I have designated you to command the whole army. You will therefore assume the enlarged duty at once, conferring with me so far as necessary. Yours truly, A. Lincoln. P.S. For the present let General Wool's command be excepted. A. L."

The same day the order was issued from the War Department.

McClellan received the news of his elevation with commendable humility. "I do not feel that I am an instrument worthy of the great task, but I *do* feel that I did not seek it. It was thrust upon me. I was called to it; my previous life seems to have been unwittingly directed to this great end, and I know that God can accomplish the greatest results with the smallest instruments—therein lies my hope." The United States was a Calvinist

[5] *Ibid.*, p. 224.

country in those days and had the strength that Calvinism gives its votaries. Stonewall Jackson also had a belief that he was an unworthy instrument in the hands of his deity. In order to ease Scott's feelings, now that Scott was out of the way, McClellan issued an order highly laudatory of the former commander of the American armies. It was intended to soothe Scott, but it came too late.

Another great event occurred just before this. On October 12, McClellan received a telegram announcing the birth of his first child, Mary. He had kept his wife at Cincinnati in this time, to be sure that she would be far from scenes of danger and undue excitement. In November he rented a house in Washington at the corner of 15th Street and H Street, to which he brought his augmented family. After that his life became better ordered and more regular.

Now came the first disaster. On December 20, 1861, McClellan was stricken with typhoid fever. The attack was severe, and a few days later he was in grave danger. For a time the army was paralyzed; Marcy, chief of staff and McClellan's father-in-law, did not know what to do in his absence. However, the commander continued to direct operations to some extent from his sickbed. He returned to his office on January 13, 1862, but it was some time before he recovered his strength and full mental vigor. Through the whole year 1861 McClellan had been working at top capacity, snatching food at any odd hour or not at all, working sometimes sixteen hours a day, and Nature was revenging herself for his excesses.

By this time criticism of McClellan was in full blast, and a sick man cannot defend himself. His biographer, Myers, states that McClellan should have attacked Johnston in November. "While he did not know as we do today, that the chances were very favorable to his success, yet these chances may have been worth taking, for the political stakes at issue were very great." Those who know the full facts will dissent, as do many military critics. The eminent G. F. R. Henderson fully approves McClellan's inaction at this time. Attack was what the Confederates at Manassas wanted, what they prayed for. There is no reason to suppose that the Unionists, assaulting powerful works, would have been any more successful than McDowell had been in the open field in July. For, if the Union army was vastly improved, the Confederate army was likewise. It was drilled and better equipped than in July, 1861, and fully capable of giving a good account of itself. Nothing in McClellan's career reflects more credit on him than his refusal to risk the cause of the Union for political reasons by attacking a strong position before his army was trained for it. If McClellan had died at this time and had been replaced by a political general, it is possible that the end of 1861 would have witnessed the conclusion of the war with a Southern victory. But, fortunately for the Union cause, McClellan's vitality and youth triumphed over the disease.

About the same time came the great disaster, the replacement of Simon Cameron as secretary of war by Edwin M. Stanton. Cameron, who was a corruptionist but a friend to McClellan, was overthrown by men not much less dishonest than he. How Stanton procured Cameron's place is not known, but it was the result of a protracted intrigue. Stanton, who had been a Democrat and a member of Buchanan's cabinet, longed to retain power. A bitter partisan, he fitted into the radical scheme of things; and the radicals in the last months of 1861 were making progress politically as the war lengthened and men's feelings grew embittered. McClellan says in his book that Stanton courted him while seeking the place of secretary of war, and there can be no doubt of this, for in the autumn of 1861 McClellan's opinions still had weight with the authorities.

To the small McClellan came the tall Stanton, impressive with his great beard and square spectacles, a strange man, wheedling and menacing by turns. McClellan says, "He at once sought me and professed the utmost personal affection, the expression of which was exceeded only by the bitterness of his denunciation of the government and its policy. I was unaware of his appointment as secretary of war until after it had been made, whereupon he called to ascertain whether I desired him to accept, saying that to do so would involve a total sacrifice of his personal interests, and that the only inducement would be the desire to assist me in my work. Having no reason to doubt his sincerity, I desired him to accept, whereupon he consented, and with great effusion exclaimed, 'Now we two will save the country.'" [6] The next day Lincoln called on McClellan to explain that he had appointed Stanton, thinking that he was a great friend of McClellan.

Almost immediately McClellan found that matters had changed for the worse. It became difficult to approach Stanton, who assumed a high and mighty air. Lincoln's impatience with McClellan's delay in attacking Johnston increased, and McClellan naturally attributed it to Stanton's influence. His free intercourse with Lincoln ceased. The government became annoying about the Confederate batteries on the lower Potomac. The evacuation of these batteries, McClellan knew, could be effected only by a movement of the Army of the Potomac, which would force the Confederates to abandon all advanced positions and fall back southward. A positive order of Lincoln's—instigated, McClellan thought, by Stanton—forced McClellan to open the Baltimore and Ohio Railroad, closed by the Confederates in western Virginia.

McClellan, for this purpose, went to Harper's Ferry in February, 1862, with the intention of occupying Winchester in force. A pontoon bridge across the Potomac could not be relied on as a permanent passageway; McClellan wished to reconstruct the railroad bridge, destroyed some time before. He delayed his advance on Winchester pending the rebuilding of the bridge. At Harper's Ferry, the general learned that Lincoln was dissatisfied with his failure to advance into the Shenandoah Valley; but, on going to Washington and laying his plan before Stanton, he received assurance that the Secretary was entirely satisfied with what he was doing. However, Stanton said nothing to the President, who was not at all assured that matters were going well until McClellan made an explanation, whereupon he expressed himself as content.

Lincoln brought up the great question that was destined to

---

[6] *Battles and Leaders of the Civil War* (New York, The Century Co., [1887-88]), Vol. II, p. 163. Hereafter cited as *B. and L.* This and succeeding quotations are included by the express permission of the publishers, D. Appleton-Century Co., New York.

divide government and general. McClellan, with the soldier's instinct to strike at the heart, had proposed a new plan for the conquest of the seceded states. This was to ignore Manassas and the overland route to Richmond and proceed against the city from the lower Rappahannock. There were advantages and disadvantages in this plan. The advantages were that Manassas would be evacuated and the Union supply base would be fully protected by gunboats on the Potomac and Rappahannock rivers; it could not be assailed. An advance from Urbanna, too, would force the Confederates to concentrate at a considerable distance from their supply lines. Disadvantages were the several rivers the Union army would have to cross on the way to Richmond; and, much more, the uncovering of Washington by a movement so far to the east. On that point the authorities were very touchy; until almost the end of the war they feared a Confederate descent on the capital city.

McClellan said of Lincoln that "it had been suggested that I propose this movement with the 'traitorous' purpose of leaving Washington uncovered and exposed to attack. I very promptly objected to the coupling of any such adjective with my purposes, whereon he disclaimed any intention of conveying the idea that he expressed his own opinion, as he merely repeated the suggestions of others. I then explained the purpose and effect of fortifying Washington, and, as I thought, removed his apprehensions." [7]

On March 8, McClellan convened his division commanders and laid his plan before them. They unanimously approved his arrangements; he thought that he had won a victory, only to find that he was mistaken. On the same day, the War Department issued an order creating army corps and assigning McDowell, Sumner, Heintzelman, and Keyes to command them. McClellan's objections were brushed aside, apparently without consideration. Of the four corps generals only one had commanded as much as a regiment before the Bull Run Campaign of July, 1861. As McClellan at this time learned that the Confederates were evacuating Manassas and desired to advance against them, he wired Stanton asking that the corps formation be postponed.

[7] *Ibid.*, p. 166.

The reply was a refusal but, on McClellan's insistence, Stanton gave way.

Lincoln, who later acquired a very considerable competence in military affairs, was a tyro in 1861, as in fact were all the civil functionaries. Determined to push the war vigorously—not understanding the thousand and one preparations necessary—Lincoln, on January 27, 1862, issued a rather quaint order directing the Army of the Potomac to advance to Manassas on February 22. The idea was that of a general movement of all the Union armies on Washington's natal day. McClellan objected in a letter of some length, and the President did not insist on the literal obedience of his order. However, there can be no doubt that McClellan lost face by not attempting to carry it out, impracticable as it was.

The Confederate evacuation of the extensive Manassas fortification was unexpected by McClellan and was not dictated by any immediate military necessity. That it was abandoned without a battle was a victory for the Union, as it could only have been carried at heavy loss. The cautious Johnston, aware that a forward movement of the Union army was at hand and that Manassas exposed him to attack far from his supply base, fell back to the Rapidan River, leaving behind quantities of stores that could not be carried for lack of transportation. As McClellan's main object in moving from Urbanna had been to compel the evacuation of Manassas, the advance from the former place lost most of its attractions while its drawbacks became plainly evident. It was then that he revised his plan, substituting a movement from Hampton Roads to that from the Rappahannock River. This was a great improvement on his first scheme, and the true line of approach to the Southern capital, especially as the Union sea power could be used in the York and James rivers.

The prime advantage of such a movement was that it obviated the necessity of giving battle to the Confederates on the Rapidan River, behind which they had taken their station. McClellan from the first appreciated the difficulties of the overland route, destined to bring grief to several Union generals. If his plan could have been carried through with the full support of the government, it would have probably resulted in ending the war.

But the authorities never believed in it, never gave it full support and, finally, wrecked it completely, at a time when it was still highly promising.

There can be no doubt that Stanton never liked McClellan, and that his dislike grew with time. The root of the trouble was the temperamental difference between the two men. McClellan was a conservative in politics, an advocate of states' rights, frank, free-spoken, expressing opinions openly and not always tactfully. Stanton was sly, smooth, underhanded, devious, and tyrannical. He liked to have subordinates crawl to him, and McClellan did not crawl to any man. Consequently, it was only a question of time before the two became acutely antagonistic, and the time was very short. That the fault did not lie with McClellan is shown by the denunciation of Stanton by Burnside when commander of the Army of the Potomac. Stanton was an able and energetic executive, justifying Lincoln's trust in him; but he was bitter and vindictive, incapable of acting in good faith toward anybody who had aroused his animosity.

Almost from the first, Stanton began to sow the seeds of distrust in Lincoln's mind. The latter paid Stanton the tribute of respect that a country attorney naturally entertains for a great city lawyer; he always considered Stanton's opinions, even when he did not follow them. Beyond a doubt Stanton had something to do with the blow that was struck at McClellan at this time.

While McClellan was near Manassas, on March 12, 1862, following Johnston, he saw in the newspapers an order relieving him of command of the armies of the United States and confining him to the Department of the Potomac, which extended from Philadelphia to Richmond and from the Atlantic Ocean to the Allegheny Mountains.[8] This was a sufficiently large empire, but McClellan was not blind to the threat involved in his demotion, especially as nothing had been said to him about it. It was his reward for not carrying out the wild plan of assaulting the Confederates at Manassas—in other words, the reward for sane and competent generalship. Other commanders have experienced the same fate. Nevertheless, George B. Mc-

[8] Bates states that he suggested this to Lincoln.

Clellan prepared for the expedition to the Virginia Peninsula with a good deal of optimism. He had accomplished a great deal; he had created the first properly organized, drilled, and equipped army ever seen in America. He had laid the foundation for Union success.

CHAPTER FIVE

EMBARKATION ON A GREAT ADVENTURE

ABRAHAM LINCOLN, contemplating the great problem of subduing the South, reluctantly consented, on March 8, 1862, to McClellan's plan of attacking Richmond by way of the James-York Peninsula. Not realizing the advantages of this line of approach, he preferred the overland advance from Washington because such a movement would prevent the Confederates from making any serious thrust against the capital of the United States. Lincoln himself and his advisers were uneasy all through the war because they could look out of the windows of the White House and see the hills of a Virginia hostile to them, with an army only awaiting a chance to cross the intervening river. From first to last the Union strategy was handicapped by the exposed situation of Washington. And in consenting to the Peninsular Campaign, Lincoln expressly enjoined that a sufficient force be left for the protection of the capital. Just how large that force should be was not determined.

McClellan felt misgivings due to the reluctance of the government to endorse his plans, but his chief uneasiness arose from Stanton's personal hostility, becoming more pronounced every day. However, Stanton knew how to conceal his feelings and to appear complaisant. Born with the intrigant's tortuous soul, he preferred to undermine an opponent rather than to overthrow him by open attack. In the absence of any apparent opposition, the commander of the army entered on the execution of his plan in a spirit of high hope. He believed he had created an army that was better than the opposing Southern host and that he could win the war with it if given the full support of the government. Everything hinged on that, the government's full support. He was not to get it; Stanton saw to that.

On March 17, 1862, the docks of the ancient town of Alexandria, opposite Washington, began to hum as long lines of blue-coated troops filed through the cobblestoned streets and came down to the great river. A part of Heintzelman's corps was the first to embark on the transports, followed by Porter's division. The troops on reaching Fort Monroe were put in position on roads leading to Yorktown.

Major General John E. Wool was in command at Fort Monroe. He was seventy-eight years old and had become a brigadier general in 1841, five years before McClellan graduated from West Point. He was suffering from a bad attack of jealousy, since he was made a major general two days after that rank was conferred on McClellan, who even now, at the beginning of the campaign, was his superior officer. The two men clashed at once and continued to disagree until Wool was sent to take command in Baltimore on June 1, 1862.

McClellan realized that he was operating in the shadow of the guillotine. In a letter to Halleck, four months before that officer was ordered to Washington, he said, "The Abolitionists are doing their best to displace me." He was aware, even at that early date, that his conservative opinions made him unpopular with the radical Republicans coming more and more to the front in Washington. Already Stanton had gained one victory over him, though a partial one. On March 11, McClellan had been relieved of his position as commander in chief (later filled by Halleck) and confined to the command of the Army of the Potomac. A second blow came when, on March 31, Blenker's division was detached from the army. At this very time Stanton was ominously writing Adjutant General Thomas, enclosing the President's instructions to McClellan and asking, "I desire you to report to me whether the President's order and instructions have been complied with in respect to the forces to be left for the defense of Washington."[1] Nevertheless, McClellan left Alexandria, on April 1, in a buoyant mood.

[1] *O.R.*, Ser. I, Vol. XI, Pt. 3, p. 57.

Arriving at Fort Monroe on April 2, he found there 60,000 men and 100 guns. He issued orders for a movement on April 4, though there was a shortage of draft animals and wagons. On April 3, Stanton struck at him again, and effectively, when McClellan received a telegram depriving him of any authority over Wool. Thus he had no control of his base of operations.

McClellan has been much censured for not moving more rapidly in the opening phases of the campaign. But right here, at the outset, came up the question of maps. The best maps obtainable in Washington were poor. Sketches made by a military officer showed the Warwick River flowing north and south, not in its true course east and west. Orders based on this erroneous map were issued on April 3 for the opening movement next day, but the officers could not carry out their orders because they could not reach the positions assigned them.

Then came the final blow, destined to rob McClellan of his chance of success in the campaign just beginning. The following message reached him:

> "Adjutant General's Office
> April 4, 1862
>
> "General McClellan:
> By direction of the President, General McDowell's army corps has been detached from the force under your immediate command, and the general is ordered to report to the Secretary of War.
> Letter by mail.
>
> L. THOMAS,
> Adjutant General."

This meant that after the plans of the campaign had been drawn and accepted by the government, 40,000 men were taken from the forces McClellan counted on and assigned to duty elsewhere, "reporting to the Secretary of War." At last Stanton had administered what was intended to be a *coup de grâce*. That it was not was due to McClellan's Scotch stubbornness of character.

Lincoln was a great and good man but he was surrounded by persons of a different character, made ruthless and unscrupulous by the necessity of carrying on a great war. The eminent historian John W. Burgess has this to say of the web of intrigue in which McClellan was involved at this period: "Whether a crushing victory over the Confederates ending at once the rebellion, before slavery was destroyed, was wanted by all those who composed the Washington government may well be suspected. And it is now clearly certain that there were some who would have preferred defeat to such a victory with McClellan in command. It was a dark, mysterious, uncanny thing, which the historian does not need to touch and prefers not to touch."

Burgess probably does Stanton an injustice in thinking that he desired McClellan's defeat at the hands of the Confederates, for Stanton, harsh and unethical as he was, was genuinely patriotic. It would seem that what he wanted, and tried to accomplish, was to goad and hamper McClellan until he resigned. He wished victory for the army but he did not wish McClellan to be the victor.

Historians have represented McDowell's detachment from McClellan as due to Stonewall Jackson's feats in the Shenandoah Valley and fear for the safety of Washington, but it should be noted that the order taking McDowell away was issued on April 4, long before Jackson had won fame or was considered a threat of any importance. At the same time Stanton must have worked on Lincoln's fears to get so large a unit detached from the Army of the Potomac. No such force was needed to man the Washington defenses.

McClellan was only rendered the more determined by this adverse stroke of fortune. But he found his advance checked by unlooked-for circumstances. Reconnaissances made under fire revealed the fact that the Warwick River, heading near Yorktown, flowed across the Peninsula, and that from Lee's Mill to Yorktown the north bank of the stream was one long line of earthworks. The British position of 1781 at Yorktown had been built up into a semi-permanent fortification.

Here was a serious situation; the Confederate line would have to be forced before the Union army could move toward Richmond. Moreover, McDowell's detachment affected the matter vitally, for it had been McDowell's part in the plan to take Gloucester Point, across the York from Yorktown, and thus turn the Confederate flank. A frontal attack was hardly possible, for the Union commander was confronted by a strong line of earthworks behind an unfordable river. What was left but a siege?

On April 7, McClellan wrote Stanton that since his plans were made, 50,000 men had been taken from his command. His present force was about 85,000 men, but detachments would have to be made for guard duty and scouting. He could assail the enemy's works and perhaps take them and he would begin the attack as soon as his siege train came up, but to accomplish this he needed the First Corps to land in the rear of Gloucester Point and capture it.

As a siege had not been contemplated in the plans drawn in Washington, McClellan now had to request the necessary equipment. Awaiting this, he was anything but idle. Engineers gathered information about the Confederate works, drawing maps of them. Landing places and docks were established, roads were constructed, and troops moved to the front. Reconnaissances showed, that, because of dams, the Warwick was impassable except on dam embankments, which were narrow and commanded by artillery.

General John G. Barnard, chief engineer of the army, thought the Confederate position could be carried only by a siege. General Keyes wrote as follows: "This army having been reduced to 45,000 troops, some of them among the best in the service, and without the support of the Navy, the plan to which we are reduced bears scarcely any resemblance to the one I voted for.... Notwithstanding the rapidity of our advance, we were stopped by a line of defense 9 or 10 miles long, strongly fortified by breastworks erected nearly the whole distance behind a stream or succession of ponds, nowhere fordable, one terminus being Yorktown and the other ending in the James River, which is commanded by the enemy's gunboats.... The approaches on one side are generally through low, swampy, or thickly-wooded ground, over roads which we are obliged to repair or to make before we can get forward our carriages. The enemy is in great force, and is constantly receiving reinforcements from the two rivers. The line in front of us is therefore one of the strongest ever opposed to an invading force in any country."

The works were indeed strong, due to the skill and energy of

John B. Magruder, the Confederate commander. However, the Confederates were in anything but force when McClellan landed at Fort Monroe; Magruder had only about 12,000 men. But, master of the art of camouflage, he made his small numbers appear to be several times their reality. It was one of the most remarkable feats of the war, but Magruder received little in the way of gratitude from his government, which did not know how to use this great artist in deception. Before long Joseph E. Johnston came down from the north with the main Southern army, taking command and interposing a formidable obstacle to the Union advance.

McClellan did not give up the various detachments without grumbling. On April 9, Lincoln wired him, "Your dispatches complaining that you are not properly sustained, while they do not offend me, do pain me very much." The President went on to say that Blenker's division had been withdrawn before McClellan left Washington, "and you know the pressure under which I did it, and, as I thought, acquiesced in it—certainly not without reluctance."

Lincoln found that McClellan had left less than 20,000 men for the defense of Washington and Manassas Junction, and some of those were scattered. McClellan had stated he had only 85,000 men present for duty, but Secretary Stanton showed that he had 108,000 with him or *en route* to him. Lincoln concluded, "I suppose the whole force which has gone forward for you is with you by this time, and, if so, I think it is the precise time for you to strike a blow. By delay the enemy will relatively gain upon you—that is, he will gain faster by fortifications and re-enforcements than you can by re-enforcements alone. And once more let me tell you it is indispensable to you that you strike a blow. I am powerless to help this. You will do me the justice to remember I always insisted that going down the bay in search of a field, instead of fighting at or near Manassas, was only shifting and not surmounting a difficulty; that we would find the same enemy and the same or equal entrenchments at either place. The country will not fail to note, is now noting, that the present hesitation to move upon an intrenched enemy is but the story of Manassas repeated."

It will thus be seen that Lincoln did not appreciate the difficulties confronting McClellan. The latter, indeed, might have forced the Confederate works at Yorktown soon after his arrival on the scene, but only at great cost. After Johnston's arrival he could not have stormed them at all. Just as McClellan had been right in refusing to assault the works at Manassas, held by the best defensive general in America and a gallant amateur army, he was right now in not making a frontal attack on the Confederate fortifications, admirably constructed by excellent engineers. It is likely that Lincoln would have seen the problem in a better light if he had not always had Stanton at his elbow telling him that McClellan had men enough, that only McClellan's slowness and reluctance to attack held him back. But McClellan, just as he had saved the Union by declining to assault Centreville, once more preserved his cause by refusing to wreck his army against the strong lines of Yorktown. Johnston, after his arrival, would have liked nothing better than to be attacked; it was what he prayed for.

The Washington authorities, in urging McClellan onward instead of settling for a siege, were playing into the Confederate hands. Barnard wrote in his report, "If we could take Yorktown or drive the enemy out of that place, the enemy's line was no longer tenable. This we could do by siege operations. It was deemed too hazardous to attempt the reduction of the place by assault." Such was McClellan's decision, and there were excellent reasons for it. The government, on the other hand, was thinking more of political effects—of bringing the war to a close before the November elections. But McClellan could not be supposed to take serious military risks for even the best of political reasons.

In spite of the incessant rains of one of the wettest springs ever known in Virginia, with the ensuing necessity of constructing roads, the Union army pressed operations with vigor and skill. It was some time before the heavy siege artillery came, but as soon as it arrived it was put in place. Earthworks of large dimensions were thrown up opposite the Confederate lines— earthworks still of size and often mistaken for those of 1781. In something less than a month McClellan had disembarked, built roads, thrown up earthworks, put his guns in place, arranged his units, made every preparation for blowing to pieces the Confederate lines at Yorktown. In that country of no real roads, halfway under water, offering every advantage to the defense, this was no mean achievement, however the authorities at Washington might view it.

Ridicule has been poured on McClellan for his delay before the Confederate lines, coming both from Union and Confederate sources. He is represented as being fubbed off by Magruder with a skeleton army which he should have pushed aside without trouble. The facts are otherwise. The Confederate defenses were, for those days, exceedingly formidable, especially with the whole country more or less submerged. What McClellan did was to conduct a campaign in a vast swamp, with every adverse weather condition, losing thousands of men from sickness; and, on the whole, he did it admirably. Only his great power of organization made it possible at all.

The opposing lines at Yorktown crept close to each other, and in the first days of May the artillery fire was constant on both sides. This was particularly the case on May 3, when the Confederates poured a storm of shot and shell on the Union earthworks until midnight. Then the fire ceased, and the weary soldiers behind the Union lines lay down to sleep.

When they awoke on Sunday, May 4, 1862, they found a change. No shots came from the opposing side, where all was silent. Loud explosions were heard in the direction of Yorktown behind the Confederate lines. The observation balloon went up in the clear air carrying the redoubtable Professor Lowe, chief of aeronauts. He reported that he saw bright lights, like houses or ships on fire. Heintzelman, accompanying Lowe on his next ascension, observed men in blue entering the Confederate works without opposition. Coming down, he sent orders to Kearny and Hooker to break camp and prepare to move. Averell's cavalry received the same notice.

What had happened was that the astute Joseph E. Johnston, Confederate commander, had waited to the last possible moment before withdrawing. Knowing that McClellan's siege guns were in position and that they would quickly blast the Confederate defenses into fragments, he pulled out of his works and was in retreat westward up the Peninsula.

It was some little time before the Unionists were ready to pursue; about midday the leading units got under way. At McClellan's headquarters all was stir and bustle, for it was no small job to issue orders for the immediate movement of 100,000 men, with all the impedimenta of an army in the field. The orders were issued, the army moved, and late that afternoon was nearing Williamsburg in spite of roads so deep in liquid mud that they were streams rather than highways. McClellan wired Stanton, "I find Joe Johnston in front of me in strong force, probably greater a good deal than my own, and strongly entrenched. My entire force is undoubtedly inferior to that of the rebels." Already, it will be seen, McClellan was vastly overestimating the numbers of his opponents, something he continued to do until the end of his military career. Actually, at that time Johnston had about 55,000 men, and his fieldworks at Williamsburg were formidable only in places.

Johnston was forced to halt and turn at bay because his wagon trains, stalled in the mud, were in imminent danger of capture. Indeed, his bony cattle and inferior wagons made the withdrawal difficult. His line, stretched in front of the ancient capital of Virginia and off to the left almost to the York River, faced the Unionists as they came up slowly through the rain and bottomless mud. McClellan at last had a chance to strike a blow at the elusive Johnston.

Stoneman, skirmishing with the Confederate rear guard, came upon the fortifications late in the afternoon of April 4. "The works consisted of a large fort (Magruder) at the junction of two roads running from Yorktown to Williamsburg, and small redoubts on each side of this, making an irregular chain of fortifications extending, with the creeks on which they rested on either flank, across the peninsula."

These works were held by two brigades. Stoneman, finding the Confederates in force, sent his cavalry forward for information and held back his infantry until Hooker and Smith should arrive. When Smith came up, Sumner advanced the brigades of Hancock and Brooks in order to carry the Confederate rifle pits. As

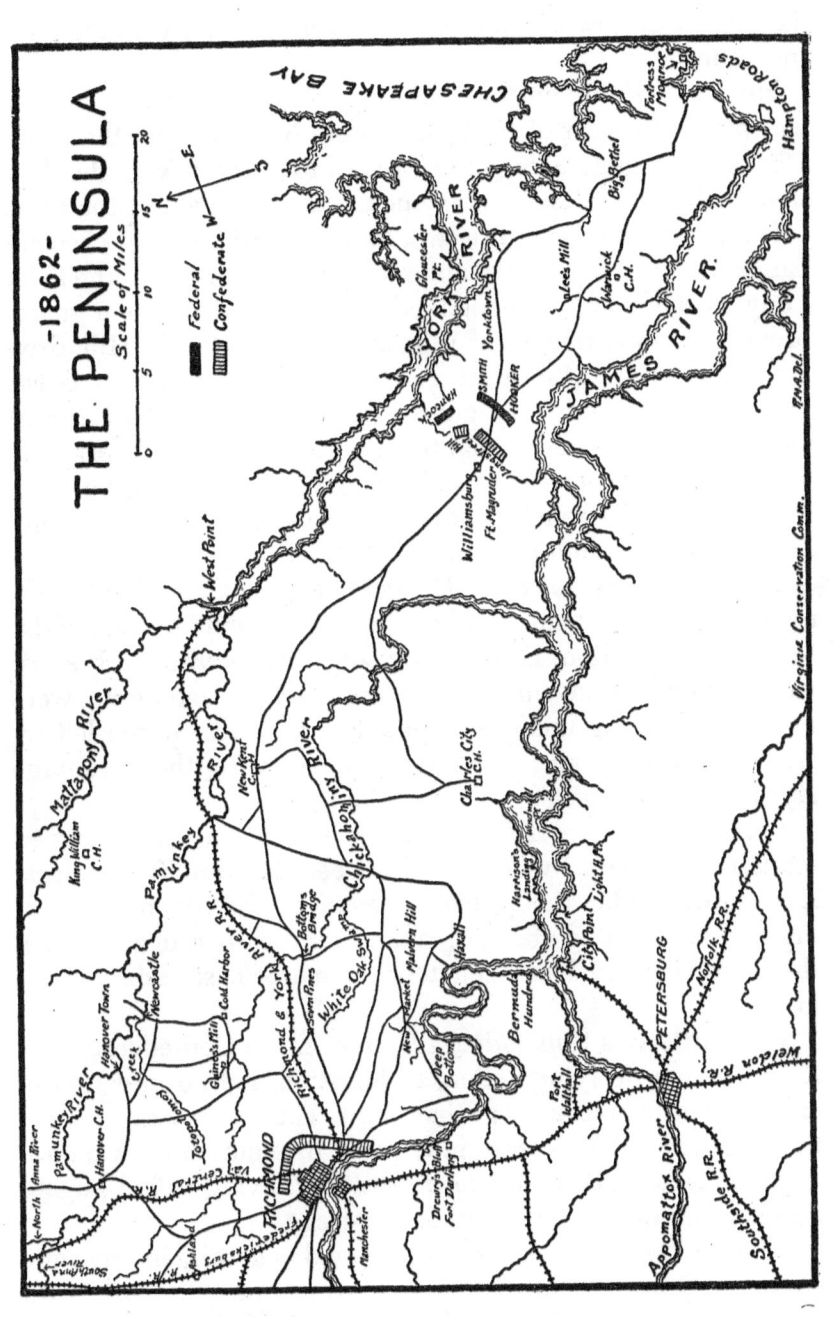

darkness was now coming on, however, Sumner withdrew for the night.

Hooker, arriving on the field in the early morning of May 5, was placed in front of Fort Magruder. Smith was on the right, Hooker on the left. Struggling forward to the field were the divisions of Kearny, Casey, and Couch, almost bogged in the mire.

Hooker, on his own initiative, sent forward a brigade accompanied by several batteries and seemed about to sweep the field. Longstreet, who was in command of the Confederate rear guard, brought up the brigades of Wilcox, Pickett and A. P. Hill, driving Hooker back after a severe conflict in which the Unionists lost many men and some guns. This was perhaps the bitterest struggle of the war up to that time. Both sides showed desperate gallantry and great steadiness, Hooker, calling for help, was reinforced by Kearny, sent by Sumner, who was in general command, as McClellan was not present.

The battle was not over. Hancock, on the Confederate left, made a vigorous advance and gained some ground in spite of determined opposition. D. H. Hill went forward with Early's brigade to stop the movement. The Confederates, coming up, were met by a blasting musketry fire and a bayonet charge led by Hancock. They were forced back; on this wing the advantage lay with the Unionists.

Kearny, moving to Hooker's aid, was held back by crowded roads, but came up, by brigades, between three and four o'clock. A confused conflict then broke out again on the Union left, ending with the coming of night. While Hancock had done well on the right, Hooker had been terribly mauled, suffering heavy losses.

The battle was thus indecisive, but on the Confederate part it had been a delaying action, as Johnston had no intention of engaging his whole army at that point. The Confederate wagon trains continued to creak and groan through the bottomless roads, halted constantly by the necessity of having stalled wagons dragged out of mudholes by man power.

All day of May 4, Franklin was engaged in getting his men and equipment aboard transports for a movement up the York River to West Point. Reaching Brick House Point (of colonial fame) on the right bank of the York just below West Point, he threw infantry and artillery into the forest to protect his landing, which was accomplished by early morning of May 7. Here he was in a position to cut off Johnston's wagon trains creeping along from Williamsburg.

The Confederates, realizing the menace, brought up troops to oppose Franklin; there took place in the woods the confused struggle known as the battle of Brick House Landing, or Eltham Landing. Franklin was plainly intimidated by his lack of knowledge of the country and of the enemy, and stood on the defensive when he might have inflicted much damage by a bold offensive. The engagement went on in a desultory fashion most of the day, without heavy losses on either side; the Confederates withdrew in the afternoon when their wagon trains were no longer in danger. Thus, for a second time, the Unionists lost an opportunity to destroy the Confederate trains and embarrass Johnston's retreat.

On the whole McClellan's movement up to this point had been as successful as might have been expected. Civilians unaccustomed to army movements and to the obstacles to be overcome in a difficult country were already accusing McClellan of delay and procrastination, but his subordinates all seem to have thought he had accomplished nearly everything possible under the circumstances.

Stanton, however, was still pouring poison into the ears of Lincoln, who was disappointed that in little more than a month of campaigning McClellan had failed to gain a signal victory and crush the secession movement. On May 8, the President wrote a sharp letter to the army commander because the latter had opposed the corps organization adopted by the government. He said significantly, "I now think it indispensable for you to know how your struggle against it is received in quarters which we cannot entirely disregard. It is looked upon as merely an effort to pamper one or two pets and to persecute and degrade their supposed rivals. I have had no word from Sumner, Heintzelman, or Keyes. The commanders of these corps are of course the three highest officers with you, and I am constantly told that you have no consultation or communication with them; that you consult and communicate with nobody but General Fitz John Porter and perhaps General Franklin. I do not say these complaints are true or just, but at all events it is proper you should know of their existence. Do the commanders of corps disobey your orders in anything?"

Lincoln concluded by saying that McClellan, in relieving General Hamilton, had lost one of his best friends in the Senate. Also army officers should cease writing unpleasant letters to Congressmen because of their remarks about the army.[2]

This letter is significant. It shows that the corps commanders were not satisfied with the situation and were carrying tales to Washington. Of them McClellan could have counted on Sumner, a good soldier of undoubted loyalty. But Heintzelman was an officer of no particular ability whom McClellan finally got rid of, while Keyes appears to have been secretly hostile to him. It was natural for McClellan, aware that he was surrounded by Stanton's spies, to place confidence only in men whom he knew he could trust, such as Porter and Franklin. Sometimes, indeed, his trust was misplaced, for he believed Halleck to be his friend, only to learn long afterward that Halleck was one of his most dangerous enemies.

Now there came a cheering piece of news. The *Merrimac*, which had so doughtily defeated a Union fleet in Hampton Roads and held off the *Monitor*, was blown up when the Confederates evacuated Norfolk, one of the consequences of McClellan's Peninsular Campaign. This meant that both the York and James rivers were open to Union gunboats, at least for a considerable extent. McClellan need no longer have any fear for his supply base because of the opposing navy. The base selected was Cumberland Landing on the Pamunkey River, near the White House, home of Washington's wife, and later the White House.

While McClellan had active enemies working against him, at this time he had some cabinet support. He had been intimate with Seward, and now Seward came to his help. The Secretary of State visited McClellan at Cumberland Landing and heard his story. From this place Seward wrote Lincoln on May 14, "The battle will be fought, probably, this side of Richmond. We think

[2] O.R., Ser. I, Vol. XI, Pt. 3, p. 154.

that you should order whole or major part of General McDowell's, with Shields, up the York River as soon as possible.... We find General McClellan confident of success. He moves to White House to-morrow morning."

This powerful interposition had some effect. At that moment Stanton and Seward were in opposition. On May 15, McClellan wired Stanton that he was detained by having to make roads. "News from front indicate enemy in large force. Raining to-day. No time will be lost in bringing about a decisive battle." On the same day Lincoln wired McClellan that he would do all he could to sustain him, but "I am still unwilling to take all our force off the direct line between Richmond and here."

The weather grew worse instead of better. On May 16, McClellan wrote Stanton, "Rain commenced again yesterday and continued last night and to-day. With utmost difficulty I have moved two divisions in advance this day and moved forward those in rear. We have to do much road-making as we go, but we are continually advancing.... Very cool, wet and dreary to-day." On the same day McClellan reported again to Stanton, "The rains during the past two days have rendered the roads so bad that the train of one division has been thirty-six hours in making 5 miles."

On May 18, McClellan wrote Stanton regretting to hear that he was ill. "Weather now very warm. My pickets within a mile of Bottom's Bridge, and as close to the railway bridge of the Chickahominy." He desired news of McDowell, whose position would influence his right flank. On the same day McClellan wrote Seward, still his friend. On May 19, he reported to Stanton that it was raining again but that he was advancing. He had put the railway between the Pamunkey and Chickahominy in good order. It was to be the supply line for the siege of Richmond.

And now McClellan seemed in luck, for Seward's petition was answered. Lincoln wrote McClellan, on May 21, that he would have control of McDowell's corps. However, it would be better to send McDowell to him by land rather than by water, as the latter could reach McClellan in five days by land while it would take two weeks by water.[3] There was a mental reservation in this

[3] *Ibid.*, p. 184.

decision; Lincoln did not intend to send McDowell beyond his reach; moving by land, he would be easy to halt. And, as it happened, he was recalled.

At the very same time McClellan was having a dispute with Lincoln over General Hamilton. McClellan had relieved the general for some breach of duty, and Lincoln, pressed by politicians, repeatedly requested his restoration. But McClellan resolutely refused; he answered that Hamilton was not fit to command a division and protested against his reinstatement.

On May 22, McDowell, at Fredericksburg, wrote McClellan that he had received orders to join him in the movement on Richmond. A Confederate force of 12,000 to 15,000 men under General Joseph R. Anderson was in his front. He wished to defeat this force and drive it back on Richmond, where McClellan could coöperate with him by cutting it off.[4]

Once more McClellan's drooping spirits were lifted by the prospect of victory offered him in the junction with McDowell, who would bring 40,000 troops to the army. The campaign was going well in spite of the atrocious weather, now fortunately beginning to be a little better. Lincoln had visited McDowell at Fredericksburg and given him his orders, promising that he would begin to move toward McClellan on May 24.

Meanwhile the Confederate commander had been watching his opportunity. He had been angrily accused of intending to back through Richmond in his retreat, but in reality he was preparing to fight and did not wish to do so with the Chickahominy in his rear. By a curious coincidence, at the same time both presidents were nettled with their army commanders for not being forward in fighting. Both of them thought the armies should have come to grips before this, but two such wary antagonists as McClellan and Johnston had no intention of fighting unless they thought they could do so at advantage.

On May 20, various detachments crossed the Chickahominy. It was evident that a collision could not much longer be delayed. On May 24-26, Naglee pushed forward to Seven Pines and, on May 25, the Fourth Corps was ordered to fortify a position near that place. It was just in the rear of the point where the Nine

---

[4] *Ibid.*, Vol. VI, Pt. 3, p. 186.

Mile road joins the Williamsburg road and where a national cemetery now stands. On the same day, Heintzelman advanced two miles west of Bottom's Bridge, covering the left and rear of the army. He was placed as senior officer in command of all the troops on the south side of the Chickahominy. On May 30, the troops on the right bank of the Chickahominy stood about as follows:

Casey's division, north of the Williamsburg road, with its center about Fair Oaks, a mile north of Seven Pines.

Couch, to the rear of Casey at Seven Pines.

Kearny, on the railroad near Savage's Station.

Hooker, on the banks of White Oak Swamp, to the left of Kearny.

Couch and Casey were so near the Confederates that picket firing was constantly going on. The Confederates were in force only a mile or two beyond the Union position.

The weather had turned bad again. All day and night of May 30 rain continued to fall. Rifle pits were filled; roads became impassable, and all the bridges on the Chickahominy were threatened by the rising water. It was evident to the closely watchful Johnston, eager for an advance, that the time had come to strike.

CHAPTER SIX

THE FIRST GREAT BATTLE

JOSEPH E. JOHNSTON was the kind of soldier who never fights except at an advantage, which does not prove that he was a fool; he was simply not a gambler. It happened that the Union army, on May 31, was divided by a raging river, while the whole Confederate army was on the south side of the stream. A beautiful situation for a scientific soldier who weighed every element in a military equation with the care of a chemist making an analysis.

In estimating the importance of the Chickahominy River as a military obstacle one must take into consideration the fact that in the past three-quarters of a century all watercourses in Virginia have to a large degree silted up; to-day we do not see by about fifty per cent the picture McClellan's engineers saw. That is, in that time the Chickahominy River was fifty per cent more of an obstacle than it is at present.

Bridging the stream was made the more difficult by its tendency to divide into several channels—sometimes, as at the Grapevine Bridge, in five—instead of flowing in a single stream. Moreover, the bottom land along the river, at an average half a mile wide, is a swampy jungle of trees and bushes through which neither man nor beast can pass except by the regular paths and trails.

On the Chickahominy, one mile above the main crossing point of Bottom's Bridge (passage of the Williamsburg road), was the bridge of the Richmond-York River Railroad. Three or four miles above this bridge was Grapevine Bridge. Three miles above this bridge was New Bridge. Four miles farther up was the Me-

FIRST GREAT BATTLE

chanicsville Bridge. These bridges were of the utmost importance in the events that followed.

McClellan, the engineer, who had seen European armies, realized the value of maps as did no other American officer except Stonewall Jackson. Finding that the ordinary maps were all exceedingly inaccurate, he took the best large-scale map of Virginia and cut it into squares. Then, selecting some of the bright young men of his large staff (among whom was George Custer, destined to later fame), he sent them out along the trails and roads to correct errors and bring the map up to date. By June, 1862, McClellan had better charts of southeast Virginia than Lee had in April, 1865.

We have seen that Lincoln had promised McClellan that he would send him McDowell's corps, so badly needed for the siege of Richmond the Union commander was planning. On returning from Fredericksburg to Washington, the President wrote that McDowell would begin his march southward on May 24. Just at that moment something happened to change the picture and frustrate McClellan's hopes.

Simultaneous with the movement being made south of the Chickahominy, the Sixth Corps under Franklin advanced along the north bank of the river; on May 23-24, Smith's division occupied the village of Mechanicsville, six miles from Richmond, after a skirmish with a small Confederate force. This movement was made in anticipation of McDowell's advance south from Fredericksburg. When that officer should join hands with the troops immediately north of the Chickahominy, Richmond would be completely enclosed on the north and east. McClellan's flanks would then be secure and he would be in a position to besiege the Southern capital.

Fitz John Porter was in immediate command of the movement on the north side of the Chickahominy. In the afternoon of May 27, G. W. Morell, commanding a division, moved from New Bridge, preceded by cavalry and artillery. Warren acted with his brigade in coöperation. Later cavalry under George Stoneman and infantry under George Sykes followed to protect the rear. In driving rain, through water and mud, the troops struggled forward fourteen miles to Peake's Station on the Virginia Central (now Chesapeake and Ohio) Railroad. Two miles short of Hanover Courthouse (noted as the scene of Patrick Henry's first great speech) they came upon a Confederate body. Berdan's sharpshooters were sent ahead to hold the Southerners until Morell, slowly pushing his way through the boggy roads, could come up.

The Confederates, who were in much inferior force, made a stout resistance and maintained their position until Martindale's and Butterfield's brigades arrived. Thus pressed, they then gave way, but a part of their force turned against the Union flank and rear under Martindale. However, McQuade's brigade had meanwhile come up. The Confederates, confronting largely superior numbers, abandoned the contest, leaving some killed and wounded.

This was on May 27. McClellan joined Porter on the battlefield and expressed satisfaction at the results of the small action, in which Porter claims he captured 730 prisoners and buried 200 killed, numbers considerably too large.

The following day, May 28, Porter pushed ahead to Ashland (associated with Henry Clay's boyhood), destroying railroad trains and bridges and tearing up tracks. The Confederate General Joseph R. Anderson was driven away, leaving this area open to the Unionists.

Meanwhile the blow had fallen that was destined to wreck the campaign. Lincoln and Stanton had always been averse to sending McDowell to McClellan and had only consented on Seward's plea. Now they were confounded by the news that Stonewall Jackson, moving northward down the Shenandoah Valley, had routed the Union troops near Winchester and was pressing onward toward the Potomac River, thus threatening Washington.

This gave Stanton the excuse he needed for withholding McDowell from McClellan; Lincoln, fearing for the safety of the capital, concurred. Even before this, Stanton had induced the President to hold a part of McDowell's force at Fredericksburg.

McDowell was beginning his movement to join McClellan when, in the afternoon of May 24, he received a telegram from Lincoln: "You are instructed, laying aside for the present the movement on Richmond, to put 20,000 men in motion at once for the Shenandoah, moving on the line or in advance of the line of the Manassas Gap Railroad. Your object will be to capture the forces of Jackson and Ewell." [1]

McDowell, thunderstruck by this sudden change of plan, wired Stanton, "The President's order has been received and is in process of execution. This is a crushing blow to us." Lincoln immediately telegraphed back, "I am highly gratified by your alacrity in obeying my order. The change was as painful to me as it can possibly be to you or to any one. Everything now depends upon the celerity and vigor of your movement." McDowell wired again, protesting that it was practically impossible to cut off Jackson and Ewell. "It will take a week or ten days for the force to get to the valley by the route which will give it food and forage, and by that time the enemy will have retired. I shall gain nothing for you there, and shall lose much for you here. It is therefore not only on personal grounds that I have a heavy heart in the matter, but that I feel it throws us back, and from Richmond north we shall have all our large masses paralyzed."

This was an eminently just view of the situation, but Lincoln was too perturbed for the capital to pay attention to it. In wrecking McClellan's plans the President inadvertently played into the hands of two men: Secretary of War Stanton and Robert E. Lee.

Lee had been for some time in Richmond occupying the position of general in chief *under the President*. He was much under the President, who fancied himself to be a general. Lee, most conciliatory and tactful of men, managed to get his way in many things, apparently by letting Jefferson Davis think that Lee's ideas were Davis's.

It was Lee's strategy that sent Stonewall Jackson down the Shenandoah Valley with the object of creating a disturbance there and possibly threatening Washington. Jackson had exceeded his expectations. In a campaign that has no superior for the rapid maneuvering of a small army against separated oppo-

---

[1] *O.R.*, Ser. I, Vol. XII, Pt. 3, p. 219. On May 24, McClellan received a telegram from Lincoln: "In consequence of Gen. Banks's critical position I have been compelled to suspend Gen. McDowell's movement to join you."

nents, Jackson won several victories, cleared the valley of Union troops, and created alarm all through the North. The immediate consequence was that McDowell was sent off on a wild-goose chase at the very moment he was needed for McClellan's plans against Richmond.

It seems to have been at this time that Stanton and Salmon P. Chase, Secretary of the Treasury, made their alliance, so hostile to McClellan. Chase went to Fredericksburg, apparently sent there to see that the reluctant McDowell, heartbroken at having the Richmond campaign wrecked, obeyed orders. Chase for a couple of days was constantly in communication with Stanton in regard to the movements to be made against Jackson in the Shenandoah Valley.

The authorities had, indeed, a fine case of nerves. Stanton, on May 25, 1862, wired McDowell, "Move a brigade to Washington as speedily as possible. Banks has been driven from Winchester; is in full retreat near Harper's Ferry. No time is to be lost." McDowell obeyed, though disgustedly. Being a professional soldier of much, if unrecognized, ability, he did not share the panic of the capital.

Lincoln, it should be noted, still thought of McDowell's junction with McClellan. On May 28, he telegraphed McDowell (then at Manassas Junction) an account of the fight at Hanover Courthouse, adding, "If Porter effects a lodgment on both railroads [near Richmond] consider whether your forces in front of Fredericksburg should not push through and join him." [2] Meanwhile, Lincoln had broken the unpleasant tidings, telling McClellan of Jackson's irruption and of sending troops from McDowell to catch him. He added, "If McDowell's force was now beyond our reach we should be entirely helpless. Apprehensions of something like this, and no unwillingness to sustain you, have always been my reason for withholding McDowell's from you. Please understand this, and do the best you can with the forces you have." [3] That this statement was true is shown by Lincoln's recurrence to McClellan's plan as soon as the panic had worn off.

[2] *O.R.*, Ser. I, Vol. XII, Pt. 3, p. 266.
[3] *Ibid.*, Vol. XI, Pt. 1, p. 32.

FIRST GREAT BATTLE

Stanton was burning the wires with fears of a Confederate invasion of Maryland. It was in his mind for days. McDowell wearily replied to one of these fits of apprehension, "I do not believe of the enemy's ability to cross the Potomac in force and go down on Washington. They are neither bold nor strong enough, and we are neither weak nor timid enough, for that."

On May 27, McClellan wired Stanton, "Very severe storm last night and this morning has converted everything into mud again and raised Chickahominy. Richmond papers urge Johnston to attack, now he has us away from gunboats. I think he is too able for that.... Every day is making our result more sure and I am wasting no time."

It will thus be seen that McClellan, though chagrined by losing McDowell, was going ahead vigorously with his plan for a siege of Richmond, from which his outposts were now distant only five miles.

Lincoln, eager for good news from the main army, wired McClellan on May 28, "What of F. J. Porter's expedition? Please answer." In the absence of McClellan, at the front with Porter, Marcy, the chief of staff, answered. Telegrams went back and forth, chiefly concerned with Jackson's movements. McClellan reported another terrible storm on May 30. "Roads again frightful." He was not aware that Johnston was about to strike him. It shows, however, McClellan's mastery of strategy that he wired Lincoln on May 25, "The object of the movement [Jackson's] is probably to prevent reënforcements being sent me." If Lee read McClellan's mind, McClellan also read his.

The Union engineers had built several temporary bridges over the Chickahominy, but they had not anticipated the mass of water that came down that stream in the evening of May 30 and all day of May 31.

On May 30, Heintzelman, in command on the south side of the river, sent word to McClellan that he had encountered sharp opposition in occupying his advance line (west of Seven Pines) and that he thought the situation was critical. He obtained authority to make such dispositions as he considered proper.

Keyes's corps was in front. Kearny was brought up from Savage's Station into supporting distance of Casey's division, which held an advanced position near Seven Pines.[4] There was tension in the air, as the officers realized that the flood gave the Confederates an opportunity to attack at advantage.

The whole country around Seven Pines and Fair Oaks was more or less under water; all streams were out of their banks and the Chickahominy was a black torrent pouring through the trees and bushes. The bridges were groaning under the strain and threatening to give way.

About 10:30 in the morning of May 31, a Confederate staff officer rode into Naglee's pickets on the Nine Mile road not far from Fair Oaks. This was an aide of Johnston's named Washington. It was at once suspected that a large troop movement was under way. Keyes ordered his men under arms. A little later Casey received warning that Confederates were approaching on the Williamsburg road from the direction of Richmond. Casey was in force on the Williamsburg road and to the north of it; Couch held the line along the Nine Mile road.

Masses of gray-brown men were seen moving in the trees and fields on both sides of the Williamsburg road, splashing through the water. The Union pickets came flying to the earthworks occupied by the line of battle. Keyes sent Peck's brigade to the south of the Williamsburg road, which had not been held by any troops and from which direction the Confederates were approaching in heavy force.

Casey was struck in front and on both flanks by masses of men, who disregarded the fire of artillery and musketry and continued to swarm forward. Keyes, seeing the crisis, sent to Heintzelman for reinforcements. The courier lost his way, with the result that Kearny and Hooker did not receive orders until three o'clock.

McClellan was at his headquarters at New Bridge, on the north side of the Chickahominy, when the sound of heavy firing came to his ears. Realizing that Johnston was making his long-threatened attack, he sent orders to Sumner to get his men under arms and move to the bridges.

Sumner's corps consisted of Richardson's and Sedgwick's divi-

---

[4] On May 31 Couch's division was at Seven Pines, Casey's division half a mile west of it. A part of Couch's division, with artillery, was at Fair Oaks.

sions, both camped on the left bank of the Chickahominy near Powhite Creek, six miles above Bottom's Bridge. Each division had built a bridge across the river near its camp.

At two o'clock Sedgwick's division advanced to the upper bridge. Shortly thereafter orders came for it to cross the stream and move to support Heintzelman, hard pressed on the south side. The causeways approaching the bridge were under water, and the bridge itself, swaying under the current which covered the planks, threatened to give way at any moment. Richardson's division attempted to cross at the lower bridge, but the water was so high that only French's brigade was able to pass over at this point. The other brigades of this division crossed at the upper bridge.[5]

Naglee's brigade, which was holding an advanced position on the Nine Mile road, had been struck in the flank by numbers of gray-brown men who came piling through the mud and water; his command was forced back toward the position occupied by Couch. Two other brigades were routed and driven from the field. Casey's position at Seven Pines fell into the hands of the oncoming Confederates, who pressed ahead in spite of staggering losses.

Just before this Keyes had directed Couch to throw forward two brigades to assist in holding Casey's right flank. In making this movement Couch was threatened by masses of Confederates on his right. Attacking, he was separated from the rest of his corps and driven back toward Grapevine Bridge. At this moment it looked as if the Confederates would be able to intervene between the Unionists in position on the right bank of the Chickahominy and Sumner's corps crossing the river and moving toward Fair Oaks. However, Couch, hearing that Sumner was coming up, formed his line facing Fair Oaks and the railroad, at some little distance back from it.

As the afternoon wore on the situation became increasingly serious for the Unionists. Casey had been defeated at Seven Pines and his various units driven from the field. But help was at hand. Sumner's brigades, moving slowly through the deep

[5] Alexander S. Webb, *The Peninsula* (New York, Charles Scribner's Sons, 1881), p. 110.

mire, came to the vicinity of Fair Oaks station, where Couch still held on with a few regiments of infantry and a battery. With infinite difficulty they succeeded in bringing up several pieces of artillery; the guns were buried to the axles in mud at every discharge.

Arriving in the vicinity of Fair Oaks station, Sumner's troops deployed in line of battle. None too soon, for they had hardly formed before the Confederates were on them in full fury. The latter charged, only to be thrown back by the steady fire of the Union infantry and artillery. Again and again they pressed forward, but each time they recoiled from the blazing line of blue. Sumner, seeing that the situation was in hand, ordered a bayonet charge, which, made against disorganized masses of Confederates, was effective. The coming on of night ended the conflict, in which the Confederates had been successful at Seven Pines and the Unionists at Fair Oaks. Consequently, the battle bears both of these names. Like so many other engagements of the war, it was entirely indecisive tactically. However, strategically it was a Union victory. Johnston had been the aggressor and he had failed to crush the part of the Union army south of the Chickahominy.

June 1 was another day, and the Confederates prepared to renew the battle with the morning. They were in poor condition to do so, however, inasmuch as their losses were heavy, the newly-formed commands disorganized, and the commanding general wounded. Johnston, exposing himself on the Nine Mile road with the recklessness characteristic of Confederate officers, had been struck by a shell fragment and was badly hurt. Consternation rather than triumph reigned in the Southern host.

In the night the Union commanders made preparations for a second terrible day of conflict. Couch's division and as much of Casey's as could be rounded up were placed in rifle pits east of Seven Pines near the Williamsburg road. Hooker, who had come up at dark, was on the north side of the railroad. Sedgwick was in the same position he had held at the end of the battle, at Fair Oaks. In the night three batteries were brought up, but only at the expenditure of vast effort; the roads were practically impassable.

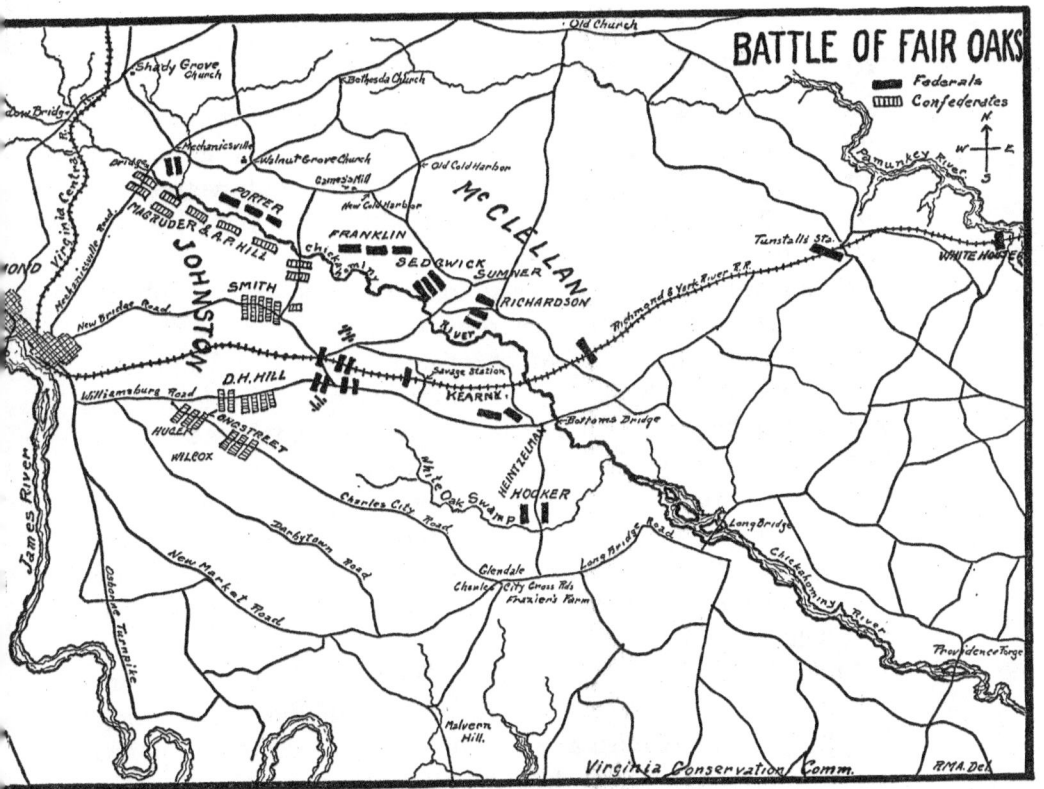

The opposing lines were now somewhat at right angles with their positions of the day before. Then the Union line had run from north to south, from Grapevine Bridge to White Oak Swamp. On June 1, the Union line lay mainly east and west along the railroad, though a part of it jutted out at Fair Oaks toward the Chickahominy. By this disposition the bridges over the river were covered as well as the all-important railroad communication with the White House.

In the morning Richardson was in line of battle near the railroad on the left of Sedgwick, and with Birney on his left. About 5:00 A.M. cavalry and a line of infantry pickets moved toward the right of Richardson's position. A battery, opening on the Confederates, dispersed them. Finding that there was a gap between French's left and Birney's right, Richardson extended his line to close it. Shortly afterwards the Confederates delivered their attack, about 6:30. Along two roads that crossed the railroad the Southerners advanced without throwing out skirmishers and as if determined to win by weight alone. Here along the railroad for about an hour the fight raged. The two lines, not far apart, blazed away at each other while the few Union cannon sprayed canister. The Confederates, outnumbered, were unable to advance. Seeing this, the Unionists charged, driving back the gray-brown men for some distance.

Meanwhile some fighting also took place along the Williamsburg road. Hooker, pressing forward, drove back the Confederates at that point. When night fell on a confused and indecisive action, the Unionists at Seven Pines occupied the lines from which they had been driven the day before. On this second day, even more than on the first, the Confederate attacks had been piecemeal, without coördination. This was possibly due to the fact that a new general was in the saddle, Gustavus W. Smith, McClellan's old crony, who before the day was over was succeeded by a third, Robert E. Lee, now really beginning his career as a field commander.

McClellan had held his own in a bitter battle where circumstances had favored the Confederates. Seldom have troops fought under more miserable conditions: roads were bottomless, fields covered with water. In some places the men stood in water up to their waists, and probably some of the wounded drowned.

Fortune had aided McClellan. The Confederate attack on May 31 had been delayed by Longstreet's passing from the Nine Mile road to the Williamsburg road, thereby upsetting Johnston's arrangements considerably. The weight of the attack should have fallen at Fair Oaks on the Nine Mile road instead of at Seven Pines on the Williamsburg road. If the Confederates had attacked in mass at Fair Oaks, they might have succeeded in intervening between Heintzelman and Sumner coming from across the river and have gained a decisive advantage. As it was, they had fought a drawn battle in which they lost about 6,000 men to the Unionists' somewhat fewer casualties. The battle demonstrated the fact that both armies were as yet raw and awkward in maneuver but that the troops on both sides were of high quality. Plunging through water, stumbling through bushes and trees, splashed with mud from eyes to feet, the men on both sides had blazed away at each other with all the courage of the race. It was essentially a soldier's battle, an infantry combat. There was little direction on the Confederate side, and not much more on the Union. Few batteries had taken part, for the guns simply could not be brought up through mud that seemed to the toiling soldiers to extend well toward China.

After the engagement of June 1, McClellan, attempting to return to his headquarters near New Bridge, found the approaches to one of the bridges used by Sumner under water for four hundred yards. He passed the river in a boat. If the battle had been delayed until June 1, Sumner could not have crossed the river and McClellan would probably have suffered a disastrous defeat. So far his luck had held. The Confederates and Richmond were plunged in gloom. The battle had not been a victory. Thousands of men had been killed and wounded. Worst of all, Joseph E. Johnston lay on a bed of pain, utterly incapable of exertion. Smith had been tried and discarded in less than a single day. Davis, making the best decision of his career, unhesitatingly assigned the command of the army to Lee, who was so entirely in the shade at that time that the newspapers greeted his appointment with grumblings. They did not know what was on the knees of the gods.

CHAPTER SEVEN

BEGINNING OF THE INFERNAL WEEK KNOWN AS THE SEVEN DAYS' BATTLES

AT NOON OF June 1 McClellan sent a report of the battle of Seven Pines to Stanton, claiming a victory. "The enemy attacked in force and with great spirit yesterday morning, but are everywhere signally repulsed with great loss.... The result is that our left is now within 4 miles of Richmond. I only wait for the river to fall to cross with the rest of the force and make a general attack. Should I find them holding firm in a strong position I may wait for what troops I can bring up from Fort Monroe, but the *morale* of our troops is now such that I can venture much and do not fear for odds against me. The victory is complete."[1] Lincoln responded: "Thanks for what you *could* and *did* say in your dispatch of noon to-day.... If the enemy shall not have renewed the attack this afternoon, I think the hardest of your work is done." This was a good guess as to the immediate situation. The Confederates were in no condition to renew the attack.

In fact, at this time the Confederate army before Richmond was in bad case; if McDowell had come to McClellan instead of being dispersed, the situation would have been desperate. Johnston had had about 55,000 men, of whom a large number had been killed and wounded. If McDowell's 40,000 men had been added at this juncture to the Army of the Potomac, McClellan would have been three times as strong as the Confederates and would have, in all probability, taken Richmond, ending the war. As the Confederates had lost New Orleans, the fall of Richmond at this time might have been decisive.

[1] *O.R.*, Ser. I, Vol. XI, Pt. 1, p. 749.

BEGINNING OF THE SEVEN DAYS

In the crisis the Confederacy was saved by Lee's strategy and Jackson's extraordinary capacity. Lee devised the Valley Campaign; Jackson carried it out. Lee at last was in command of the Southern army and possessed the confidence of President Davis to a far greater degree than the secretive and petulant Johnston. He began bringing troops from the South in large numbers, until in the end he had concentrated a force of 60,000 men in front of Richmond. The days immediately following Seven Pines, or Fair Oaks, offered great opportunities to the Union if the government had realized it. But the authorities were tugging in different directions. While Lincoln sincerely desired McClellan's success and wished to aid him, Stanton hoped to be able to get rid of him before a decisive battle was fought. Stanton also desired success, but under a new commander.

For some days McClellan was embarrassed seriously by the divided condition of his army. He reported, on June 2, that the bridges and causeways over the Chickahominy had been washed away, "leaving us almost cut off from communication" with the White House, the base of supply.

Stanton, still immovably hostile, wired McClellan, on June 2, declaring his joy over the victory. Troops would be sent him from Fort Monroe, now under his jurisdiction. When Frémont and McDowell should have disposed of Jackson, another large body of troops would join him. He concluded, "All interest now centers in your operations, and full confidence is entertained of your brilliant and glorious success." McClellan read this with pleasure. Was it possible, after all, that Stanton was not his determined enemy?

Then came a caution from Lincoln not to let the Chickahominy cut his communications. McClellan replied that every effort was being made to complete his communications. There was no certainty about this, however, as the weather continued to be appalling. On June 4, McClellan reported, "Terrible rain storm during the night and morning. Chickahominy flooded, bridges in bad condition.... I have taken every possible step to insure the security of the corps on the right bank, but I cannot re-enforce them here until my bridges are all safe.... I have to be very cautious now." The mention of caution was a sour note for the administration. At the same time McClellan reported that his casualties in the late battle amounted to 7,000 and wished to know what reinforcements he might expect at Fort Monroe or the White House. "After the losses in our last battle I trust that I will no longer be regarded as an alarmist. I believe we have at least one more desperate battle to fight."

Stanton answered that he was sending five new regiments and that he would dispatch a part of McDowell's corps when it returned from the Shenandoah Valley.

Continued rain kept the Chickahominy raging and caused McClellan to remain inactive in front of the Confederates on the Williamsburg road. He reported, on June 7, that the river was so high that the bottoms were flooded to a depth of three or four feet and that the bridge builders were working in water up to the waist pushing the bridges to completion. "The whole face of the country is a perfect bog, entirely impassable for artillery, or even cavalry, except directly in the narrow roads." He declared that he would push forward the moment McCall reached him and the ground was dry enough to admit of the passage of artillery. There is a note here reminiscent of Waterloo, where Napoleon delayed because of the difficulty of getting up his guns through the mire. On June 10, it was raining again. Once more McClellan declared he would attack as soon as the weather and ground permitted. He suggested that troops be detached from Halleck's army in Mississippi to join him in the advance on Richmond. This sound suggestion was not considered by the authorities.

If McClellan had had better information he would probably have advanced in the week following Seven Pines, in spite of the terrible weather and the bottomless roads, for, after all, he was very near the Richmond defenses. His information, however, was incredibly bad and continued to be so—particularly as to the numbers of the Confederates. That army, now huddled in camps in or near Richmond, was in a favorable position to be viewed by the spies with which the Southern capital swarmed. But the spies, who were Pinkerton detectives, were not trained military observers; they confirmed McClellan's opinion that the Confederate army was vastly larger than it was. The reinforce-

BEGINNING OF THE SEVEN DAYS

ments pouring into Richmond made estimates difficult. At all events, McClellan was led to believe that the Southern government had concentrated at least 200,000 men at Richmond to oppose him.

It is a good rule in war, and in all other conflicts, to suppose that your adversary will do what he should do; the wish should never be father to the thought. Occasionally, however, the rule fails to work, and then the consequences will be strangely different from anticipation. McClellan thought the Southern government had done what it should have done and could have done, but did not do. It could have concentrated 200,000 men at Richmond by stripping all other points; and, if it had done so, Lee might, and probably would, have won a decisive victory. But Lee, while he did bring many troops to the capital, could not overcome Davis's habitual caution to the point of inducing him to make the gamble. The consequence was that Lee in front of Richmond was always inferior in numbers to McClellan, though not greatly so. The two armies were more evenly matched in June, 1862, than they ever were again.

Under the impression that he was vastly outnumbered, waiting for reinforcements that came slowly or did not come, McClellan continued inactive except for the work on the bridges, which was vigorously pushed. The "long season in May," a Virginia expression for spring rains and freshets, was still on. Rain fell nearly every day up to June 20, and the Chickahominy was continually in flood. McClellan was never free from the fear that he would wake up one morning to find his bridges washed out and his communications cut. The roads were so bad that Burnside, who visited McClellan, reported that he was four and a half hours in going nine miles.

Stanton replied to the request for troops from the West that he would refer it to Halleck, and that McCall would soon be at hand. He concluded, "Be assured, general, that there never has been a moment when my desire has been otherwise than to aid you with my whole heart, mind and strength, since the hour we first met; and whatever others may say for their own purposes, you have never had, and never can have, any one more truly your friend, or more anxious to support you, or more joyful than

I shall be at the success which I have no doubt will soon be achieved by your arms."

This may not have been entirely insincere. At that moment, June, 1862, when it was believed that McClellan had won a victory in front of Richmond and would probably be able to take the city, Stanton's grim dislike may have lessened somewhat. After all, he worshipped efficiency.

It is easy to see, too, that these days of comparative inactivity turned the government against McClellan. True, weather conditions were unspeakable, and weather conditions have a large part in war; but beyond doubt the authorities thought that McClellan played up the weather for all it was worth in order to avoid attacking Richmond. There is some truth in this suspicion. McClellan, in his mistaken impression that he was vastly outnumbered, was waiting for more troops to join him before advancing. And if he had known of Lee's quality, it would have been pardonable in him to hesitate, for Lee was shortly to reveal himself as one of the ablest and most audacious of modern commanders. But McClellan did not know this. He did know that the Confederates had suffered heavy losses at Seven Pines and might have deduced that they were in poor condition for another battle. An advance toward Richmond might have forced them to attack him again, and that would have been to his advantage. It was to his advantage to force an action before the Confederates could be fully reinforced. All this time, while McClellan was building bridges and waiting for recruits, the Confederates were working with furious energy to build up an army adequate to meet him on even terms. The worst period of his military career were these days between June 3 and June 20 when he made no move of importance—except one. That was the Change of Base.

Luck was still with McClellan, however. On June 12-13, McCall from McDowell's corps joined the army, giving it another good division. On June 13, Captain Royall, commanding two squadrons of the 5th United States Cavalry, near Old Church (in Hanover County, on the north side of the Chickahominy) was suddenly attacked by a column of gray and brown horsemen which came galloping through the woods. The Union riders were scattered, and the Confederates continued on their way eastward.

Sent out by Lee to reconnoiter the Union forces on the north side of the Chickahominy, this cavalry had one of the most romantic of experiences. Mounted on race horses not yet ruined by hard service and poor feed, headed by Stuart of the plumed hat and an immense Prussian on a gigantic steed, these boys rode joyously along the leafy lanes, singing and shouting. The iron of privation and defeat had not yet entered their souls.

Stuart was sent out on a reconnaissance, but he thought it would be great fun to ride all around the Union army and go back to Richmond triumphant. He did encircle the Army of the Potomac, crossing the swollen Chickahominy with difficulty but having no other trouble. He came, laughing, into Richmond, which greeted the feat with ribald merriment at McClellan's expense. The gray-brown riders had fired few shots and had done only a little damage, but they had created a sensation in the Union army. Messages went back and forth; cavalry attempted to intercept the bold raiders. Anger and recrimination.

It was a glittering deed, but it had an adverse effect on the fortunes of the Confederacy. McClellan, uneasy before over his communications, was impressed by the danger to them of a raid—a raid that might break the railroad from the White House to his army and thus cut his supply line. He began to make arrangements to change his base to the James River. The initial order was issued on June 17.

He was in a bad humor, too, over the failure of McDowell to be put definitely under him. On June 14, he reported, "The stampede of last night has passed away. Weather now very favorable. I hope two days more will make the ground practicable. I shall advance as soon as the bridges are completed and the ground fit for artillery to move." McDowell should be under him. As it was, McDowell expected to take back McCall at pleasure.... "General McDowell, and all other troops sent to me, should be placed completely at my disposal.... In no other way can they be of assistance to me. I therefore request that I may have entire and full control."

He was at last preparing to advance. He had moved his headquarters to the south side of the Chickahominy, "so that I can reach any point of attack or advance." Always ready for new ideas, he was using an observation balloon with considerable results, even in that wooded country. On June 18, he telegraphed the War Department that deserters reported a troop movement from Richmond to Jackson in the Valley. In another dispatch to Stanton he added, "Am at a loss to understand the reported re-enforcements to Jackson, unless the enemy are in great strength here." This was in answer to a wire from Lincoln, which said of the troops that had gone to Jackson, "it is as good as a re-enforcement to you of an equal force. I could better dispose of things if I could know about what day you can attack Richmond, and would be glad to be informed, if you think you can inform me with safety."[2] Lincoln again wired McClellan, "I do not see how re-enforcements from Richmond to Jackson could be in Gordonsville as reported by the Frenchmen and your deserters. Have not all been sent to deceive?"

This was a shrewd guess. Lee was again playing on the fears of Washington by ostensibly sending troops to Jackson, preparatory to bringing Jackson's whole command to Richmond for an attack on McClellan. Indeed, McClellan's days of grace were passing rapidly. Now, past the middle of June, it would be a desperate adventure to attack Richmond. Soon it would be impossible to attack with any chance of success. Lee's energy and his influence with the government in Richmond had entirely altered the situation.

On June 20, McClellan sent a dispatch to Lincoln that had great bearing on his later troubles. He said that Jackson had been reinforced from Richmond but that other troops had arrived. "There is not the slightest reason to suppose that the enemy intends evacuating Richmond; he is daily increasing his defenses. I find him everywhere in force, and every reconnaissance costs many lives, yet I am obliged to feel my way, foot by foot, at whatever cost, so great are the difficulties of the country; by tomorrow night the defensive works covering our position on this side of the Chickahominy, should be completed. I am forced to this by my inferiority in numbers.... I would be glad to have

---

[2] O.R., Ser. I, Vol. XI, Pt. 3, p. 233.

permission to lay before your excellency, by letter or telegraph, my views as to the present state of military affairs throughout the whole country." This dispatch brought forth the letter of July 7, memorable in its consequences.

Lee was now rapidly completing his arrangements to take the offensive. So far events had worked in his favor. At his order Jackson was coming to reinforce him while McDowell was still absent. He had decided to throw the mass of his army on Porter holding the north side of the Chickahominy and guarding McClellan's communications with the White House. He would have a good chance to crush Porter before McClellan could rescue him from the south side of the river.

Yet even before he began his advance, Lee's strategy had been frustrated. Stuart's raid, alarming McClellan for his dangerous line of communications, had determined him to change his base to the James River below Richmond, where gunboats could insure safety. He had begun to move stores and supplies from the White House, a process halted by the happenings of the following days.

McClellan was too acute to be greatly deceived by Lee's strategy. Already, on June 24, warnings were sent to Union commands of indications that the Confederates threatened to pass the Chickahominy at Meadow Bridge. They were planning to cross there and at other bridges.

Both commanders were preparing to advance: Lee to strike McClellan's right wing; McClellan to move south of the Chickahominy in readiness for regular siege advances against Richmond. Lee had settled on June 26 for the beginning of his movement. On June 25, McClellan pushed a force westward along the Williamsburg road. A sharp action followed in which the Unionists succeeded in advancing their picket line to King's Schoolhouse, quite close to the city.

The day before Lee moved, McClellan had penetrated his intentions. On June 25, he notified Burnside, in North Carolina, that Negroes and deserters reported Jackson as coming to Richmond. On the same day he informed Casey, at the White House, "It is said that Jackson is coming from Gordonsville with the intention of attacking our right flank soon; therefore be vigilant."[3] That night McClellan telegraphed Stanton that his information confirmed the impression that Jackson would soon attack his right and rear. "Every possible precaution is being taken. If I had another good division I could laugh at Jackson. ... Indications are of attack on our front to-morrow. Have made all possible preparations." This dispatch illustrates in a striking way McClellan's military intuition. The next day McClellan wired Stanton, "A contraband servant in the Twentieth Georgia came in this morning, and confirms in a remarkable manner the story of Jackson being on our flank and his intention of attacking our communications. ... There is no doubt in my mind now that Jackson is coming upon us, and with such great odds against us we shall have our hands full." Pinkerton, a man of imagination, had just boosted the Confederate forces in Richmond by 120,000; McClellan cannot be blamed for thinking that the odds were heavily against him. He wired Lincoln that the Confederates were 200,000 strong.

McClellan's complaints and pleas for reinforcements and his prophecies that he was about to be attacked by overpowering numbers annoyed Lincoln, who told him on June 26, "I give you all I can, and act on the presumption that you will do the best you can with what you have, while you continue, ungenerously, I think, to assume that I could give you more if I would." This statement was true from Lincoln's point of view but not from McClellan's. There were thousands of Union troops in northern and eastern Virginia, many of whom could have been sent to the Army of the Potomac without risk, but the President was still so obsessed by the picture of Jackson's descending on Washington that he thought it necessary to keep them from McClellan. Stanton was, of course, glad enough to prevent McClellan from being strengthened. The net result of Stanton's hostility and Lincoln's mistaken view of the situation was to place the Army of the Potomac, divided by a dangerous river, in a position of great peril. If Lee's tactics had been equal to his strategy, if the various parts of the untrained Southern army could have been brought to act in harmony, McClellan would have ended his career on the Chickahominy; and the Southern republic, in all

[3] *Ibid.*, p. 253.

probability, would have won its independence. Only the difficulty of securing unity of action in a wooded country and McClellan's own remarkable skill as a defensive general and master of logistics saved him. For this peril the government was mainly responsible. McClellan had every reason to call for heavy reinforcements, which were available if the government dropped its timid policy of keeping large bodies of troops near Washington. In leaving him exposed to attack before Richmond the government was guilty of an error that might well have lost the war. True, early in June McClellan could have advanced with considerable chances of success; but in the last days of the month the possibility of an offensive had been taken from him, and he was soon to be thrown on a desperate defensive.

Lee launched his attack on June 26. His plan was elaborate, and in the absence of anything resembling an adequate staff offered large chances of misadventure. Jackson was coming from Ashland, fifteen miles north of Richmond, to the right flank of Porter's position, which was on the north bank of the Chickahominy at the hamlet of Mechanicsville, six miles northeast of Richmond. Jackson sent Lee word that rain, falling heavily again, would delay him. He was due to reach his position in the morning of June 26, but his men toiled along narrow woods roads, deeply rutted, in the intense heat of a typical tidewater summer day, breaking through tree obstructions left by retiring Unionists and waiting while cavalry drove off squads of opposing horsemen. Jackson, with the advance, reached Polly Hundley's Corner, three miles from Mechanicsville, about 3:30 in the afternoon, and concluded that it would be impossible to continue his march for that day. His troops were stretched out for miles along the narrow roads; the rear probably did not come up until after dark. Lee's troops, grouped at the various bridges to cross from the south side of the Chickahominy, waited in vain to hear from Jackson.

One of the strangest contradictions of this singular war was the fact that Lee, when he launched his offensive on June 26, 1862, within less than ten miles of his capital, was almost entirely ignorant of the country in which the operations were to take place, while McClellan and his staff had an intimate acquaintance with it. This illustrates the difference in outlook between a man who had been with great armies and studied their methods and another soldier whose experience of war had been parochial. Lee, who had never seen a real army, did not appreciate the value of maps.

Lee indeed had a map, if a wretched scrawl in which nearly every location was wrong, and many points were omitted, may be called a map; McClellan made maps that are good even today, allowing for the changes effected by time. Yet Lee, in the multiplicity of his duties in organizing and equipping an army with little to go on, may be forgiven for neglecting a single item, even if that item was all-important.

Everything in the Confederate army was makeshift. The troops were half drilled and untrained (except Jackson's command), and they were clad in every style of uniform or none; some went into battle wearing frock coats and top hats, while others had nothing better than the rough clothing dished out to plantation slaves. Their food seems to have consisted of rancid bacon and flour, which was made into paste and toasted on ramrods. Their arms included flintlock muskets and fowling pieces. Their antiquated cannon were dragged by bony horses. Their wagon trains embraced every species of vehicle existing in the South.

Opposed to them was the army that McClellan had created and trained. It was well organized and drilled. It was neatly, if sometimes a little unusually uniformed—one New York regiment wore white straw hats—and its rations were generally good. The commissary, like everything else in McClellan's army, was efficiently administered. Its wagon train was large, with good draft animals. Its ordnance was the best to be obtained at that time. The army counted many excellent surgeons and had adequate medical supplies. If it was a somewhat raw army, it was a real army. The Confederates, opposing it, were rather a collection of commands than an army in a technical sense.

Still, in this early summer of 1862, the dice were less heavily loaded against the South than at any subsequent time. The actual numbers of the combatants were nearly equal; for if McClellan had a far larger total than Lee, some of his men were noncombatants, while others had been detailed for duty behind the lines. In the engagements of the Seven Days, Lee sometimes attacked with superior numbers, something that never happened again. Moreover, though the Union rank and file were better developed physically and better nourished than their opponents, they were not as inured to exposure and hardship as the primitive small farmers who filled the Southern ranks, accustomed as these were to outdoor life without comforts. Still more important was the superiority at this period of the Southern company officers. The Union company officers (except the few regulars) were drawn from the same classes as the privates. The Confederate army, on the other hand, was officered by young sportsmen, country gentlemen who passed their time in riding and hunting and were accustomed to command slaves—as good military material as the world afforded. It was these company officers who inspired Lee's army with desperate courage and made possible such success as he gained in the Seven Days. As the war went on most of them were killed or invalided, and then the opposing armies became much the same in quality. But in 1862 they were there—splendid, handsome, spirited young men who carried girls' pictures next their hearts and counted it a privilege to charge batteries. They were romanticists all.

Why was it that McClellan, with an army little larger than Lee's, was expected to walk into Richmond, over earthworks and in the face of batteries, thus ending the war at a blow? It seems absurd, and yet this was the case. The truth was that the Washington authorities underestimated the fighting qualities of the Confederates, now that the latter were far from Washington. Although the Union army had been routed in July, 1861, the authorities could see no reason why McClellan, with the troops he had, did not win a decisive victory. The soldiers at the front had a very different opinion of the Confederate infantry, dirty, ragged and half-starved as it was. They knew well the valor, endurance and marksmanship of the tattered legionnaires. Indeed, at the end of June, 1862, McClellan could not reasonably have been expected to defeat the Confederate army and take Richmond with the force at his disposal. He needed, at the least, 50,000 more men, and the government would not give them to him. It left him high and dry, with his army divided by a treacherous river, expecting him to perform something in the nature of a military miracle. This was due to the enmity of Stanton and to Lincoln's failure to understand the situation.

The terrible problem that faced Lee on this hot June day was to overthrow with his armed mob, just beginning to be an army, the well-drilled and well-equipped, if new, Union army. And he was groping in the dark. At that time neither side made regular reconnaissances with patrols. All that Lee knew of his opponents was that the right wing, north of the river, was smaller than the left wing south of the stream. In a vague way he knew of Beaver Dam Creek near Mechanicsville and of Powhite Creek, some miles beyond it. He did not know of the existence of Boatswain Swamp, destined to be the scene of his first great battle. He was dependent for information on his cavalry, and the cavalry had limitations.

Lee stood on the high hill where the Mechanicsville turnpike from Richmond turns downward to the Chickahominy bottom. In that wooded country his field glasses revealed little. He could see a balloon aloft on the other side of the river, a few horsemen at Mechanicsville, and the blue ascending smoke of enemy campfires.

Still an amateur, if an amateur of genius, Lee had evolved a complicated tactical arrangement, one demanding a trained staff. Standing on the hill, he waited to hear from Jackson, whose part it was to come up in Porter's rear and cut the Union communications with the White House. When Jackson drew near, four commands were to cross the Chickahominy at various bridges and advance, catching in the widespread net the Union troops on the north side.

Porter, a most capable soldier, knowing that he was about to be attacked, had taken up his position on the ridge east of Beaver Dam Creek, which bends around Mechanicsville and runs into the Chickahominy a mile or so south of the hamlet. He had thrown up earthworks to protect his line, but, as a matter of fact, his position, while strong against a frontal assault, had its right flank in the air, quite open to attack. When Jackson came up behind him, he would have to withdraw.

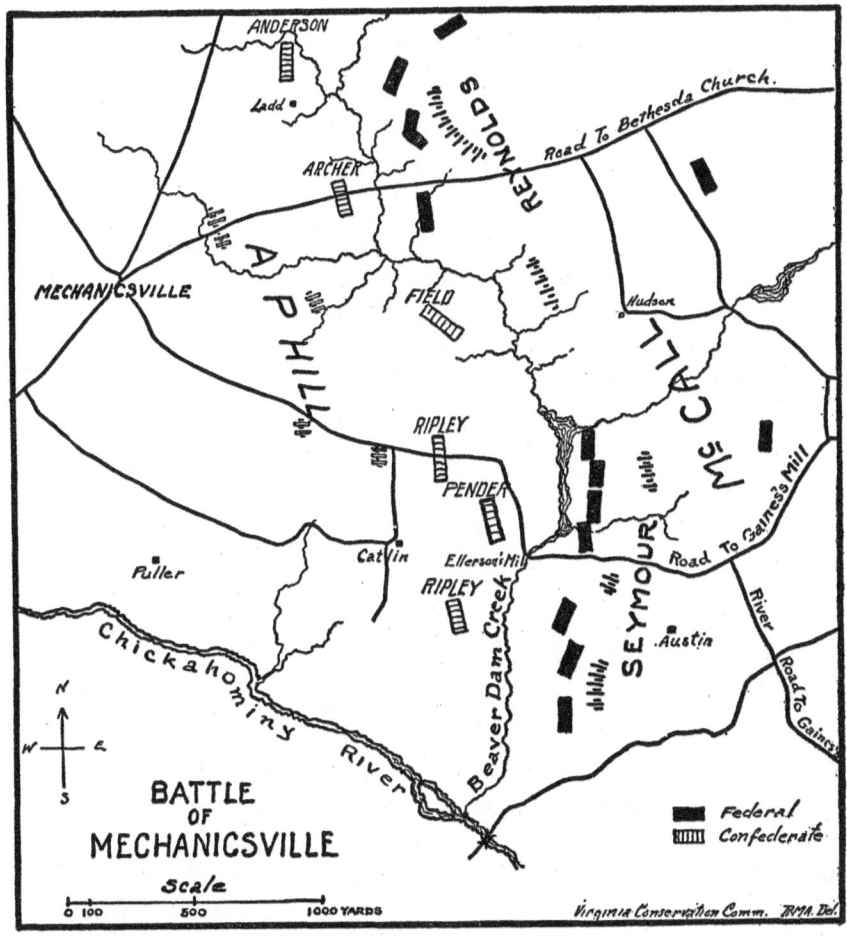

But Jackson had not come up, and the June day was passing into afternoon. A. P. Hill crossed the river and came down the north bank to Mechanicsville. A Union picket in the village was brushed aside. The Confederates, unused to war, imagined they had gained an advantage. What they did was to uncover a strong position. It was then that Lee, having discovered Porter's position, sent Hill an order not to advance. Hill did not get the order or ignored it; he seems to have feared to delay.

Porter was well prepared. Early in the afternoon of June 26, McClellan, on hearing from him that Jackson was in contact with his advance posts, went over to Beaver Dam Creek and remained there until 10:00 P.M., supervising arrangements and watching the action that presently followed.

The troop positions were: Martindale of Morell's division was on the right; Reynolds was on the left of Martindale and Seymour on the left of Reynolds; Meade and Sykes were in reserve.

In the morning of June 26, Meade was brought up to support Reynolds. All the morning Porter was receiving news from his advance troops of Jackson's movements; his cavalry, with infantry detachments, was in constant contact. About 3:30 word came that the outpost at Meadow Bridge, upstream, had been driven back and part of it captured.

Shortly afterward the pickets in Mechanicsville reported that columns were advancing along the road leading south from Meadow Bridge. Presently shots were fired in Mechanicsville itself, and gray-brown figures were seen there through the smoke. The outpost in the hamlet fell back hurriedly to the position behind Beaver Dam Creek. The Confederates were deploying in fanshape formation on the flat terrace to the south of the village.

Hill, determined to attack, spent little time in reconnaissance. His men, advancing from Mechanicsville to the creek, came under a terrible fire of artillery and infantry and were driven back with loss. But the officers who led them were the bravest of the brave, and the gray-brown line went ahead again in the face of a storm of canister and bullets. The ground was strewn with their dead and wounded. At length the Confederates fell back to cover, all except one regiment, which crossed the creek and established itself on the east bank. All in all, the attack here was a complete failure.

Lee had not wished to make an assault on a strong position, but he was committed and could not well withdraw. He now took charge himself. To outflank the Unionists he sent brigades from D. H. Hill's division to turn the Union left near Ellerson's Mill. As the Union line extended nearly to the river, this attempt was foredoomed to failure. The Confederates, rushing downhill to the stream (there a millrace), faced a hail of lead, and recoiled. Again and again they were rallied and brought forward against the Union line at Ellerson's Mill, protected not only by

BEGINNING OF THE SEVEN DAYS

artillery and infantry behind log breastworks but by a waist-deep stream. Led by their reckless officers, the unfortunate Southerners displayed the most heroic gallantry and did not give up the hopeless effort until nearly nightfall. Then they fell back toward Mechanicsville, leaving hundreds of their fellows on the slope and in the mill bottom.

McClellan was with Porter all through the engagement. He was not a little elated at the result. The Confederates, with faulty generalship due to their lack of reconnaissance of the ground, had attempted to storm a very strong position and had lost about 2,000 men killed or wounded, while the Union loss was trifling. Lee's first battle had ended in bloody failure.

When the shots died away and there was silence except for the cries of the wounded, McClellan and Porter discussed the situation. Knowing that Jackson was at hand and that McDowell would not come, the Union commander decided not to attempt to hold the position on Beaver Dam Creek. He even doubted that he could maintain himself on the north bank of the river, though he hoped to do so. He was preparing to abandon the north side and transfer Porter to the south side, a movement that had become practicable now that his change of base was nearly effected. What weighed most with him was the peril of his divided army and his obsession of Lee's superior numbers. If it had not been for the latter delusion, he might have elected to strengthen his right wing and fight it out at that end of the line. A third course was open to him in the night of June 26, though a risky one. He could have withdrawn his right wing to the south side of the river and then have attacked the Confederate defenses with his whole army while Lee was still on the north bank of the Chickahominy. Lee had foreseen this possibility but had to take the risk.

Probably McClellan made his wisest choice when he decided to fight at a new and stronger position on the north side of the river. His only mistake was in not holding the new position in sufficient force. This was on a hill behind Boatswain Swamp, four miles down the river from Beaver Dam Creek.

McClellan left Porter without deciding how long he would hold on at Beaver Dam. But at 3:00 A.M. Porter received orders to abandon it and fall back to Boatswain Swamp. He obeyed this order in the early hours of June 27, leaving a rear guard. When the Confederate pickets, creeping forward in the morning, came close to the Union position they found it deserted except for a small force that withdrew when fired on.

CHAPTER EIGHT

GAINES'S MILL
June 27

The Unionist rear guard fell back slowly along the road running eastward. The men were confident, buoyed up by their easy victory of the day before. A. P. Hill's troops followed the retiring bluecoats; Lee was a little way behind them. A mile and a half from the position on Beaver Dam Creek, Lee came to Walnut Grove Church, where he found no less a person than Stonewall Jackson awaiting him. Jackson, who had been ordered by Lee to "turn" Beaver Dam Creek and take the direction of Cold Harbor, had been brought to the south of Gaines's Millpond by incompetent guidance, possibly by one of Lee's staff officers. As a result, D. H. Hill's command, coming from Mechanicsville, was athwart Jackson's column, which should have been to the north.

The two generals, whose partnership was to become so noted, had here their first meeting in the field. Lee's staff officers craned their necks to get a glimpse of the soldier whose Valley Campaign was already famous. They saw a heavily bearded young officer (most Confederate generals sprouted enormous beards), shabbily uniformed and wearing an old fatigue cap, certainly no impressive figure. Lee, then as always, was immaculate in dress and striking in appearance.

Nothing is known of this conference. Jackson was, no doubt, grim and taciturn as ever. Probably he had no excuses to offer for not being able to come up the day before; he was not given to apologies. Lee was probably nervous, though almost certainly he did not show it, possessing wonderful self-control.

He set Jackson right about his route (around Gaines's Millpond and toward Cold Harbor), and then the two men must have discussed the situation at some length. Mechanicsville had been Lee's first battle, and it had been sadly mismanaged. Infantry had been sent to charge infantry that was under cover and protected by rows of guns. The losses had been heavy, the gain nothing. Beyond doubt the commander was eager to retrieve the errors of the day before and destroy Porter; he was still seeking to cut the Union communications, having no inkling of the change of base under way. His stout heart had been discouraged by the reverse of Mechanicsville; it made him all the more determined to do better the next time.

Jackson now went off on his march around Gaines's Millpond and A. P. Hill pressed forward along the road taken by the retreating Unionists. The Confederates were so ignorant of the Union dispositions that Lee had expected to find Porter in position on Powhite Creek, the stream flowing out of Gaines's Millpond, two miles east of Walnut Grove Church.

Hill's men constantly skirmished with the Union rear guard, which was engaged in retarding the pursuit while Porter was completing his preparations at his new position. When the Confederates neared Gaines's Mill, on Powhite Creek, they came under artillery fire from across the stream but found no frowning breastworks confronting them. Lee and his officers now learned that the Union position was not where they had expected to see it; they were indeed engaged in a bewildering game of hide and seek.

The Union rear guard, giving way slowly before Hill's eager men, continued to retire eastward along the sandy road. The Confederates, following a mile farther, discovered another stream, not on Lee's map—Boatswain Swamp. Coming to a steep hillside, the graybacks looked across a little valley and saw the opposite hillside swarming with men behind felled trees and bristling guns. Here, then, was the new Union position, even more formidable than Beaver Dam Creek.

The place selected by the skilled engineer, Barnard, for Porter's stand was on the hill behind the circling Boatswain Swamp, forming an arc from east to west. The stream itself was small, but its bottom was marshy and covered with dense thickets through which assailants would have to force their way. The trees on the hilltop had been cut down, giving the bluecoats a good field of fire. All in all, it was the best defensive position in this whole area. Its one defect in that sphere was that the right wing was "in the air," since it would be possible to work around that end and take the position in rear; but the Confederates did not discover this fact until too late. The left wing rested on the Chickahominy and was safe. The position was about two miles in length and a mile and a half in depth, an open plateau. It was perhaps too strong for a counterattack to be made from it, its only offensive defect.

Porter had at first about 25,000 men. Sykes and the regulars held the right, Morell the left, McCall was in reserve. Porter's headquarters were at the Watt house, near the center of his line. This house still stands, little altered from its appearance in 1862. Indeed, the battlefield of Gaines's Mill is perhaps the best-preserved in America.

Lee's plan, hastily formed of course, seems to have been to attack Porter in front and drive him into the arms of Jackson and D. H. Hill, who were off to the northeast confronting the Union right. It was a good plan if Porter had to retreat eastward to the White House instead of southward across the river, but it meant another frontal assault on a strong position, a repetition of Mechanicsville.

A. P. Hill did not halt to reconnoiter. His men, plunging down the hill on the west side of Boatswain Swamp, came under a furious fire from the Unionists on the opposite slope. Courageously, even rashly, the Southerners dashed through the bog and attempted to breast the hill beyond, but so terrible was the fire that poured from the crest that brigades crumbled away until the swamp and the slope were covered with the dead and wounded. Hill fell back after his repeated charges had failed, continuing the fight at a distance.

It was Longstreet's turn to attack. His command was on Hill's right and near the Chickahominy. His men charged with equal bravery but with no better luck. They could not face the hail of bullets and canister poured into them at close range. Meanwhile Jackson and D. H. Hill, waiting to the northeast for Porter to be driven across their front, had not entered the action.

The situation was critical. The afternoon was waning and so far no impression had been made on Porter's position. Every moment it looked more and more like another Mechanicsville. The anxious Lee, however, knew that he could not afford a second repulse. If he could not dislodge Porter, night would see the Confederates falling back toward the Richmond defenses, defeated and disheartened, his fine strategy a failure. Thus far the Union right wing was successfully holding out; and McClellan, at his headquarters at the Trent house, just south of Grapevine Bridge, troubled as he was by the reports of desperate fighting, was not dismayed. Thus far everything had played into his hands, even if McDowell had not been sent to him.

Porter was holding out but he had felt the weight of Longstreet's attack. McCall was moved up to the firing line and couriers rode across Grapevine Bridge carrying requests for reinforcements. Slocum's division of Franklin's corps was sent over the river, only to be recalled. However, when Porter repeated his appeal for aid, Slocum was sent back across the Chickahominy. Porter had taken up his station at the Watt house at 2:00 P.M. At four o'clock his line still held firmly, and his confidence increased.

Lee felt that something decisive had to be done. He sent into the still raging battle Whiting's division, which included a notable Texas brigade under John B. Hood, destined to fame. The few Confederate batteries that had been brought up had been disabled by the superior Union ordnance and stood silent, surrounded by dead gunners and horses. Thus everything had to be done by infantry alone. But Lee had at last succeeded in getting a coördinated attack. As Whiting's men charged the center of the Union line near the Watt house, Jackson and D. H. Hill to the northeast joined in the assault. All along the line from east to west the gray and brown men surged uphill against the defenders. Up the slope they came, seen through the smoke clouds like wraiths, their fierce eyes gleaming, their cries rending the air.

Whiting had given his men orders not to fire but to speed at double quick through the bog and up the hill. The Confederates, conspicuous among them the gallant Texans, floundered over the marsh and the bodies of their dead comrades and through the dense bushes and felled trees, breasting the slope under such a fire as had never been known before on an American battlefield. The Unionists, not waiting to come to grips with these desperate men, broke when the clambering graybacks came close, and sought safety in flight. In a moment the Southerners were among the guns on the crest and the battle was practically won. Whiting's charge, which could not have taken more than a few minutes, cost a thousand men, killed and wounded.

At this moment, in the late afternoon, with the Confederates on the plateau, Porter was in dire need of reinforcements, which came in insufficient numbers. To his repeated calls for aid, McClellan responded, sending French's and Meagher's brigades across the river about 6:30, the time when Porter's line was broken. These troops arrived too late to save the day but rendered invaluable service in covering the retreat.

Why were not more troops sent to Porter, and why not earlier? Here, it would seem, McClellan lost an opportunity of winning a victory by failing to take a risk. It was only late in the afternoon, and after desperate efforts and immense losses, that Lee was able to break the line and gain a victory; he came perilously close to defeat.

It would appear that Magruder, south of the Chickahominy, had much to do with saving the day. This prince of military play-actors had been making an imposing display of force all the afternoon. Not satisfied with feinting, and against his orders, two Alabama regiments actually emerged from the defenses and launched an attack on the Union line that is known as the action of Golding's Farm. They were easily repulsed, but they gave the impression that Magruder was about to assume the offensive. Before this McClellan had asked his corps commanders if they could spare men to aid Porter, and they had replied that they could not. Now, more than ever, the Union commanders south of the river stood on the defensive, leaving Porter to his fate. If McClellan had taken matters in his own hands, despite the generals, and sent reinforcements in time, he might have won a victory at Gaines's Mill and thrown Lee in disorder back on the Richmond defenses. Instead, this day was the decisive one in Lee's career. He won at Gaines's Mill, not because of superior generalship but because of superior nerve; taking every risk, he opposed unlimited audacity to the caution of McClellan and his subordinates.

As evening came on, the Unionists gave way all along the line. Union cavalry, after a repulse, riding recklessly back into the ranks, confused them and caused the loss of guns. Still at places the bluecoats resisted furiously. Only with great reluctance did Sykes's regulars, on the right, give ground; they considered it a disgrace for regulars to retire before volunteers. Gloriously they upheld the reputation of the United States army, this June 27, 1862.

At last, the Confederates, converging on the crest at the Watt house from every quarter, planted their red flags in triumph and made the woods resound with their shouts. Twenty-two guns fell into their hands and a number of prisoners. They had lost 8,000 men but they had won a victory, if a costly one. Costly it was beyond all precedent; the best men of the South, the beautiful boys from the plantations, the foxhunters and sportsmen who had led the most determined assaults ever made in America lay dead or wounded by hundreds. Only through their desperate courage and unflinching self-sacrifice had victory been possible.

Porter now fell back in the growing darkness to the vicinity of Grapevine Bridge, that bridge of five sections reached by a half-mile causeway through the swamp. The Confederates were too shattered and disorganized to pursue effectively. Porter had lost heavily himself but he was safe.

McClellan had followed the course of the engagement with mounting anxiety as confidence gave way before the unremitting assaults of the Confederates and the casualties grew beyond anything in his previous experience. He had been disappointed that his corps commanders had not seen fit to detach troops for Porter's aid, though he believed, as they did, that the Confederates on the south side of the Chickahominy were in superior force instead of being, as they were, far inferior. It was a clear case of the gods smiling on audacity. Lee had attacked north of

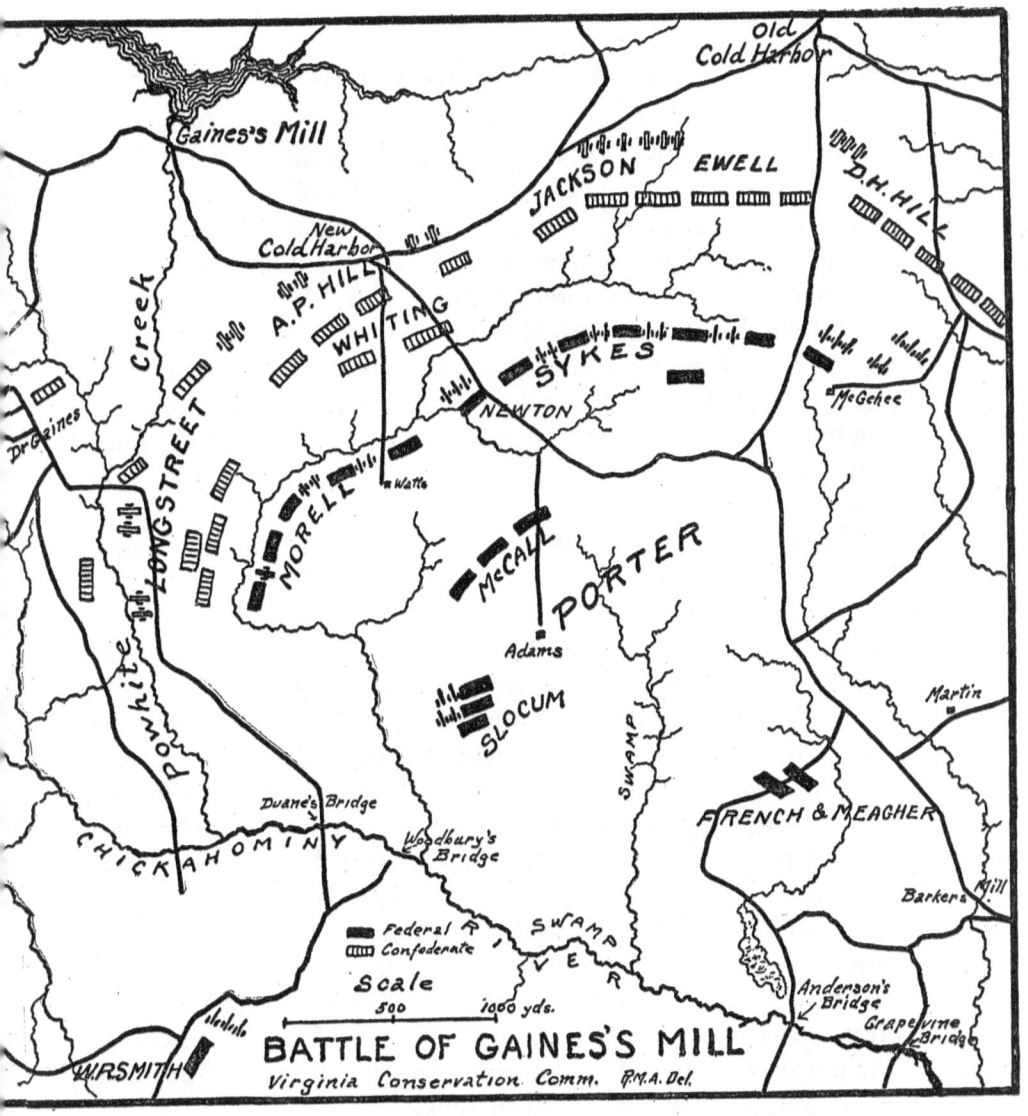

BATTLE OF GAINES'S MILL
Virginia Conservation Comm. R.M.A. Del.

the river with 55,000 of his 80,000 men, leaving only 25,000 to hold the Richmond defenses. McClellan had defended the north-bank position with 35,000 of his 90,000 men, keeping 55,000 comparatively idle on the south side.

McClellan has been somewhat unfairly criticized for not attacking Richmond while the battle of Gaines's Mill was going on. This could have been done only at great risk, since the Confederate defenses, even at that early period, were comparatively formidable. What he should have done, but did not do, was to send Porter 10,000 more men before the position on Boatswain Swamp was stormed; 10,000 more men would probably have spelled the difference between victory and defeat.

McClellan remained south of the river, at the Trent house, in constant contact with Porter all through the battle. No doubt he would have been on the battlefield itself if he had not feared a Confederate attack south of the river and considered it necessary to be at the center of his line. After nightfall he summoned Porter to a conference at headquarters, attended by all the corps commanders. The general listened to the reports and then announced his purpose of withdrawing Porter to the south side and completing his change of base to the James River, an operation that had begun some days before. Under the circumstances, cut off as he was from the White House, he could not have acted otherwise.

Porter was not dismayed by his defeat, regarded by himself as a rear-guard action. But McClellan was shaken by the reckless gallantry and grim determination shown by the Confederates—a determination that had stopped at no sacrifice. He was in a bitter mood, too, with the government, which had forced him to divide his army by a dangerous stream and then had failed to send him the needed support. Moreover, he was chagrined that Porter had been unable to hold off Lee's attacks. McClellan seems to have expected that the Confederates would meet the same fate at Boatswain Swamp that had attended them at Mechanicsville. But at the latter place Lee had attacked with only a part of his force, while in the battle of Gaines's Mill he had put in all he had. Thus he had succeeded in taking a position even stronger than that at Mechanicsville.

McClellan had every reason to be worried. He was in a false position and he knew it. He could not retain his old base at the White House without crossing the Chickahominy and fighting a desperate battle for it. But the base had lost all value, now that McDowell was not coming to him; it was no longer necessary to hold out a hand to McDowell, off to the north. The alternative was a march across the Confederate front to the James River, since a new base had to be established before McClellan could proceed against Richmond again. He had been preparing for the change, but he expected to evacuate the old base at his leisure, not to be driven from it. Still there was no occasion for despair. His army was intact and had given a good account of itself. The Confederate losses had been far heavier than his own; consequently, the odds in his favor were that much increased.

McClellan, however, was too much upset in the evening of June 27, too unstrung by the battle and its casualties to reason clearly. If he had been himself he would never have written the letter to Stanton he penned at midnight while still under a great emotional strain.

"Headquarters Army of the Potomac
Savage Station, June 28, 1862—12:20 a. m.

"I now know the full history of the day. On this side of the river (the right bank) we repulsed several strong attacks. On the left bank our men did all that men could do, all that soldiers could accomplish, but they were overwhelmed by vastly superior numbers, even after I brought my last reserves into action. The loss on both sides is terrible. I believe it will prove to be the most desperate battle of the war.

"The sad remnants of my men behave as men. Those battalions who fought most bravely and suffered most are still in the best order. My regulars were superb, and I count upon what are left to turn another battle, in company with their gallant comrades of the volunteers. Had I 20,000 or even 10,000 fresh troops to use to-morrow I could take Richmond, but I have not a man in reserve and shall be glad to cover my retreat and save the material and *personnel* of the army.

"If we have lost the day we have yet preserved our honor, and no one need blush for the Army of the Potomac. I have lost this battle because my force was too small.

"I again repeat that I am not responsible for this, and I say it with the earnestness of a general who feels in his heart the loss of every brave man who has been needlessly sacrificed to-day. I still hope to retrieve our fortunes, but to do this the Government must view the matter in the same earnest light that I do. You must send me very large reenforcements and send them at once. I shall draw back to this side of Chickahominy, and think I can withdraw all our material. Please understand that in this battle we have lost nothing but men, and those the best we have.

"In addition to what I have already said, I only wish to say to the President that I think he is wrong in regarding me as ungenerous when I said that my force was too weak. I merely intimated a truth which to-day has been too plainly proved. If, at this instant, I could dispose of 10,000 fresh men, I could gain a victory to-morrow. I know that a few thousand more men would have changed this battle from a defeat to a victory. As it is, the Government must not and cannot hold me responsible for the result.

"I feel too earnestly to-night. I have seen too many dead and wounded comrades to feel otherwise than that the Government has not sustained this army. If you do not do so now the game is lost.

"If I save the army now, I tell you plainly that I owe no thanks to you or any other persons in Washington.

"You have done your best to sacrifice this army.
"Geo. B. McClellan.
"Hon. E. M. Stanton."

May the gods preserve us from candor! This mad epistle was the beginning of the downfall of McClellan. He wrote it without any thought of the consequences. He wrote it with a heart torn by an agony of grief over the dead and wounded, honorable to his humanity, to the sympathy and compassion so prominent in his nature; but a commanding general has no business with humanity and compassion; these things belong to surgeons and chaplains. He was insane enough to pour out his tortured soul to the cold-blooded, unhuman Stanton, who valued nothing but efficiency.

McClellan had ability, courage, a nature singularly noble and high-minded (all in all, he was one of the noblest figures in American history), but he did not alas! have the lion's heart. In the night before, the night of June 26-27, after Mechanicsville, it had been Lee's turn to agonize in the hours following a humiliating defeat—a far worse defeat than McClellan's—but Lee's proud nature had not known despair or dreamed of retreat. He had spent the night in planning for another attack on the morrow, and he had retrieved disaster by brilliant victory.

McClellan had done what no general can afford to do: he had frankly acknowledged defeat. "I have lost this battle," he wrote. He should have made no such damaging admission; he should have written that a part of his army had fought a delaying action and had withdrawn in good order to the south side of the river as a part of the change of base. Above all, he should never have attempted to saddle the government with the responsibility, writing such words as, "You have done your best to sacrifice this

GAINES'S MILL

army." Is there any wonder that Stanton, disliking him before, became his implacable enemy?

It did not help the case that nearly everything that McClellan wrote was true. He had been imperilled by his government, which, in its anxiety for Washington, had left him with insufficient force to take Richmond. No Union commander produced by the war could have beaten Lee on Lee's own ground with an army of approximately the same size; no Union commander could have taken Richmond without a siege; Grant took it only after a siege of nine months and after Lee's army had dwindled to half its strength.

McClellan had been left in a perilous position, a position in which nearly any other Union commander would have lost his army, while 60,000 Union troops were doing nothing in northern Virginia. In an emergency McClellan was at his best, and here was a grave emergency.

CHAPTER NINE

GLENDALE

June 30

McClellan, on the morning of June 28, had a problem to solve. He had to take his great army, with thousands of wagons and hundreds of guns, across the front of the Confederate army to the James River and a new base, by narrow, muddy roads along which progress could only be slow and uncertain. It was a problem that would have tested the mettle of any general on earth; most of them would have failed. Not only were the Confederates flushed by their victory at Gaines's Mill but they were led by a combination of commanders in Lee and Jackson that has no counterpart in American history and few parallels in any history.

McClellan, however, was ideally equipped for such a task. When it came to logistics he was in a class by himself; no other American soldier has ever approached him in a field in which the Germans in modern times have been supreme. His talent for organization was remarkable. In spite of the wretched roads (which were merely trails) and a dangerous swamp, McClellan succeeded in the next few days in conveying his five thousand wagons and ambulances and all his artillery to his new base, frustrating all attempts to intercept him and inflicting a severe defeat on his opponents at Malvern Hill. No other general then in the Union service could have done this. In the whole war there was no greater feat. Grant indeed in the end defeated Lee, but only after Lee's army had disintegrated to such an extent that it was eventually outnumbered three to one.

McClellan made his arrangements with exactitude. At the

conference at the Trent house, June 27-28, he furnished each corps commander with a map showing the positions to be held until the army moved toward the James River. Directions were in detail.

In the night and early morning of June 28, Porter's command crossed the Chickahominy, destroying Grapevine Bridge and its causeway behind them. Morell led, followed by Sykes and McCall. The troops south of the river moved ahead, leaving a large rear guard to ward off pursuit; thus McClellan's elaborate earthworks were deserted after all the labor expended on them. They would have been invaluable if he had been able to hold the north side of the Chickahominy.

Keyes was ordered to move in advance and cross White Oak Swamp in order to cover the passage of the stream by the rest of the army. Before daylight on June 28, McClellan himself left the Trent house for his new headquarters at Savage's Station, where he could direct the movements of his army. Porter was withdrawn from guarding the bridge crossings of the Chickahominy late in the afternoon of June 28, following Keyes and taking up a position to guard the roads leading to Richmond at a point named Glendale. McCall's division, in the night of June 28, crossed White Oak Swamp to protect the moving trains. In the evening of June 28-29, Sumner's and Heintzelman's corps fell back to the vicinity of Savage's Station on the Richmond-York River railroad, where the field hospitals had been established. These troops were ordered to hold this position until the night of June 29 and then cross White Oak Swamp in the wake of the preceding column.

Lee spent the day of June 28 in attempting to determine the direction his opponents had taken. Still an amateur, though learning fast, he did not know whether McClellan would double back to his old base at the White House or move over to the James River. Stuart of the plumed hat rode off to the White House, to learn that the Union supply depots were in flames and the base totally abandoned. Dashing along the roads with his gentlemen jockeys, he enjoyed himself hugely, firing on Union gunboats in the Pamunkey, but not accomplishing much of importance.

Lee, amateur though he was, was acute, and by the late afternoon of June 28 he knew that McClellan was making for the James River and the protection of the gunboats, not recrossing the Chickahominy or retreating down the Peninsula to Hampton. He at once arranged the pursuit. Unfortunately, he attempted evolutions that would have been difficult for a trained army, let alone a volunteer army of no long existence. He proposed to spread out his troops on the roads leading from Richmond to the James River below the city, the direction in which McClellan was moving. A. P. Hill and Longstreet were sent on a wide turning movement; Jackson, Magruder, and Huger were to follow on the heels of the retiring Unionists and attempt to hold them until the other commands could hit them in the flank.

Jackson was to cross the Chickahominy at Grapevine Bridge, just destroyed by the Unionists. He was then to unite with Magruder and Huger, on the south side, in an attack on the Union rear guard. These troops would follow the roads nearest the Chickahominy while A. P. Hill and Longstreet were curving off toward the James.

In this plan it was not taken into consideration that Grapevine Bridge had been destroyed and would have to be replaced before Jackson could cross. His trained engineering corps, toiling rapidly, completed their work in time for Jackson to cross on June 29 but not in time for him to join Magruder and Huger in the projected movement. Huger was sent down the Charles City road, which was greatly impeded. Magruder waited in vain for both Jackson and Huger. Then, realizing that the prey was escaping, he advanced on the Union position at Savage's Station.

In the forenoon of this day (June 29) he had attacked the retiring Unionists at Allen's Farm, not far from Fair Oaks, and had been driven off by a part of Franklin's corps. Continuing down the Williamsburg road, he came to the vicinity of Savage's Station in the late afternoon of June 29.

A singular scene met his gaze. Here was a wide open space in that forest country. In hospital tents, around the houses and outhouses of a large plantation 2,500 of the sick and wounded of McClellan's army were receiving care. Supplies were burning at the station. On the railroad a train of cars carrying stores

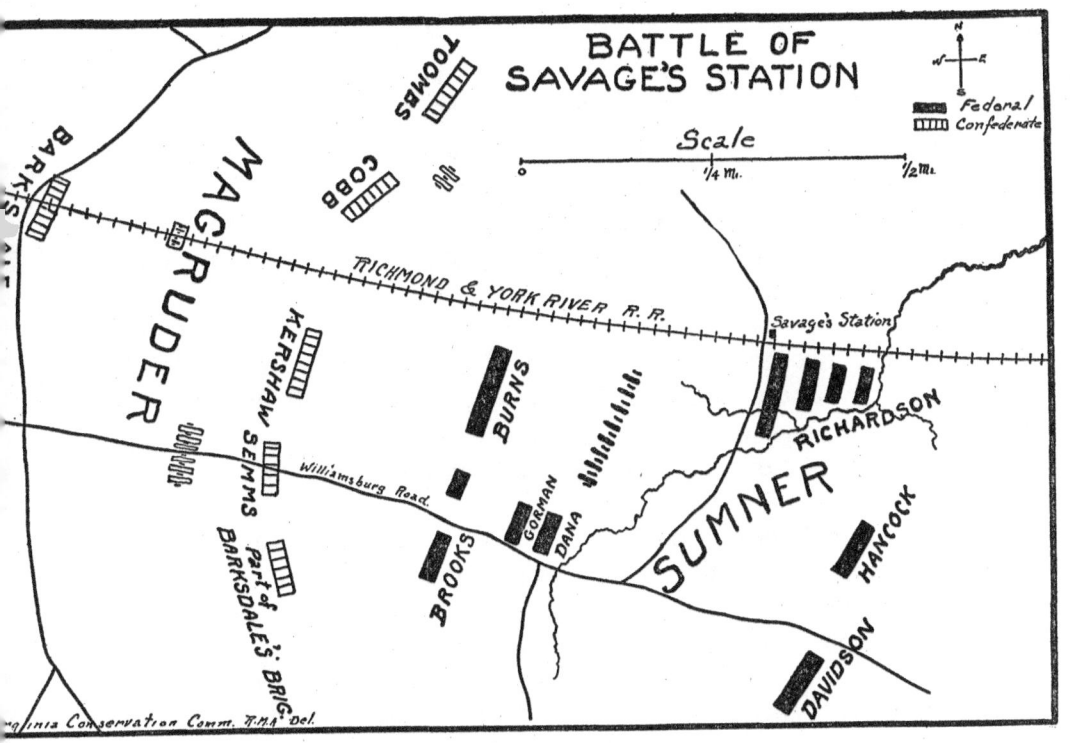

careered along in flames and finally plunged hissing into the river at a ruined bridge. In the space about the plantation houses and in the adjacent meadows 50,000 men of McClellan's were crowded, not only a rear guard but actually the major portion of the army. Sumner's corps held the line between the railroad and the Williamsburg road, Burns's brigade in advance. Richardson's division was to the right. Three batteries were on the left. The day was oppressive, the soldiers worn and hungry.

The wagon trains had gone on ahead and were crossing the dangerous White Oak Swamp, which lay between Savage's Station and the James River. Heintzelman, finding his men packed in like sardines at the station, pulled out in the afternoon of June 29, taking the road to White Oak Swamp. Magruder, drawing near the place, realized that Lee had assigned him a terrible task in view of the absence of both Jackson and Huger. Jackson was still pegging away at the bridge, and Huger was somewhere south of the Williamsburg road, not knowing exactly what was expected of him in the way of coöperation.

The afternoon of a hot day was advancing when, about four o'clock, Franklin and Sedgwick rode over to the hospital at

Savage's Station to inquire for friends. From the hospital they started off to call on Heintzelman, supposed to be still in the position he had occupied in the morning. As the two generals rode across the open fields, they saw troops emerging from a wood to the north of the railroad.

Sedgwick, stopping, exclaimed, "Why, those men are rebels." The two generals then galloped back toward the main Union body under fire from a Confederate battery. The signal men announced the approach of a body of infantry and a car on the railroad carrying a cannon. It is believed that this was the first railroad battery.

Franklin sought Sumner, senior in command, whom he found sleeping. Sumner, awakening, sent two regiments of Burns's brigade to attack the graybacks, who were beginning to appear in the woods near the Williamsburg road. Burns extended his line to the railroad. Confederate batteries opened on him but were silenced by the heavier Union guns. Confederates, charging madly, broke Burns's line. Sumner, placing himself at the head of the two regiments, moved to the support of Burns's endangered command. The Confederates fell back. On the left Brooks's brigade of Smith's division moved forward against a Confederate force south of the Williamsburg road. Here, after a hot fight, the Southerners also retired. About a thousand men were killed and wounded on both sides.

What had happened was that Magruder, instead of confronting a rear guard, found himself in the immediate presence of a large part of the Union army. He could not hope to hold such a force for any length of time with his small command and wisely withdrew before he was annihilated. If Jackson and Huger had been with him, the situation would have been very different, but he had only his own brigades to depend on. It seems, however, that Lee did not understand what happened and blamed Magruder for not accomplishing the impossible. Sumner was so elated by this success that he wished to remain at Savage's Station and was only persuaded with reluctance to carry out McClellan's orders.

McClellan spent the day of June 29 in making a personal examination of Charles City Crossroads (Glendale) and Malvern

Hill. Glendale was a point where his army would be exposed to attack from the direction of Richmond, and Malvern Hill, an eminence not far from the James, was essential to the safety of his army. He realized that he was of more use directing movements than on the battlefield itself. In this he anticipated the duties of modern commanders, who are seldom anywhere near the scene of actual fighting. McClellan's function after Gaines's Mill (admirably performed) was to arrange for the movement of troops and trains and select positions for defense.

Keyes was directed to move in the night of June 29-30 to Malvern Hill and take position on the left. Porter was to follow and extend the position to the right (east). The wagon trains were to be pushed ahead behind these troops to the protection of the gunboats. One by one the commands crossed White Oak Swamp.

A sharp cavalry brush on the Quaker road near Willis Church (not far from Glendale) showed that the Confederates were on the alert and would attempt to obstruct the Union army. Keyes, in advance, moved to James River, where he took position below Turkey Creek Bridge, near Malvern Hill.

Heintzelman had crossed White Oak Swamp at Brackett's Ford in order not to impede troop movements on the White Oak Bridge road. Coming out on the Charles City road west of Glendale, he went to McClellan's headquarters and reported, remaining there for the night. In the morning of June 30, he destroyed the bridge at Brackett's Ford and felled trees across the Charles City road, effectually blocking it.

By midday of June 30, the Union wagon trains were getting well out of danger. At Glendale a part of the trains took the direct way (Willis road) to Malvern Hill, while another section turned off on a road leading to Haxall's Landing, two miles east of Malvern Hill. By this time the advance of the Union army had reached Malvern Hill, but the greater part of it was on the Willis road or back at Glendale holding that vital position.

Jackson, crossing the Chickahominy in the morning of June 30, reached Savage's Station, which he found abandoned by all Unionists except the dead and wounded. Here he met Lee and the two commanders held a conference, of the proceedings of which we have no knowledge. It is supposed, though, that Lee directed Jackson to follow the retiring Unionists across White Oak Swamp and join in the attack to be launched by A. P. Hill, Longstreet, and Huger. We have no actual information, and Jackson's instructions may have been otherwise.

Lee then rode off to join Longstreet and A. P. Hill. These two had spent the night of June 29-30 at Newmarket Heights, not far from Malvern Hill. In the morning of June 30 they might have pushed on to that place, where they could have attacked the Unionists to advantage, as the greater part of the Union army had not arrived. But whether ordered by Lee or through some mistake, A. P. Hill, in the absence of Longstreet, who was with Lee, took the Long Bridge road, leading away from Malvern Hill and northeast to Glendale. The Union wagon trains were traveling south on the Quaker (Willis) road. Longstreet's and Hill's commands moved in the opposite direction, and about midday of June 30 the two came to the vicinity of Glendale, which they found held by the Unionists in force.

Things were not going well with Lee's plan. A. P. Hill and Longstreet were up, but the rest of the army was scattered on various roads. Jackson, coming about midday of June 30 to White Oak Swamp, found the bridge destroyed and the hills on the south side of the stream occupied by Union troops in considerable numbers. He studied the situation for several hours but did not attempt any movement, for which he has been severely censured; indeed, his inaction at White Oak Swamp has been more criticized than any other event of his military career. D. H. Hill, who was with Jackson, long afterward joined in these reflections.

It is easy to condemn. The fact is that White Oak Swamp is an awkward military obstacle. It is narrow but rather deep, and the bottom is quicksand in places; McClellan took the trouble to build several bridges over it. Its worst feature is the dense jungle that fills the narrow swamp on both sides of the stream itself. Jackson could only have crossed in column and must have met with severe losses in so doing. Evidently he did not think he would be compensated for his casualties in forcing a crossing. In the light of the awful slaughter next day at Malvern Hill, he may have been mistaken, though it is difficult to see that victory at Glendale would have prevented a battle at Malvern Hill. The error of nearly all historians lies in thinking that Lee attacked McClellan's flank at Glendale. When the battle was fought there, in the late afternoon of June 30, the wagon trains and the greater part of the army had passed; the conflict at the crossroads was more of the nature of a rear-guard action than a flank attack.

The Union rear guard, consisting of 25,000 men, was arrayed along the Quaker (Willis) road from the Charles City road to a point about two miles south. Slocum, on the right, was north of the Charles City road; next was Kearny between the Charles City road and the Long Bridge or Newmarket road (by which Longstreet and A. P. Hill had come); south of the Long Bridge road was McCall, and on the extreme left, Hooker. The field of fire was obstructed by the woods, which afforded the Confederates cover in which to form. It was vital for the Unionists to hold this Quaker road, since it was the highway to Malvern Hill where their troops were concentrating.

About 10:30 A.M. of June 30, McClellan and Franklin came to Glendale. Slocum was posted there. McClellan sent Franklin to take command of the troops detailed to guard the crossings of White Oak Swamp. As Franklin approached the swamp, he heard the roar of a terrific bombardment. Jackson had massed his artillery on the hill overlooking White Oak Swamp and was attempting to blast a way across the stream. Franklin states that the cannonade was such as he never heard equaled, lasting for half an hour and then dying away. Its chief effect was to hasten the exodus of wagons parked in the vicinity of the swamp. About 4:00 P.M. the Confederates, having failed to gain anything by the bombardment, made a movement toward Brackett's Ford, which Franklin met by sending two brigades to that point. These brigades, finding that Jackson did not cross, went off to take part in the battle of Glendale. Before this the road east of the Quaker road was discovered; Franklin used it after nightfall of June 30 to move toward Malvern Hill.[1]

Meanwhile McCall had taken position at the Glendale crossroads, together with Kearny and Hooker, reinforcing Slocum,

[1] *B. and L.*, Vol. II, pp. 178-79.

who had been there since early morning. Longstreet states that his troops were in position at 11:00 (probably too early) and that he waited some time for the signal from Jackson and Huger to begin the attack. About 2:30, hearing artillery firing to the north, he thought it was Huger's signal; in reality it was Jackson's bombardment. Longstreet returned the signal with a blast from his batteries.

The Confederates were too scattered to hope to accomplish much. A. P. Hill and Longstreet were ready, but where were the other commands? Jackson, as we have seen, had found White Oak Swamp an obstinate obstacle. Huger was so effectually blocked by the trees on the Charles City road that he never reached Glendale until after the battle. Magruder was kept moving from point to point by contradictory orders. Holmes, on the River road near Malvern Hill, was too deaf to be fit for field service; he accomplished nothing whatever. Thus the battle had to be made by Longstreet and Hill alone. Lee was with them and President Davis also. Davis was wild with anticipation as he gazed at the bluecoat line, hoping that the day would see the destruction of McClellan's army and the realization of the dream of Southern independence. Lee was quiet and possibly dubious. His plan was not working well. A Union battery opened fire on the group of leaders, whereupon Hill insisted on the notables taking cover, which they reluctantly did. It was a point with high-command Confederates to expose themselves.

Longstreet, attempting to silence this troublesome battery, brought on the engagement, probably about 3:30 P.M. The Confederates, advancing from the cover of the woods with wild yells and waving flags, came under the fire of infantry and batteries but pressed onward, capturing a battery at the bayonet's edge and making a break in the Union line. They were thrown back, in turn, by the reserves hurried forward by Sumner and Heintzelman. The fighting was especially severe at the center, where McCall was. The Southerners, charging through the trees and over the open ground immediately in front of the Union line, were torn by canister and bullets, but time after time came to grips with the Unionists. The lines intermingled at some points; bayonets and gunbutts were freely used in the fiercest hand-to-

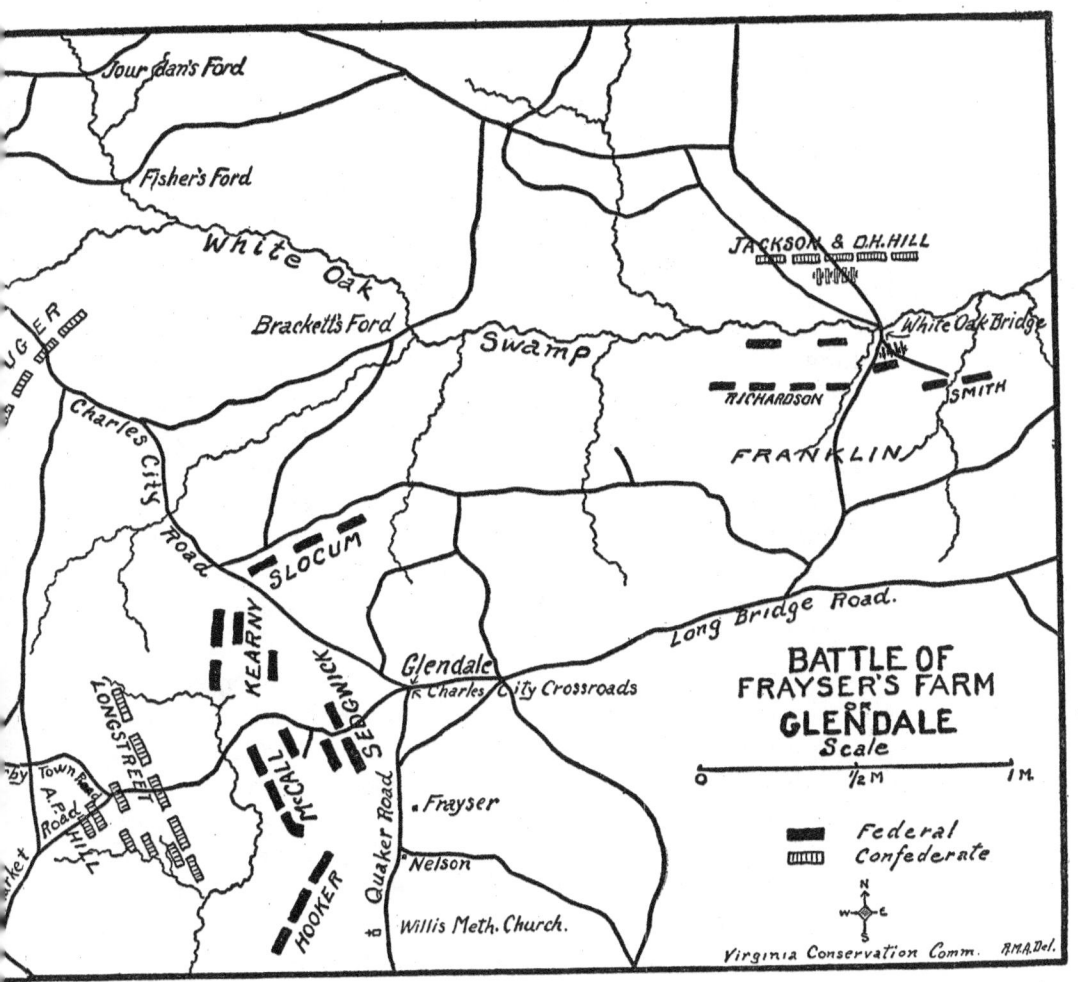

hand conflict of the war up to that time. In fact, in the whole war there was no harder fighting at close range.

The Union reserves, coming up in numbers, lent weight to the Union resistance; gradually the battle began to go against the madly struggling Confederates. Longstreet, using his own division and part of Hill's, was considerably outnumbered; his batteries were overpowered by the superior Union guns. McCall's line, after being broken, was restored by fresh troops. On the extreme left, Hooker threw back the Confederates and later angered Longstreet by claiming a victory over him.

The Southerners, though fighting bitterly, were making no headway and evening was coming on. The resistance of the Unionists had been stubborn and effective. Night fell on an inferno of yelling, screaming figures firing and thrusting at each other in the dense smoke, a scene for Doré. Longstreet now threw into the conflict 10,000 men of A. P. Hill's that he had been holding back for pursuit. If the Union line was not broken there could be no pursuit.

These fresh troops turned the tide. They shattered McCall, making a gap in the Union line. McCall's men were scattered to the winds, and, in trying to rally them, he himself rode among the Confederates and was captured. Hooker extended his right and Kearny his left, closing the gap made by McCall's break. The Union line of battle then withdrew slowly and in good order from the field, continuing the fire of the batteries as they retired. McCall's stampede was the only rout.

In this struggle, in which about 10,000 men were killed and wounded on both sides, the Union loss, for the only time in the Seven Days, seems to have exceeded that of the Confederates. The reason for this was that at Glendale the bluecoats did not occupy a prepared position as at Mechanicsville, Gaines's Mill, and Malvern Hill and so were not protected by breastworks or favored by the nature of the ground.

The Confederates claimed a victory, and it was true that they held the field. However, they had failed in their design to take McClellan in flank or crush the rear of his army. The Union rear, in fact, had held off the Confederates until the wagon trains were out of danger, and McClellan, at Malvern Hill, had made arrangements for defense there. Nevertheless, the retirement of the Unionists from Glendale to Malvern Hill was somewhat precipitate and marked by muskets, canteens, and clothing strewn along the road. This abandoned material gave the Southern leaders the impression that the Union army was demoralized, which was far from being the case.

Lee's design had failed; his disappointment must have been intense. For this result Jackson, Huger, Magruder, and Holmes were blamed, though the trouble was rather due to the difficulty of securing the coördination of commands, widely separated, in a country most imperfectly known by the generals. Moving by narrow roads, sometimes obstructed, through dense woods and over swampy streams, the Confederates did not accomplish all that Lee had hoped and expected. An amateur staff made it difficult for the commander to keep in communication with the various units. Still, in spite of all failures, Lee had frustrated the campaign against Richmond, and that was much—under the circumstances a great success.

McClellan now occupied Malvern Hill, a defensive position than which no general could ask anything better; it may be called the perfect position. Lee apparently knew little about it, or he would have hesitated to assault it. Instead he would have sought to flank it, to get at the Union army from another angle.

Porter, with the Union advance, came to Malvern Hill in the morning of June 30. If Longstreet and Hill had advanced to that point instead of Glendale, Porter would have found himself outnumbered and forced to fight for life. As it was, he established himself on the hill after a skirmish at Turkey Creek at the foot of the eminence. Here he waited while the various commands came toiling to the hill and took up their positions across its northern face.

CHAPTER TEN

MALVERN HILL
July 1

MALVERN HILL is a hill, or hills, rising sharply on the southern face from the James River plain and affording a wide outlook over fields and forests. The northern face is a long and gentle incline ending in a jungle marsh at the foot. The spur occupied by the Union army was called Crew Hill, from the house used by Porter as his headquarters; it directly faced the Quaker road by which the Confederates would approach. In the many decades since 1862 the scene has changed little. Then as now the hill consisted of meadow and field, and then as now one looked down on the swampy forest at the foot. At that season of the year some of the wheat was shocked, affording the Union sharpshooters some slight cover.

Across the field from east to west Porter arranged his troops, consisting of Morell's, Sykes's, and McCall's divisions of his own command; Couch's division of Keyes's corps; and brigades from Sumner's and Heintzelman's corps. Couch, Kearny, and Hooker were east of a road that splits the hill, Morell to the west, and Sykes in reserve. Behind the line of battle stood, hub against hub, a hundred guns or more of the fine Union artillery, placed by Henry J. Hunt, greatest of American artillerists. In the wheatfield far down the slope Berdan's sharpshooters, excellent and highly trained marksmen, spread out to impede the Confederate advance.

"Here for miles our delighted gaze surveyed a country which had not yet been devastated. There were fields covered with tall rows of graceful corn. Here were fields of almost ripe wheat, rich with the promise of the coming harvest, while at our feet meandered the gentle James River."[1]

The arrangements could not have been bettered. Looking northward from their position on the crest of the hill, the blue-coated infantrymen and artillerymen saw in front of them a long and gradual slope on which approaching enemies would be exposed to fire for half a mile. McClellan had outdone himself in the choice of a position. Gaines's Mill had been good, but for a frontal attack Malvern Hill was all that a general on the defensive could desire.

In the morning of July 1, Lee had conferred at Glendale with several of his officers, including Longstreet, as to the next move. He knew that the opposing army was in position on Malvern Hill but did not understand the strength of that eminence. D. H. Hill, who had learned something of it from a native, cautioned Lee about assaulting it, but Longstreet, in excellent humor, told him not to be frightened, "now that we have McClellan on the run."

Jackson seems to have proposed a flanking movement to the Union right, but Lee determined to attack the hill, apparently on Longstreet's assurance that he could find a place in which to put sixty guns. There was no such space, for the Confederates had to form in the marshy bottom that furnished no gun positions whatever. The few Confederate batteries that opened on the Union line were blown to pieces by the massed ordnance on the hill, leaving the attacking force almost without artillery support.

Impressed by this, Lee, according to Longstreet, changed his plan, ordering Longstreet and A. P. Hill to move around the Union right, eastward. Some time before this, however, he had issued a battle order; in the absence of an adequate staff, the various commands were to advance from the woods when a shout was raised. Lee did not succeed in revoking his first order. Troops, rushing forward from the protection of the trees, brought on the battle despite his efforts to avoid what he saw must be a sanguinary affair. Ill, he had little influence on the

[1] J. J. Marks, *The Peninsular Campaign in Virginia* (Philadelphia, 1864), p. 289.

events that immediately followed. So far as anybody directed them, Longstreet did, but the Confederate attacks were disjointed, certainly until late afternoon.

McClellan, with his staff, came on the field in the morning and approved Porter's arrangements, making a few changes. Then he went on to Harrison's Landing, to get in touch with the gunboats and prepare for the last leg in the change of base. Porter was left to fight the battle; there was not a more competent man for it in the army. McClellan, having seen that all was well on the field of the expected battle, went on with his work as commanding general. In all these arrangements he left the fighting to his capable subordinates, confining himself to the choice of positions and the movements of the army and the wagon trains. Due to this division of functions, he was able to carry his army across the Confederate front to his new base.

About ten o'clock the Southern skirmishers began to feel out the position, keeping up a desultory fire, to which the Union infantry made little reply. Confederate artillery fire, however, was quickly suppressed. It must have been in this period that Lee came to the conclusion that it would be better to flank the hill and gave directions to that effect. Single brigades of Confederates emerged from the woods and attacked Morell and Couch, though without accomplishing anything. They were repelled by artillery fire. Probably these isolated advances committed Lee beyond recall.

Up to 4:00 P.M. the Confederate attacks were made by detachments and in small force. Then fell a silence as the assailants prepared for their main effort. About 5:30 new batteries that had been brought up opened on the Union position, followed presently by waves of infantry. "As if moved by a reckless disregard of life, equal to that displayed at Gaines's Mill, with a determination to capture our army, or destroy it by driving us into the river, regiment after regiment, and brigade after brigade, rushed at our batteries; but the artillery of both Morell and Couch mowed them down with shrapnel, grape and canister, while our infantry, withholding their fire until the enemy were within short range, scattered the remnants of their columns." [2]

[2] *B. and L.*, Vol. II, p. 417.

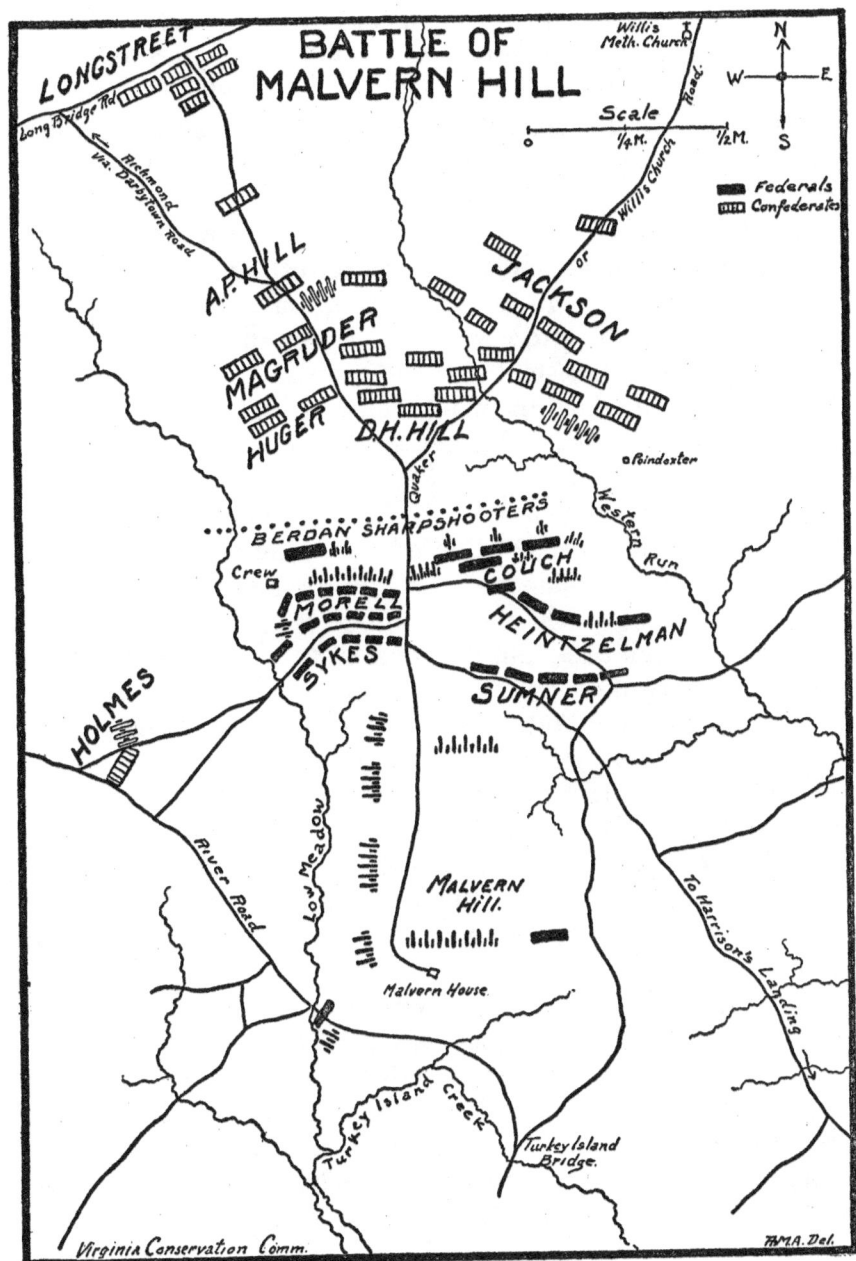

The execution done by the Union artillery firing at close range was fearful; the whole surface of the hill was dotted with the dead and wounded. Still the Confederates continued their attacks, with a heroism seldom equaled. They came on, wave after wave, dissolving under the storm of canister, only to charge again.

The Unionists, stirred by success, pressed forward to meet the Confederate advance and to pursue retreating men, suffering many casualties, though in small proportion to those of the assailants. Late in the afternoon Porter feared that his line might break under the persistent and furious assaults and called for help. Morell, on whom the main attack had fallen, was shaken. Sumner sent Meagher, and Heintzelman sent Sickles; they came up just as the battle was at its height. This reinforcement assured the success of the Union defense, if that had actually been endangered. While squads of Confederates clung to hollows near the Union line, the main body had been repulsed at nearly all points, and with great loss. The Confederates, broken and badly disorganized, fell back into the cover of the woods from which they had emerged.

Early in the night Porter sent word to McClellan, who was at Harrison's Landing, informing him of the successful defense and expressing a hope that the withdrawal was at an end. Before the messenger could have reached McClellan, orders came from the general directing the army to withdraw to Harrison's Landing. The order was promptly obeyed; by daylight of June 2, the various units were well on the way to Harrison's Landing on James River.

It is possible that McClellan would not have continued his withdrawal if he had been fully aware of the magnitude of the success gained by his troops at Malvern Hill; but, not being on the field most of the day, he did not realize what had happened. The Confederate army was shattered; it had lost 5,000 men, while the Union loss was only about 2,000. Besides, in its rapid advance the army had shed many stragglers. Lee was seldom in worse case than in the night of July 1-2, 1862. Owing to faulty tactics, his brilliant strategy had been largely frustrated. It is possible, even probable, that if McClellan had assumed the offensive on July 2 he would have won a great victory. Still it is difficult to say what would have happened. While half of Lee's army was in wretched condition for another combat, Jackson, who had taken little part in the battle of Malvern Hill, was fairly fresh and able to give a good account of himself.

McClellan, on board a gunboat, was deeply apprehensive. However, in the afternoon a dispatch came from Chief of Staff Marcy stating that the army held the enemy at bay. Cheered by this news, McClellan's spirits rose buoyantly, though he did not change his order to withdraw. Later he rode to the field, but apparently did not remain long.[3]

It was Jackson who read McClellan's mind. When someone expressed apprehension that the latter would renew the battle next morning, Jackson said curtly, "No, he will clear out." It was true. When Confederate pickets cautiously crept through the wheatfield and approached the Union position, they found it deserted. The Union army had won a victory but had retreated as a part of the withdrawal to the James River base. McClellan was never again to have an opportunity so pregnant.

All night of July 1-2, relief parties roamed over the battlefield with lanterns, picking up the wounded, who were to be found in every hollow. Stragglers covered the country. July 2 was a day of summer tempest, with a devastating rain. A Union chaplain at one of the hospitals says, "During the entire day of Wednesday, there came in the broken fragments of the Confederate army. The Williamsburg road for miles was dark with straggling, wandering bands: without guns, shivering in the cold rain, destitute of overcoats and without food, they presented themselves at our hospitals the most pitiable objects I ever saw. ... Hundreds of these broken bands and gunless men came in during the day, and great numbers were seen wandering toward Richmond, cowering under the shadow of trees and sleeping in the storm by the wayside. When met or aroused, they all eagerly inquired for their regiments or divisions."[4]

The condition of the Southern army at this time was wretched. The chaplain goes on to say, "On the heights over the swamp

[3] Marks, *op. cit.*, p. 298.
[4] *Ibid.*, p. 300.

[White Oak Swamp] we came upon strong bodies of the Confederate army. They were free and familiar with us; uniformly supposing me to be a Confederate surgeon, I was never challenged. There was in their camps none of the air of comfort and abundance seen in ours; the men were poorly clad in the coarsest homespun, such as I have seen formerly worn by the slaves in the South; the greater part of them were without tents and sheltered under booths.

"They had nothing of food but the dirtiest bacon sides and flour—salt was an unknown luxury.

"They were without knapsacks and overcoats, and many of them had no blankets; their sufferings in storms and in the chilly nights must have been well nigh unendurable.

"Everything on which I looked was immeasurably inferior to the equipments of our army. The horses were poor and fed on corn only; the army wagons were of the fashion in use when I was a boy.... The harness of the horses was old and dried in the sun....

"The gun-carriages and caissons had evidently passed through trying scenes, and looked as if they would soon shake to pieces. The artillery horses were quite as poor as those already mentioned.

"In the camp there was little of that order and military discipline which we could have seen even in the newest regiments in our service....

"In the fields were encampments of General A. P. Hill's troops; some of his regiments were on parade, and presented lines of men in all conceivable costumes—some dressed in gray, others in the blue cloths of our troops, others in brown; many were ragged, some sleeveless, and a multitude I thought were shirtless."[5]

In the morning of July 2, Lee faced the problem of pursuing the lately victorious Union army to its new base and attempting to strike it another blow before it escaped. According to the historians McClellan was safe after Malvern Hill, but this is not entirely true. He was still in danger.

If the Southern army had been in condition to follow, his peril

[5] *Ibid.*, pp. 309-11.

would have been great. But it took time to gather the shattered commands in the drenching rain, and, finally, when the army was set in motion it covered little ground. This is not to be wondered at. The wonder is that the army should have been able to advance at all after the terrible experiences of July 1.

The Confederate cavalry upset the apple cart for Lee. The Unionists, on reaching the flats on the river in the vicinity of Harrison's Landing, exhausted by fighting and marching through knee-deep mud, many of them shaking with malaria, felt that they were at last safe from pursuit. They spread out over the fields near the river, pitching tents and seeking some degree of comfort and repose after their toils and hazards. Thus occupied, they neglected to seize the hill overlooking their camp grounds, known as Evlington Heights.

Stuart had not accomplished much in the Seven Days, partly because he had been sent to guard the roads leading down the peninsula, partly because of the wooded and difficult nature of the country. Now, at last, he was out in front of his army, following the Unionists. In the morning of July 3, the plumed cavalier with a few squadrons came to Evlington Heights, entirely unoccupied, and gazed down with interest on the bluecoats in the flats below as they went about their camp duties. Here was an opportunity. If Confederate infantry and artillery could be hurried up and placed in position on the hill, the Unionists would have to fight a bloody action to dislodge them. A telling blow might, even then, be dealt McClellan's army.

Stuart did not visualize all this. Boylike (he was under thirty), he brought up a tiny howitzer and opened fire on the host below. Their attention called to the threat, troops soon advanced up the heights, driving off Stuart's handful of cavalry and establishing themselves on the hill. Union engineers went busily to work laying off lines for the extensive fieldworks that still in part remain, the most interesting relics of the year 1862 in America.

At length, in the afternoon of July 3, the Confederate infantry columns drew near Evlington Heights, only to find them held by the Unionists in force. Longstreet, senior in rank in Lee's absence, suggested to Jackson that he advance on the Union works. Jackson declined to commit himself to an engagement without Lee's knowledge. When the commander arrived, July 4, he and Jackson surveyed the Union position with care. Lee longed but abstained; he could afford no more frontal assaults on prepared positions. Jackson concurred with him in the decision that it would be too risky to attack.

The weary and bedraggled Confederates reversed their march, turning their faces toward Richmond. Falling back to Newmarket Heights, they went into camp, exhausted, hungry, and many of them ill. McClellan was left to establish himself at Harrison's Landing in peace. The Peninsular Campaign, greatest in American history up to that time, was over.

That campaign remains to this day misunderstood. McClellan had failed, it is true, but the failure was not due to defeat in battle but to the false position he was in. It was not McClellan that Lee had beaten, but the Union government, which, in its fear for the capital, had wrecked the campaign at its most critical period by keeping from the army 50,000 men McClellan should have had. In reaching out for that promised reinforcement, he had been compelled to divide his army by the Chickahominy, thereby laying himself open to attack. Since McDowell did not come—was, in fact, never designed to come—McClellan could not have maintained himself in front of Richmond with a supply base on the Pamunkey River. He did the only thing possible under the circumstances in moving to the James River. He accomplished that movement with extraordinary success. It was entirely too much to hope and expect that he should defeat Lee and capture Richmond with an army only slightly larger than Lee's. Left in the lurch by his government, he had done all that could have been reasonably expected of any commander; he should have been congratulated instead of censured. And yet government and North had expected him, with what he had, to overthrow Lee and enter the Southern capital in triumph.

His new base on the James River was far better than that on the Pamunkey, open to attack from several sides. Here, in the absence of an adequate navy, the Confederates could trouble him little; cut off his supplies they could not. Here he was in the true position to besiege and capture Richmond. It took three years of disaster to teach the Washington government that Richmond could not be taken by the overland route from the north. McDowell, Pope, Burnside, Hooker, Meade, and Grant all failed in the effort. It was not until Grant, in the summer of 1864, adopted McClellan's strategy that he captured the city and won the war.

Yet in justice to the Washington government it should be noted that its apprehensions for the capital were by no means groundless. Jackson would probably have taken the city if given sufficient force. It was in dire peril after the Second Manassas. Early, with only 10,000 men, threatened it in July, 1864; with a larger force he would have entered it. This was the penalty the United States government paid for having its capital on the border line. Not to be outdone in self-penalization, the Confederate government established its capital at Richmond, also near the border line. Tit for tat.

The great lesson of the Peninsular Campaign was that Richmond could be taken only by a siege. If McClellan had approached with 200,000 men, Lee would have been pinned to the city as he was in 1864-65; Richmond would probably have fallen in the early part of 1863. McClellan would have erected massive siege works, too strong to assault. He would have extended his left to cut the Confederate communications with the South. An engineer of great skill, he would have done all that Grant did, and maybe more. Lee, chained to fortifications instead of exerting his marvelous skill in field maneuver, would have been robbed of his strength and would have lost, as he finally did, a war of attrition in which the Union could afford to sacrifice two men for one.

CHAPTER ELEVEN

THE PLOT MATURES, BUT PROVIDENCE
(OR, FROM THE OTHER POINT OF VIEW, SATAN)
FRUSTRATES IT

THANKFULNESS fell on the Union host when it realized that it was at least temporarily safe in the lines of Evlington Heights. It had faced a terrible enemy with great courage and with a degree of success it could hardly have hoped for under the circumstances; but the men were hungry and dirty, suffering from malaria and dysentery, sun-blistered, and desperately tired. However, they had escaped the serpent coils of Lee and were grateful, for while civilians might disparage the Confederate army, the soldiers who fought against it did not. They knew the quality of the ragged men in gray and brown.

McClellan made his headquarters at Berkeley, a colonial house with a history. There generations of Harrisons had lived and propagated, the most notable of them William Henry Harrison, President of the United States for a month. This Harrison, anticipating Greeley's "Go West, young man, go West," had settled in Ohio and become an Indian fighter. By a queer quirk of fate, this man of ancient colonial lineage had been, in the presidential campaign of 1840, pictured as the poor man's candidate against the innkeeper's son, Van Buren, representative of the vested interests. McClellan did his best to spare the place from the ravages of soldiers, as he always did, wherever he might be. Of all things, he detested vandalism most. He never warred on noncombatants.

McClellan's first emotion was an intense thankfulness that he had saved the army, mixed with pride over the victory at Malvern Hill. If Lee had had the 200,000 men with which Union information credited him, McClellan would have been indeed fortunate to escape; but, if Lee had had the 200,000, it is most unlikely that McClellan would ever have reached the James.

The first reaction in Washington was relief, for, following the defeat at Gaines's Mill, there had been harrowing anxiety in the capital. Lincoln had doubted in those dark hours whether success lay ahead—whether, after all, he would not have to admit defeat. It was one of the crises of the war.

On July 1, the President sent McClellan word that reinforcements were not available; if he was not strong enough to face the enemy he must find a place of security, even, if necessary, at Fort Monroe. The next day the President told McClellan that he did not think he was strong enough to take Richmond. "Try just now to save the army." And on July 3, when the news came of the arrival at Harrison's Landing, Lincoln frankly expressed his gratification. "All accounts say better fighting was never done." Again, "Be assured the heroism and skill of yourself and officers and men is, and forever will be, appreciated."

McClellan's spirits were reviving, his estimate of events more optimistic. In the night of June 28 he had admitted defeat, but, on July 4, he wrote Lincoln, "We were not beaten in any conflict. The enemy were unable by their utmost efforts to drive us from any field."

McClellan, hope renewed, was thinking of another advance against Richmond from a far better base than before. Here was the place, he realized, for operations against Richmond, for the strangle hold of a successful siege.

He knew that all was not well in Washington, that Stanton was working against him; but he did not realize the full extent of the danger and that only extreme caution could save him. But, open-hearted, straightforward, he could not keep his thoughts to himself, even when prudence demanded it.

On July 7, McClellan wrote Lincoln a letter that had much to do with sealing his fate. It is curious to reflect that at this time everybody in high position found it necessary to advise Lincoln, believing still in the incompetence of the chief executive. "The Constitution and the Union must be preserved," McClellan wrote, "whatever may be the cost in time, treasure and blood."

This must have bored Lincoln but could not have displeased him. The general went on to say, however, that while slaves employed by the army should be freed, and the slaves in certain states might be liberated on the plea of military necessity, "a declaration of radical views, especially upon slavery, will rapidly disintegrate our present armies." To Lincoln, face to face with the grim realities of the situation and pressed by the abolitionists —thinking of abolition as the remedy for many ills, the probable regeneration of the drooping Union cause—the sentiment could not have been welcome. McClellan concluded his rather condescending advice with a plea for a consolidation of forces and the appointment of a commander in chief, which office he did not ask for himself. He might have spared his ink; he was not thought of for the place. Possibly he knew that Halleck was being considered at this very time. Indeed, even before McClellan came to grips with the Confederates at Richmond, the authorities were casting about for a successor. He was too outspoken, too free with political opinions, too independent, too impolitic. He did not take off his shoes and salaam when he entered Stanton's presence. He was even blunt with Lincoln, who, tolerant as he was, preferred deference. The plot revolved around John Pope, who had come to Washington from the West. Pope was related to Mrs. Lincoln and was intimate with the President. He persuaded Stanton, bitterly hostile to McClellan, that Halleck was the military genius needed for the army chief and that he himself was qualified for command. Stanton considered the possibilities.

Many good officers were with the Army of the Potomac, but none of them had held independent command. There was Ambrose E. Burnside. Yes, he had headed a sea expedition to North Carolina and had won some success. Then eyes were turned West. Fortunately for himself, Grant was not called to Virginia to face Lee and Jackson at their best. And Pope? Pope had won a victory over the Confederates at Island No. 10 in the Mississippi River. Yes, Pope might be the predestined savior of the cause.

Lincoln and Stanton still feared for Washington, the more so that McClellan was now twenty-five miles southeast of Richmond and in no position to intervene between the Confederates and the capital. The thing to do was to unite all forces in northern Virginia and try the overland campaign once more. So Lincoln thought. Stanton emphatically agreed. Chase chimed in. Such a combination would stultify McClellan and make easier his discharge.

On June 26, when Lee was launching his attack, Lincoln issued an order consolidating the troops in northern and western Virginia in the Army of Virginia, to be commanded by Major General John Pope. Pope was assigned the large order of protecting Washington, disposing of Stonewall Jackson, and aiding McClellan to capture Richmond. Even before the Seven Days he was designed to succeed McClellan.[1] The latter did not immediately perceive the threat. He had all along preached consolidation; now his advice seemed to be on the point of being taken. If a great army should be put together, Richmond would surely fall.

Lincoln visited McClellan at Harrison's Landing and seemed satisfied with what had been done. His gaunt frame stretched in a field chair, he gazed at the James River and listened to the dapper McClellan's account of his trials and triumphs, but did not have much to say. His manner carried no prevision of disaster to the army commander, who was pleased by the visit.

McClellan attempted to establish friendly relations with the commander of the Army of Virginia, applauding the concentration of troops and declaring that lack of it had caused his troubles. He said he was in a strong position and hoped to be able to seize the right bank of the river, putting him in a situation to maneuver freely. "As soon as Burnside arrives I will feel the force of the enemy and ascertain his exact position." If the Confederates advanced against Pope, he would try to take Richmond.[2]

This was July 7, the day on which Little Mac cooked his own goose. Burnside was coming back from North Carolina and McClellan expected him to come to the James. The Washington authorities had not broken the unpleasant news to McClellan

[1] *O.R.*, Ser. I, Vol. XII, Pt. 3, p. 435.
[2] *Ibid.*, Vol. XI, Pt. 3, p. 306.

that Burnside was not for him. Burnside was intended for Pope's new army.

Lincoln was preparing to get a general in chief, but it was not to be McClellan. Politics were coming into the game. William Sprague, little manufacturer-politician, recently elected senator from Rhode Island, had seen Lincoln and urged that Halleck was the man of destiny. Also, no doubt, he put in a word for Burnside, that notable Rhode Island product. This confirmed Pope's advice.

On July 6, Lincoln communicated with Halleck, then at Corinth, and presently brought him East. Halleck, everybody thought, was a Big Brain. With Halleck in Washington, everything would go well.

Already steps were being taken to supersede McClellan. General R. C. Marcy wrote him that he had seen Lincoln and that the latter expressed a desire to help him. Idle words. On July 10, General John A. Dix, commanding at Fort Monroe, was halted as he was preparing to reinforce McClellan by an order from Stanton to send no more troops to him. The same day Halleck informed Lincoln that Senator Sprague had seen him, and that he advised that all troops in the Virginia-North Carolina area be put under one commander. That move would make McClellan subordinate, even if he were retained at all.

McClellan, at the same time, was being betrayed by his lieutenants. At that period the idea prevailed that tidewater Virginia was very unhealthy—one of the causes of the withdrawal from Harrison's Landing. Keyes wrote Lincoln (without notifying McClellan) that the army could not remain at Harrison's Landing, as heat and sickness would destroy it. To advance on Richmond 100,000 more men would be needed. The army should be removed to Washington. "To shut up this army on the James River is to make certain its destruction or its neutralization within the next two months."

Thus was McClellan knifed by older officers jealous of him, though his real friends stood by him loyally until the end. He was the kind of individual who makes zealous partisans and bitter enemies. The idea of the unhealthiness of the James River pleased Stanton, another argument to advance for the with-

THE PLOT MATURES

drawal of the army from Richmond and the getting rid of McClellan.

On July 11, Halleck was made general in chief, and on July 23 he assumed command, though the order appointing him was not published until August 11. Everything was preparing for McClellan's elimination.

A message from Lincoln, on July 13, first showed McClellan, still hopeful, how far he had lost the confidence of the government. Lincoln, tart and sardonic, asked McClellan what had become of the 160,000 men of his army. Of them 80,500 remained, leaving 75,000 to be accounted for. Lincoln thought 23,500 would cover casualties, leaving at least 45,000 unaccounted for.

"If I am right, and you had these men with you, you could go into Richmond in the next three days. How can they be got to you, and how can they be prevented from getting away in such numbers for the future." [3]

McClellan answered that he had never had 160,000 present for duty. On July 15, he had present 88,665, and absent by authority, 34,472, a total of 144,407. The sick numbered 16,619. The number actually absent was 40,000. He had called the attention of the War Department to the evils of absenteeism. The men escaped in various ways, many on pretense of illness.

What he said was true enough. The wastage in volunteer armies, not under the sternest discipline, is always large. McClellan fared no worse than Lee, who sometimes had twice as many men on the rolls as present for duty. Men sick and half sick, men suffering from nostalgia, deserters and malingerers had slipped out of the army by thousands in its progress from Yorktown to Harrison's Landing. But the authorities made no allowances. The only way the evil could be remedied, under the circumstances—even if then—was by wholesale executions. McClellan would never have favored that.

McClellan, understanding how the wind blew but still hoping against hope, was now anxious about Burnside, ordered back from North Carolina. "What of Burnside?" he asked Lincoln. The answer came that Burnside was at Newport News, ready

[3] *Ibid.*, p. 319.

to move one way or another. Meanwhile Hunter arrived at Fort Monroe with more troops, and Stanton wired Dix to keep him there. Stanton had turned thumbs down on McClellan and he usually had his way. He was becoming more powerful every day.

Pope was now in the saddle and was moving southward in a way that McClellan must have considered incautious. By July 17, his pickets were twenty-five miles south of Fredericksburg, and troops were at Gordonsville on the way to destroy the Virginia Central Railroad, one of Lee's supply lines. Culpeper was occupied. Pope was enterprising and full of confidence, not having encountered Lee and Jackson. He imagined they were on a par with Southern generals in the West. Boylike, he is said to have indulged in bombast that later he was to regret. "My headquarters are in the saddle," he had announced. "In the West we are familiar with the backs of our enemies," or some such stuff. Lee, hearing, began to be interested. The newcomer promised to be better game than McClellan.

Burnside came up from Fort Monroe to see McClellan. The two were great friends. No doubt McClellan told Burnside that important changes were impending, for Burnside telegraphed Stanton for an interview, not hankering for McClellan's place. But at this very time Stanton was considering Burnside for the command.

The army, rested and full fed, was rapidly improving instead of degenerating as Keyes had predicted. On July 20, 101,000 men were present for duty. There were still thousands of sick, but new cases were fewer. McClellan began to hope again, standing there at Berkeley house looking out at the river that represented opportunity.

Burnside's troops still ate their rations and played poker at Fort Monroe. Stanton had determined that they should not join McClellan for a new movement on Richmond, but Lincoln does not seem to have made up his mind for some days. He informed McClellan that Burnside's destination would soon be decided.

McClellan still hoped against hope that Burnside would come to him. Lee and Jackson in Richmond watched intently, for Burnside's movements would determine their own. If Burnside came to Harrison's Landing, an advance on Richmond by Pope could be more or less ignored. If Burnside went north, McClellan would be harmless and Pope would be the fox to hunt.

The crisis was coming, had almost come. Southern fortunes were in the hands of these two keen strategists, alert, audacious, lion-hearted. Davis was not interfering, for Richmond was still in danger.

On the other side was nothing but uncertainty. One thing only had been decided: McClellan must go. Who would succeed him? Nobody knew exactly. In the washing for diamonds several stones were being examined: Halleck, Pope, Burnside, possibly others. Surely one of them must be a true jewel.

The Washington authorities were still militarily ignorant; they were just learning the game. If they had understood, they would have appreciated McClellan's ability in escaping decisive defeat at the hands of Lee and Jackson, commanding probably the best amateur army the world ever saw and one approximately as large as McClellan's own. Two years later Grant, with twice as many men as Lee and with the great Jackson gone, escaped decisive defeat only by the skin of his teeth. In 1862 he would have been a morsel exactly to Lee's taste.

Lee sent Jackson northward to oppose Pope and perhaps defeat him. Lee still watched in Richmond. McClellan, whose intelligence was now better, informed Lincoln of Jackson's movement. At the same time Pope notified McClellan that Ewell was at Gordonsville and Jackson not far away. Pope was still confident, still unafraid.

Each day that went by saw McClellan's chances lessening, the chorus against him swelling. Wool now joined in, prompted by his resentment at being subordinate to a man half his age. Wool had been in the army a lifetime and was still of little importance; he would never be an army commander. His feeling was perfectly natural and human. Rank with gall, he went, of course, to Stanton, damning not only McClellan but Grant as well. It was the same old song; the army would die in the Virginia climate. It took Grant to dissipate the prejudice. Wool concluded: "I do not mention these things because I desire the command of an army." [4]

[4] *Ibid.*, p. 331.

Keyes joined in, writing to Meigs, quartermaster general and another enemy of McClellan. (Apparently, poor McClellan had no friends at headquarters in Washington.) The army would die on the James. Keyes urged Meigs to use his influence to have it removed. "If the movement begins to-morrow or next day," Keyes raved, "or even one week hence, I think the army could be removed in safety; after that its removal would be of doubtful possibility."[5]

This was pleasant for Stanton, who needed all the authority he could get to overthrow McClellan, still supported by Lincoln.

Halleck had written quite a love letter to McClellan, assuring him of eternal friendship and the desire to help him. He, Halleck, had not, of course, sought the position of general in chief; it had been forced on him. He had wished to leave the West. Soon he wished himself back there.

McClellan knew how to evaluate such apologies; all generals utter them. What he did not know was that Halleck was hostile to him, that the latter had been brought East really to supersede him. He thought Halleck was a friend, as if he could have had a friend at headquarters in Washington. Halleck was perhaps friendly at first, but, being a man of weak character, he was brought over to the side of the conspirators who were seeking to ruin McClellan.

Under the delusion that Halleck wished to help him, McClellan, on July 26, asked for Burnside's and Hunter's troops, still at Fort Monroe. "I am sure," he said to Halleck, "that you will agree with me that the true defense of Washington consists in a rapid and heavy blow given by this army upon Richmond."[6]

Halleck, on July 25, abandoned his desk in Washington to visit McClellan on the James. An armchair strategist of the first water, he did not have brains enough to value McClellan's searching insight, his scientific knowledge of war. For Halleck made, deprecatingly, to Stanton a statement that is the supreme vindication of McClellan as a general. "He [McClellan] said that he proposed to cross the James River at that point [vicinity of Berkeley], attack Petersburg, and cut off the enemy's com-

[5] *Ibid.*, p. 333.
[6] *Ibid.*, p. 334.

munications by that route south, making no further demonstrations against Richmond. I stated to him very frankly my views in regard to the danger and impracticability of the plan, to most of which he finally agreed." [7]

What must have been McClellan's disappointment as he realized the impossibility of convincing the general in chief of the soundness of his strategy, the utter futility of attempting to oppose the fallacy of the overland campaign from the north! How bitter must have been his reflections two years later when he saw Grant carry out the identical plan he had proposed in 1862! Grant was merely the executive who put through McClellan's idea.

Lee was in these August days becoming more and more hopeful, for the Confederate commander began to see that the opponent he feared most of all of those he faced was out of favor at Washington.

Halleck not only refused to countenance McClellan's plan, but he brought exceeding bad news. For the decision had been made to abandon all that McClellan had won and fall back on Washington. It was not McClellan that Lee had defeated, but the Washington government. It was now about to admit defeat. Halleck said that McClellan's army would be united with Pope to cover Washington unless he felt strong enough to take Richmond with his present force. Halleck offered 20,000 more men as the maximum reinforcement. McClellan agreed to the terms. With 20,000 recruits, he would actually have about 115,000 combatants. But at the same time Keyes wrote Meigs that Halleck underestimated the Confederate army, that it was 200,000 strong. Still that 200,000 visualized by Pinkerton detectives!

Despite McClellan's offer to attempt Richmond if given 20,000 more men, the Washington government had now, after long hesitation, decided finally to abandon the effort. Stanton had won.

On July 30, Halleck ordered McClellan to prepare to send his sick North. At the same time he assured him of support, asking McClellan's in return. He also alluded to the rumors hostile to McClellan with which Washington resounded.

[7] *Ibid.*, p. 337.

"There seems to be a disposition in the public press," he said, "to cry down any one who attempted to serve the country instead of party. This was particularly the case with you, as I understood, and I could not doubt that it would be in a few weeks the same with me." [8]

It was in answer to this letter that McClellan finally ruined himself. Most indiscreet and undiplomatic of men, he poured out his confidential opinions at a time when such opinions could only damn him. Wise man, Grant. He merely grunted and smoked cigars, whence there came to him opportunity and supreme fame. McClellan talked and talked. And fell.

McClellan told Halleck (July 30) that he felt no jealousy at being under him. Then he went on to say: "I think that the question of slavery should enter into this war solely as a military one; that while we do our best to prevent the rebels from making military men of their slaves, we should avoid any proclamation of general emancipation, and should protect inoffensive citizens in the possession of that as well as of other kinds of property...

"The people of the South should understand that we are not making war on the institution of slavery, but that if they submit to the Constitution and laws of the Union they will be protected in their constitutional rights of every nature." [9]

This message must have come as a shock to Lincoln. That most astute of men knew that the war to save the Union was failing, that some new stimulus was essential. He was already considering the Emancipation Proclamation, which turned the war into a crusade and aroused the ardor of the radicals. And here, as the moment approached for such an announcement, he found that the commander of the main army was opposed to "making war on the institution of slavery!"

How could a government with one opinion and a general with the opposite go in harness together? From that hour McClellan's fate was settled. Only a question of time.

It was decided to disregard him altogether and to withdraw

[8] *Ibid.*, p. 343.
[9] *Ibid.*, p. 346.

the Army of the Potomac to the vicinity of Washington. When Secretary Welles, on August 7, was told by Halleck of the decision made, he protested, declaring that troops and naval vessels should be maintained at Harrison's Landing to force the Confederates to keep their army at Richmond. He adds, "strange that this change of military operations should have been made without Cabinet consultation, and especially without communicating the fact to the Secretary of the Navy, who had established a naval flotilla on the James River by special request to coöperate with and assist the army. But Stanton is so absorbed in his scheme to get rid of McClellan that other and more important matters are neglected." [10]

The impending blow fell on August 3, when Halleck wired McClellan, "It is determined to withdraw your army from the Peninsula to Aquia Creek. You will take immediate measures to effect this, covering the movement the best you can.... The entire movement is left to your discretion and judgment." Troops were to be kept at Fort Monroe and Norfolk.

McClellan replied the next day: "I must confess that it has caused me the greatest pain I ever experienced, for I am convinced that the order to withdraw this army to Aquia Creek will prove disastrous to our cause. I fear it will be a fatal blow.

"The army is now in excellent condition and discipline. We hold a debouche on both banks of the James River, so that we are free to act in any direction....

"It may be said that there are no re-enforcements available. I point to Burnside's force; to that of Pope, not necessary to maintain a strict defensive in front of Washington and Harper's Ferry. ... Here, directly in front of this army, is the threat of the rebellion. It is here that all our resources should be collected to strike the blow which will determine the fate of the nation. All points of secondary importance elsewhere should be abandoned, and every available man brought here; a decided victory here and the military strength of the rebellion is crushed.... Here is the true defense of Washington. It is here, on the banks of the

---

[10] *Diary of Gideon Welles*, Vol. I, p. 83. (Boston, Houghton Mifflin Company, 1911.) Extracts used by special permission of the publishers.

James, that the fate of the Union should be decided. . . . I entreat that this order may be rescinded.

"If my counsel does not prevail, I will with a sad heart obey your orders to the uttermost of my power."

This was sound advice, the soundest advice given the government during the war. The removal from James River was a retrograde step of the utmost importance, one that cheered the Confederates and relieved their fears for Richmond. McClellan, at Harrison's Landing, was in a position to begin that siege of Richmond which Grant undertook two years later. The siege, if begun in 1862, would have robbed Lee of his greatest resource, his skill in maneuver. The abandonment of James River gave Lee the opportunity to conduct the campaigns of the Second Manassas, Maryland, Fredericksburg, Chancellorsville, and Pennsylvania—that is, it afforded a scope for his superior generalship that McClellan never would have allowed. In other words, by abandoning the grip on Richmond which McClellan had obtained, the Washington government, all unwittingly, gave the Confederates a chance to win the war. But the fear of Robert E. Lee had entered into the hearts of the rulers of the capital; they were more concerned with the defense of Washington than the capture of Richmond.

Halleck's explanation of the change of policy, in which he had concurred after all his assurances to McClellan, was somewhat lame. It was the old story that the government could not give the required reinforcements (McClellan had asked for 35,000 more men instead of the 20,000 offered), that the health of the army would be ruined if it were kept on the James in August and September, that most of the officers desired the removal. As pointed out before, the health of Grant's army was not ruined by being in the same position. And at that time the health of the Union army was improving. McClellan was broken-hearted as he saw all the fruits of his labor thrown away by authorities too lacking in understanding to appreciate what he had accomplished. But what saved the Washington government was the parallel lack of understanding in Richmond. Exchanging blunders, the two governments kept at the game until Richmond blundered fatally and finally. But no one could have foreseen that Davis would out-blunder Washington, and the withdrawal of the Army of the Potomac from before Richmond gave the Confederates their best opportunity to win the war.

Halleck, however, was disingenuous, indeed actually insincere. On August 7, he raised McClellan's fallen hopes by telling him that he expected McClellan to command all the troops in Virginia, and that, with this army, he could take Richmond. But it was necessary for him to withdraw his troops from Harrison's Landing. "I must beg of you, General, to hurry along this movement.... I cannot regard Pope and Burnside as safe until you re-enforce them. Moreover, I wish them to be under your immediate command for reasons which it is not necessary to specify." [11] Thus was the pill sugar-coated.

Burnside had gone to Aquia Creek. His movement, when it came to Lee's knowledge, decided the issue of the campaign. Lee felt that McClellan, without reinforcements, would not attack Richmond, that Pope was to be the threat. He prepared to move.

The end had now come to McClellan's hopes, but he obeyed. It is an evidence of Halleck's stupidity that he expected McClellan to evacuate a great army, with immense stores and thousands of sick, in the very presence of the enemy, in a day or two. In the first place, McClellan had to make sure that Lee would not descend on him while he was in the act of embarkation. Consequently, on August 5, he pushed a large force westward to Malvern Hill, which he reoccupied. Lee moved forward to confront him, but there was no battle. McClellan was no longer advancing on Richmond, and Lee had had enough of Malvern Hill. The Confederates therefore fell back toward Richmond while the Union troops returned to Harrison's Landing. McClellan felt certain that there would be no interference with his departure.

In this movement from Harrison's Landing material was discovered for McClellan's condemnation; he did not move fast enough to suit Stanton and, therefore, did not move fast enough for Stanton's echo, Halleck. The great difficulties in the way were entirely overlooked.

[11] O.R., Ser. I, Vol. XI, Pt. 3, p. 300.

In the first place, there were not enough transports, and again, on several occasions, the transports were tied up by storms. Some of the commands had to tramp to Yorktown while others went by water to Fort Monroe. There was, moreover, a perfectly human reluctance on McClellan's part to abandon a great and promising plan for a movement of dubious utility, and a still more human unwillingness to give up the command of the army he had created and trained, an army so different from the mob of Bull Run.

If, therefore, McClellan hesitated a little, who shall blame him? He did not hesitate long. He says himself, "I proceeded to obey the order with all possible rapidity, firmly impressed, however, with the conviction that the withdrawal of the Army of the Potomac from Harrison's Landing would, at that time, have the most disastrous effect upon our cause." [12]

McClellan, while shipping off the sick and supplies, made one last, despairing effort to persuade Washington. On August 12, he told Halleck that the Confederates at Richmond were weakened by detachments and that Longstreet, with only 18,000 men, occupied a position near Malvern Hill that could be turned. He could advance on Longstreet and in forty-eight hours drive him into the Richmond defenses or destroy him. This success would enable him to push on into Richmond, but he would have to retain his army and be reinforced. It was the last gesture. There was no response.

Pope, on August 12, informed McClellan that Jackson had fallen back on Gordonsville and that he himself would move forward to Louisa as soon as Burnside arrived. Showing the uncertainty prevailing, Pope added: "Do I understand that he takes the chief command when he joins?" [13] It is evident from this that Pope knew McClellan was to be relieved but suspected that he himself was not destined as successor. Apparently the government (possibly as a result of Sprague's activities) was already seriously considering Burnside and would have, except for the disaster of Second Manassas, elevated him then instead of waiting until November. At all events Burnside, now at Fal-

---

[12] *Ibid*, Pt. I, p. 81.
[13] *Ibid*, Vol. XII, Pt. 3, p. 565.

mouth, across the river from Fredericksburg, was ordered to make a junction with Pope. This, however, was never completed. Burnside remained guarding the lower fords of the Rappahannock and out of touch with the Army of Virginia until the Second Manassas.

Meanwhile Pope, with a rashness that showed his ignorance of the situation, crossed the Rappahannock and advanced to the Rapidan. Halleck sent him the sound advice not to cross the latter river, though neither he nor Pope knew what was being prepared.

On August 9, Jackson struck Pope's advance under Banks at Cedar Mountain, not far from the village of Culpeper. A bitter fight followed in the fields along the little mountain; Jackson was hard pressed to win. Win he did in the end, driving the Union advance to Culpeper. But on Pope's approach he fell back, and the Unionists claimed a victory.[14]

As a matter of fact, Pope was in great danger. Lee had made the most daring decision of his life. Feeling that McClellan, still at Harrison's Landing, would not advance again on Richmond, Lee, in company with Longstreet, audaciously went off to join Jackson, leaving only a small force to protect the Southern capital. Concentrating his troops behind Clark's Mountain near Orange, Lee prepared to fall on the unsuspecting Pope, who had no idea that he was in the immediate presence of the whole Confederate army. It was Lee's simple and excellent plan to attack Pope while the latter was between the Rappahannock and Rapidan rivers, giving the Confederates a chance for a decisive victory. In other words, the abandonment of the advance on Richmond was already offering Lee great opportunities.

A mere accident apparently frustrated the scheme. Lee ordered cavalry to lead the advance, and the cavalry was slow. Jackson wished to go ahead anyway, but Lee demurred. Several days passed. Then, Lee, going to his signal station on Clark's Mountain, had the mortification of seeing Pope's host—wagon

---

[14] As early as August 10 McClellan foresaw Pope's defeat. "I have a strong idea that Pope will be attacked during the coming week, and very badly whipped he ought to be—such a villain as he is ought to bring defeat on any army that employs him."

trains, guns, troop columns—heading northward. Pope had learned of the trap he was in and was making tracks. He fell back to the north side of the Rappahannock. Lee advanced to the south bank, and the two armies confronted each other across the stream, here narrow and easily fordable in August. Thus matters remained until the last days of the month. The Confederates pushed a force across the river, which rose after a storm and cut off the return. When the Southerners finally regained the south bank, Pope thought he had gained a success. He was simply pausing now for the arrival of McClellan's army. Apparently he had no plans, and Halleck had none. Micawber was waiting for something to turn up.

McClellan pushed the evacuation of Harrison's Landing with skill and speed. Scores of transports were loaded with sick and with the army impedimenta. In contradiction to the belief that McClellan did not loyally coöperate with Pope is the evidence of General Lorenzo Thomas: "The army is in fine spirits and splendid fighting order, and only wish they may be attacked. No one could have made the movement more skillfully or in less time." [15] McClellan informed Halleck, on August 17, "I have seen Burnside. Now that we are committed to the movement, you may be sure that it will be carried out without the delay of a moment. Not an hour has been lost thus far. Count on my full coöperation." [16]

The next day McClellan reported that the last of his rear guard had crossed the Chickahominy. "I will now push everything to Yorktown and Monroe with all possible dispatch." On August 19, he added, "I will now move leisurely, but will be sure to have the troops ready to embark as fast as transports are on hand. Please hurry horse transports and those for batteries."

On August 19, Halleck wired McClellan that the Confederates were moving across the Rapidan in force. "It is of vital importance that you send forward troops as rapidly as possible, leaving the material which is not absolutely necessary to follow more leisurely. We want immediately all the men that can possibly be sent."

[15] *O.R.*, Ser. I, Vol. XII, Pt. 3, p. 579.
[16] *Ibid.*, p. 590.

THE PLOT MATURES 139

Halleck was, again, disingenuous. At that moment Pope was not in danger, and, if threatened, could have fallen back to Centreville. The hurry was to get hold of McClellan's troops and relieve him of command. The authorities were afraid to dismiss him summarily; they were trying to ease him out of the saddle, for they knew his immense popularity with the rank and file. In their dealings with him they were indirect, underhanded, insincere.

On August 20, McClellan reported that Sumner's corps was at Williamsburg; Heintzelman and Franklin at Yorktown; Porter at Fort Monroe. Porter would have all his corps embarked the next day. "No time shall be lost in pushing off the troops as rapidly as possible." Ordering Heintzelman to use every vessel at Yorktown, day and night, he enjoined, "Not one moment must be lost in carrying out this order." To Franklin he said, "It is highly important that you should reach Newport News with your command to-morrow evening if possible." On August 20, Halleck informed Pope that Burnside's corps was arriving at Aquia Creek on the Potomac. All troops there would be under Burnside for the time being. In other words, McClellan's army was being transferred to Burnside.

On the same day, McClellan wrote confidentially to Burnside, beginning "My dear Burn," stating that he had received messages from Halleck that Pope was in danger and that he was pushing the troop movements. He added: "Yesterday and to-day I have received intelligence from confidential sources leading me to think it probable that Halleck either will not or cannot carry out his intentions in regard to my position, as expressed to you. This shall make no difference with me. I shall push on everything just as if I were to remain in command." [17]

Halleck's attitude toward McClellan had changed, as the latter wrote Burnside. Arriving in Washington with friendly feelings for McClellan, he came into contact with the coterie led by Stanton that was trying to jettison McClellan, and fell into their way of thinking, being a man of small independence of

---

[17] *Ibid.*, p. 605. McClellan wrote, on August 10: "Halleck is turning out just like the rest of the herd. . . . I see more clearly every day their ulterior purpose to force me to resign."

character. Stanton was telling him that McClellan was delaying the departure from James River, and Halleck was wiring McClellan to hurry. Every day he was becoming more and more hostile to the latter.

At last McClellan remonstrated. Halleck answered that he did not wish to be harsh, but that "I did feel that you did not act as promptly as I thought the circumstances required. I deemed every hour a golden one, the loss of which could not be repaired. I think you did not attach so much value to the passing hours; but perhaps I was mistaken." Unless McClellan's troops could join Burnside and Pope, Washington would be in actual danger.

The troops were being transferred with McClellan's usual skill. Rufus Ingalls reported, "The Harrison's Landing depot was abandoned with great success. The fleet was withdrawn with much system and without any material loss. The march of the army was conducted with great deliberation and good judgment. I accompanied the general by land. Our immense trains were taken through without accident." [18] So goes all the evidence. McClellan's withdrawal from Harrison's Landing was conducted with admirable precision and without loss. There was no real basis for the attacks being made on him in Washington. These were simply a part of the plot.

On August 21, Morell's division was at Falmouth and Porter's entire corps was arriving at Aquia. Heintzelman was to go from Aquia Creek to Alexandria, where there were better docks.

McClellan, having made all arrangements, left Fort Monroe for Aquia on August 23, arriving the next day. He was in a painful state of uncertainty as to his future. He wired Halleck, "I took it for granted that I was to come here to receive orders and am ready to move in any direction, having my staff, etc., still on the steamers." Halleck replied that he hoped to be able to give orders the next day, but the orders never came. Halleck added that he was trying to hold the line of the Rappahannock until all the Union forces could be united. At the same time (August 24) Burnside at Falmouth wanted to know where Pope was, having heard that he was retreating northward. Porter was

[18] O.R., Ser. I, Vol. XI, Pt. 3, p. 614.

feeling his way to Pope, who did not furnish sufficient information to enable troops to find him.

On August 25, Jackson crossed the Rappahannock west of Pope. The latter learned of the movement the same day from his signal station, which reported moving columns of troops. But Pope, without strategic insight, imagined that Jackson was retreating to the Shenandoah Valley. He had no prevision of his own peril. On the same day McClellan suggested to Halleck that Porter, on his way to join Pope, be left where he was, as the lower Rappahannock line might be in danger. He was thinking of a flank movement around Pope's left, but Lee instead was making it around the right. McClellan himself was still at Falmouth. Did Halleck wish him to stay at Aquia or go on to Alexandria? He had received no orders. Porter reported to Burnside instead of to McClellan, who was being more and more ignored as the plot against him ripened. He was now practically a general without a command.

Pope was getting touchy about the situation, as the idea was filtering through the brains of the authorities that he was a feeble general and that the capital was in danger. Halleck had to assure him that there was no dissatisfaction with him. He added, "The main object has been accomplished in getting up troops from the Peninsula, although they have been greatly delayed by storms."[19] In other words, the main object was McClellan's deposition.

On August 26, McClellan was inquiring about facilities for sending troops from Alexandria to Pope's army. He was informed that there were no cars and that the troops would have to march. McClellan was not sending orders to any troops, since Burnside was in actual command. Porter had become somewhat bewildered, being ordered both by Burnside and by Pope, who wanted him immediately. On August 26, Halleck wired Franklin at Alexandria to march toward Warrenton, reporting to Pope. On August 27, McClellan reached Alexandria and so informed Halleck, who had no message for him. McClellan wanted to know if Sumner and Franklin should not move to Centreville to join Pope, or if Sumner should not come to Alexandria for the de-

[19] *Ibid.*, Vol. XII, Pt. 3, p. 666.

fense of Washington, now seen to be in peril. Also should not Burnside leave Falmouth to cover Pope's retreat if he fell back that way?

Halleck was upset at a daring raid made by Stuart to Pope's rear and reflected in conversation on unnamed officers. McClellan, stung by repeated slights, demanded to know if the comments applied to himself, stating that he had just arrived at Alexandria and had no orders.

Halleck answered: "No remark was made by me, or in my hearing, reflecting on you, in relation to Manassas," but it was strange that 500 of the enemy could make such a raid with 20,000 Union troops nearby. "It would have been perfect nonsense to have referred to you when you had just arrived and knew nothing of the disposition of the troops. Indeed, I did not blame any particular person."

By this time the situation was growing serious and the authorities in Washington were biting their nails. Fighting was going on but nobody in the capital knew anything about it. Pope had fallen back from the Rappahannock but his whereabouts was unknown. It did not appear that he was the appointed savior, or anything but a badly fuddled commander.[20]

Halleck himself was at his wit's end to know what to do. With disaster pending, McClellan's merits were remembered. In the absence of information from Pope, the whole situation was clouded, and the head general was learning the difficulties of conducting campaigns from a desk chair.

As the problem was evidently becoming too big for Pope—even the fog of war could not conceal that—and as Burnside had nothing to offer, Halleck fell back on McClellan. On August 27, he wired him to bring up Sumner and Burnside, if necessary. He had sent General Barnard to confer with him. "From your knowledge of the whole country about here you can best act. I have had no time to obtain such knowledge.... As you must be aware more than three-quarters of my time is taken up with the raising of new troops and matters in the West. I have no time

---

[20] McClellan wrote on August 24: "Pope ran away from the Rappahannock last night, shamefully abandoning Porter and Burnside without giving them one word of warning."

for details. You will, therefore, as ranking general in the field, direct as you deem best; but at present orders for Pope's army should go through me." [21]

On the same day Halleck wired McClellan, "All orders sent to General Pope will be sent through you." McClellan replied that he would come to see Halleck at once. Lincoln was asking McClellan for news from the front, where great things were going on about which no information could be obtained. McClellan was once more giving orders, trying to bring up troops from Aquia to Alexandria. Circumstances were working for him.

Full reinstatement of McClellan to command might have staved off disaster. But it was not to be. Stanton, enraged by the ineptitude of Halleck and the evident incompetence of Pope, now attacked McClellan in a query to Halleck. He demanded the date when McClellan was first ordered to evacuate James River and whether the order was promptly obeyed; also whether the order for the movement of Franklin's corps from Alexandria had been promptly complied with. [22]

At this moment Halleck was again on good terms with McClellan, informing the latter that he could learn nothing from the front except through him and Burnside. The two conferred the whole evening of August 28, McClellan not leaving until 2:00 A.M. About midday McClellan had informed Halleck that the Confederates were in force at Manassas and were said to be between Pope and Alexandria. Movements from Alexandria should be made in force, or troops might be beaten in detail. He suggested that Pope should fall back to the Occoquan, a good suggestion indeed. At 3:30, McClellan wired that no time should be lost in pushing troops toward Pope. This did not look like a disinclination to support that general.

Just then McClellan changed his tune, saying that Franklin's and Sumner's corps were in poor condition to fight a battle.

---

[21] *O.R.*, Ser. I, Vol. XII, Pt. 3, p. 691. McClellan wrote on August 28: "I find Halleck all dispirited.... I shall keep as clear as possible of the Presdt. and Cabinet.... Pope is in a bad way, his communications with Wash. cut off and I have not yet the force to relieve him." Again he wrote: "Now they are in trouble they seem to want the 'Quaker,' the 'procrastinator,' the 'coward,' the 'traitor.'"

[22] *O.R.*, Ser. I, Vol. XII, Pt. 3, p. 706.

Halleck replied that there must be no delay in sending Franklin to the front. At 10:00 P.M. of August 28, McClellan told Halleck that Franklin was ordered to march early next morning. Reports were that the enemy, 120,000 strong, were moving toward Arlington and the Chain Bridge.

McClellan now stationed Sumner in the vicinity of the Chain Bridge and wished to keep Franklin also for the defense of Washington. Indeed, he and Halleck were at odds about Franklin; Halleck was trying, unsuccessfully, to get Franklin to Pope, even going over McClellan's head to order him. Franklin finally left Alexandria but was stopped at Annandale by McClellan. The latter has been greatly blamed for this action. It would seem, however, that there was reason for it.

Franklin, according to McClellan, had only about 10,000 men. The defenses around Washington were at that time so thinly garrisoned that the authorities feared that Stuart would ride into the city, which he, no doubt, would have done if he had known. McClellan had taken Pope's measure and felt that he would fail against such opponents as Lee and Jackson, that his defeat was certain. But what would that defeat mean? Suppose that Lee intervened between Washington and Pope and drove Pope away from the city; what would prevent his taking Washington? Certainly not the handful of raw troops in the forts and Sumner's small corps. That was why McClellan strove to keep Franklin near the capital: to save it if Lee came. He put the capital before Pope. The consequence was that Franklin did not join Pope until after the Second Battle of Manassas, and this was possibly a good thing. Franklin could not have prevented the defeat and would have been involved in the rout. Halleck answered that McClellan's dispositions were judicious and that what was to be feared was a night raid into Washington. He was enraged, though, that Franklin had not gone on to join Pope. "This is contrary to all my orders; investigate and report the facts of this disobedience." McClellan answered that he desired definite instructions, as he disliked to be accused of disobeying orders when he was only exercising the discretion given him.

Halleck finally answered Stanton's query, stating that he had

THE PLOT MATURES 145

directed McClellan, on July 30, to send his sick away preparatory to moving his army. (McClellan did not understand it in this sense; he thought he was merely to be relieved of a burden.) The order was not carried out as promptly as Halleck expected. Then Halleck went on to make a statement that reflected on the authorities. "The object of pushing General Pope forward to the Rapidan was simply to gain time for General McClellan's army to get into position somewhere in rear of the Rappahannock.... When General McClellan's movement was begun it was rapidly carried out; but there was an unexpected delay in commencing it." (McClellan says he had to push troops westward to make sure of not being attacked while embarking and that he had 12,000 sick, with only a few transports for moving them.) Then came the dispute over Franklin's movements. Halleck had tried to push him forward to Pope, but McClellan had held him back. (McClellan stated that he halted Franklin because he feared that the enemy in force were moving on the Chain Bridge.) All in all, Halleck, who knew his cue, made out a bad case against McClellan without doing anything more than failing to give McClellan's reasons for his course. Stanton was now merely awaiting an opportunity to get rid of McClellan, who he, mistakenly, thought was no longer needed. The plot was ripe, but Fate defeated it.

The period of uncertainty, so deplored by Halleck, was rapidly approaching an end. Heavy detonations in the direction of Manassas informed McClellan, near Alexandria, that serious fighting was in progress. Halleck ordered Franklin and Sumner to use their legs to reach Pope, even if without rations. McClellan wired Halleck that both commands were moving forward, that he had sent every soldier to the front.

While the fighting went on, and the rumble of the cannon echoed across the hills, McClellan waited in an agony of impatience and impotent desire. In the evening of August 30, he wired Halleck: "I cannot express to you the pain and mortification I have experienced to-day in listening to the distant sound of the firing of my men. As I can be of no further use here [near Alexandria], I respectfully ask that if there is a possibility of the conflict being renewed to-morrow, I may be permitted to go to the scene of battle with my staff, merely to be with my own men, if nothing more; they will fight none the worse for my being with them. If it is not deemed best to entrust me with the command even of my own army, I simply ask to be permitted to share their fate on the field of battle. Please reply to this tonight." Halleck replied next morning, "I cannot answer without seeing the President, as General Pope is in command, by his orders, of the department." [23]

This dispatch (omitted from the *Official Records*), should dissipate the idea that McClellan was reluctant, that he held back. He was eager to go forward to the fight, even if not permitted to command. But the conspirators, desiring to disgrace him, were determined that he should gain no laurels in the field. It was not until the full news came of the battle, and it was evident that no laurels had been gathered by the Union army, that McClellan was once more considered. In the hour of danger, following Pope's failure, he would do. He would be permitted to halt the rout and restore confidence to the disheartened army and the demoralized government.

Pope announced—the first dispatch from him for days—that Jackson was defeated and retreating. He himself had lost 8,000 men, the enemy many more. Glorious news indeed! The formidable Jackson defeated and retreating! As late as 8:30 in the night of August 30, McClellan thought that Pope might have been successful.

Then, later, came the thundering news. In the morning of August 31, Halleck learned something of the truth. He wired Pope: "You have done nobly. Don't yield another inch if you can avoid it. All reserves are being sent forward. With Franklin and Sumner, who must now be with you, can't you renew the attack?" Pope could not; he was heading for the Washington defenses.

It was Porter who told the whole truth, stating that he "was whipped, as was the whole army, badly—that is, I was over-

---

[23] *B. and L.*, Vol. II, p. 149. On August 30, McClellan wrote his wife: "They have taken all my troops from me. I have even sent off all my personal escort. I have been listening to the distant sound of a great battle—my men engaged in it and I away! I never felt worse in my life."

THE PLOT MATURES 147

powered.... We were driven from the field, and here we are [Centreville] after marching all last night. The men are without heart but will fight if cornered. Pope sent in a flag of truce today to get our wounded." [24] At 7:30 McClellan reported there were 20,000 stragglers between Centreville and Alexandria.

The facts were out. Pope had not only been beaten but routed. More than his army was in danger. Washington and the government were face to face with a crisis of the utmost moment. Everything depended on the decision then made. Was McClellan to command, or would the authorities gamble once more with an inexperienced general and perhaps lose the war? They thought of Burnside, but, fortunately for themselves, they passed him by. It was McClellan's destiny to save the situation.

Now comes the story of what Lee and Jackson were doing while Halleck and the authorities in Washington were trying to ease McClellan out of his command and find a general more in accord with current political opinions. That dangerous old game: appointing generals for politics instead of for military efficiency. It nearly ruined the Union.

Lee, that astute judge of opponents and a commander who feared McClellan, did not fear Pope. He prepared, literally, to play rings around him, to take liberties with him that he would not have dared to attempt against McClellan. He read Pope as a routine officer without strategic imagination, easily confused, and readily duped. And in the next few days he carried into execution the greatest strategic movement in American history. Lee by now had graduated. All that he had needed to bring out military talents second to few in history was experience, and the Seven Days had given him a great deal of experience, generally unpleasant. Thereafter he avoided frontal attacks on fortified positions. At Gettysburg, he ventured once more on such a movement and lost. When he stood gazing at Cemetery Ridge and Round Top, the ghost of Malvern Hill must have risen before him. But in August, 1862, Lee and Jackson and the gray-brown army were all at their best—entirely too good for a mediocre soldier who had just combined disjointed bodies of troops into an army.

[24] *O.R.*, Ser. I, Vol. XII, Pt. 3, p. 768.

For several days Lee and Pope confronted each other along the Rappahannock. Jackson, sending a force across the river, was obliged to recall it, giving the Unionists the chance to claim a success. Then Lee launched the ubiquitous Stuart on a raid to Pope's rear; Stuart gleefully returned with Pope's headquarters papers.

Given this information, Lee prepared to use it, knowing that he must act before McClellan's and Burnside's troops reached Pope. He now decided to attempt to cut Pope's communications and intervene between the Union army and Washington, the possibility of which McClellan had foreseen.

On August 25, Jackson was launched on this great adventure while Lee prepared to follow with Longstreet. Jackson crossed the Rappahannock west of Pope. He was now in his own country, the lovely piedmont of Virginia, with open meadows in which fine cattle grazed and with the pleasant little Bull Run Mountain on his right and the higher, hazy Blue Ridge on his left. In the whole United States there is no more beautiful terrain, now the paradise of thoroughbreds and fox-hunters.

To reach Pope's rear Jackson had to sweep in a wide circle and pass the Bull Run Mountains, which might be blocked. But Jackson's dirty, ragged men marched fast under the chief's eye and, coming to Thoroughfare Gap, in the low mountain range, passed through without meeting resistance.

The movement was observed but misinterpreted. Pope's signal men told of long columns of troops and wagons and artillery moving to the west of him, and he concluded that Jackson was retreating westward. Then, on the morning of August 27, he heard, to his astonishment, that Jackson had struck his supply railroad at Manassas. There's Pope's vast stores went up in smoke while ragged Southerners guzzled champagne and canned lobsters from the sutlers' shops.

Pope turned troops toward the raider, only to learn that the audacious Jackson had disappeared. He was shaken but, thinking the movement only a raid, made preparations to join forces with Franklin and with Burnside from Falmouth. If both these commands reached him, he would far outnumber Lee. Meanwhile Lee, following in Jackson's footsteps, passed through

Thoroughfare Gap with little resistance and was soon in touch with Jackson.

Jackson, to be near Lee, had fallen back to the battlefield of Bull Run, or Manassas, and had concealed his troops in the woods north of the Warrenton Turnpike, along which the battle of Bull Run had been fought. Tramping eastward, through the hot and dusty August afternoon, King's division of Pope's army appeared in front of Jackson. Jackson might have let them go on to join Franklin, who was then a little out from Alexandria. But it was Lee's plan to prevent just such a combination. Jackson thought fast and decided quickly.

Suddenly the weary Union soldiers, trudging along the high road, heard a commotion and turned to see a line of gray and brown men emerging from the woods north of the road. On they came, shouting, their red flags flapping in the light breeze. Lee's strategy was reaching fruition.

Quickly the Union column turned into line and spread out across the fields, awaiting the advancing Southerners. Presently the two lines came close and began to blaze away at each other while the cannon spattered grape and canister. On they fought, the lines swaying backward and forward, while the afternoon waned and the harvest moon arose, yellow and immense in the smoky air. The carnage was great, for the troops on both sides were marksmen. Killed and wounded lay in rows across the field; many high officers were struck, including Ewell and Taliaferro. Jackson's loss was heavy, and the contest remained in doubt until the Southern commander threw in his reserves and swept the field. The Unionists fell back southward toward Pope instead of eastward toward Franklin.

The fat was now in the fire. The groping Pope could no longer doubt where Jackson was, for Jackson had advertised his presence. Pope hurried his forces toward Manassas, ordering up Porter, then on his way from Falmouth. Jackson, meanwhile, fell back to an unfinished railroad a couple of miles north of the Warrenton Turnpike, since the railroad bed furnished some cover for his men.

On the morning of August 29, the massed Union troops attacked Jackson. Heintzelman's corps (including Hooker and

Kearny) held the right of the Union line. Sigel was next and then Schenck. Reynolds held the extreme left. Reno's command arrived and was put into the battle. McDowell and Porter were coming up from Manassas Junction. The fighting was severe, the losses on both sides heavy.

The Union troops went forward rather mechanically, fighting without much direction or enthusiasm, for the army was a collection of commands thrown hastily together. Besides, the men had little faith in Pope.

It was otherwise with the Confederates. The gray and brown men, standing in their lines behind the railway embankment, rammed their cartridges home with frantic haste but took time to aim. They stood there, ragged, dirty, hollow-eyed: cursing, shouting, laughing, jesting, supremely confident because Jackson were there—Jackson who drove them like dogs and fought them without mercy, but on whose flags victory always rested. It would be so again they knew. Jackson, watching his blazing line and hearing the shouts and loud laughter of his followers, relaxed his grim features into a smile. He knew his gray-brown men. At last the fire died away, and the worn-out troops on both sides could rest for a while beside the dead.

In the night Jackson withdrew his men to the cover of the woods, giving Pope the impression that he was defeated and retiring. The next morning Pope, wholly misunderstanding the situation, prepared to pursue. He did not know that Lee and Longstreet had come up and made contact with Jackson, that he was in the presence of the whole Confederate army.

Porter had known it for some time. Ordered by Pope to attack Jackson's right, he found masses of troops in his front and on his flank, Longstreet's command. Only some queer quirk had kept Longstreet from joining in the battle, leaving Jackson to bear it alone. If Porter had gone forward he would have been caught in a vise and crushed; but for not obeying Pope's order he was court-martialed and cashiered, to be reinstated years later on Confederate testimony.

Moving forward in the morning of August 30, Pope still found Jackson in his front. The Confederates, emerging like wood nymphs from the forest, deployed in line, and the battle was renewed. The Unionists, advancing, poured volleys into the gray-brown men, receiving volleys in return that drove them back. The Unionists made some ground on their right but felt increasing pressure on their left. In places the Confederate ammunition gave out, and the gray-brown men repelled charges with stones, shouting like schoolboys in a rock battle.

About midday Pope sent forward Porter's corps, supported by King's division, Sigel's corps, and Reynolds' division, in an attempt to beat Jackson's right. The attack failed; Porter fell back. Then it was that Lee decided to throw in Longstreet. The latter turned the tide of battle by artillery. Many batteries were lying idle behind Longstreet's line; these now discharged a perfect storm of grape and canister upon Pope's left flank. No troops on earth could have endured such punishment. The Union line began to recede, slowly and then more rapidly. At this moment Lee ordered an advance of his whole army. It was magnificently made. Far to the right and left, enveloping the Union flank, the gray-brown lines swept out of the woods, and forward with a gigantic chorus of triumphant voices, the red battle flags gleaming in the late afternoon sun.

Before such an assault Pope's army crumpled and fell back eastward, though here and there squads of men continued to resist. At that moment it seemed that Lee had won a decisive, even an annihilating, victory.

He was cheated of it by one thing alone—Sykes's division of Porter. These regulars, the equals of any troops on earth, held Henry Hill, just south of the Warrenton turnpike and near Bull Run; all that Longstreet could do failed to dislodge them. They held out while the shattered army passed Bull Run. Night ended the pursuit. Thus Porter and Sykes saved Pope's army, for which they never received the smallest thanks. Indeed Porter was saddled with the blame of the defeat.

The next evening, August 31, after a halt at Centreville, the army continued to fall back. It had never had much confidence in Pope or liking for him; it had fought bravely enough but as if preordained to defeat. Weariness and disgust were the mood of officers and men alike.

In the starlight one officer said, incredulously to another, that he thought he recognized McClellan in a group of men standing on the road side.

"Nonsense," said the colonel. "What would General McClellan be doing out in this lonely place, at this time of night, without an escort?"

Then some one came running and crying out, "Colonel, Colonel, General McClellan is here!"

"The enlisted men caught the sound! Whoever was awake aroused his neighbor. Eyes were rubbed, and those tired fellows, as the news passed down the column, jumped to their feet and sent up such a hurrah as the Army of the Potomac had never heard before. Shout upon shout went out into the stillness of the night; and as it was taken up along the road and repeated by regiment, brigade, division and corps, we could hear the roar dying away in the distance. The effect of this man's presence upon the Army of the Potomac—in sunshine or rain, in darkness or in daylight, in victory or defeat—was electrical, and too wonderful to make it worth while to give a reason for it." [25]

Thus the soldiers themselves, if not the government, recognized with clear vision where the hope of the Union lay, the Union that McClellan was to save in spite of itself.

[25] *B. and L.*, Vol. II, p. 490.

CHAPTER TWELVE

HE SAVES THE UNION IN SPITE OF ITSELF

IN THE MORNING of August 31, McClellan wired Halleck: "My aide just in. He reports our army as badly beaten. Our losses very heavy. Troops arriving at Centreville. Have probably lost several batteries." That evening McClellan added that he understood there were 20,000 stragglers between Centreville and Alexandria. Evidently the Army of Virginia had gone to pieces.

It was characteristic of Halleck, at his wit's end, to call on the lately deposed McClellan "to assist him in this crisis with his ability and experience." McClellan promptly answered, "I am ready to afford you every assistance in my power, but you will readily perceive how difficult an undefined position, such as I now hold, must be." Asking when he could see Halleck, McClellan was told that any hour would suit.

As the magnitude of the defeat began to dawn on the authorities, Halleck suggested to Pope that he fall back to Fairfax or even towards Alexandria. At the same time Halleck directed McClellan to stop retreating troops and retain them where he could best establish an outer line of defense. "I am fully aware of the gravity of the crisis and have been for weeks."

Even on September 1, the authorities did not entirely realize the seriousness of the situation. They were too full of their animosity for McClellan to understand what faced the Union, with the defeat of its main army and the spreading demoralization, made evident by the thousands of stragglers who filled the roads and fields in the vicinity of Alexandria. The cabinet members were more concerned with getting rid of McClellan than with taking measures to save Washington.

Only a few days before, the conspirators, hoping that Pope had defeated Jackson, thought that the time had come to dispose of McClellan. Secretary Welles, when leaving his office in the evening of August 30, was stopped by Salmon P. Chase, who showed the naval secretary a protest, addressed to Lincoln, against continuing McClellan in command. Welles refused to sign the paper, saying, "I did not choose to denounce McClellan for incapacity or to pronounce him a traitor, as declared by this paper," though he favored McClellan's dismissal. Chase said "that was not sufficient, that the time had arrived when the Cabinet must act with energy and promptitude, for either the Government or McClellan must go down." [1]

This conspiracy, in which facts were distorted or falsified, was frustrated for the time by the course of events. The midday of August 31 brought news of Pope's defeat, not confirmation of his victory; McClellan's enemies had struck too late, for Lincoln was unwilling to let go the single competent army commander.

In the evening of August 31, Welles went to the War Department for news from the front. Stanton and Caleb Smith were closeted when Welles entered. Stanton, ignoring the military plight, launched out in a tirade against McClellan, from whom he said he could get no information as to plans. He went on and on, raking up everything he had against the general, until Smith left. Then Stanton whisperingly asked Welles if he did not think McClellan should be got rid of. Welles answered that he thought so but that he disliked the underhand method adopted, that it was discourteous to Lincoln (not consulted) if nothing else. Stanton grumblingly returned that he was under no obligation to Lincoln, who had put on him an unbearable burden. [2]

Welles himself was not alarmed by the military situation on that Sunday (August 31), for Pope had minimized his defeat. Halleck, however, who knew more, did not conceal his uneasiness. He said (Welles states) that "we overrate our own strength and underestimate the Rebels'—a fatal error.... This has been the talk of McClellan, which some of us have believed."

---
[1] Welles, *op. cit.*, Vol. I, p. 94.
[2] *Ibid.*, pp. 97-98.

At midnight of August 31, McClellan, near Alexandria, telegraphed Halleck that Pope should retreat at once. "I have no confidence in the dispositions made as I gather them. To speak frankly—and the occasion demands it—there appears to be a total absence of brains, and I fear the total destruction of the army.... The occasion is grave and demands grave measures. The question is the salvation of the country.

"It is my deliberate opinion that the interests of the nation demand that Pope should fall back to-night if possible, and not one moment is to be lost." [3] He wrote his wife: "I have a terrible task on my hands now—perfect imbecility to correct. No means to act with, no authority—yet determined if possible to save the country and the capital."

His sound advice was followed, though somewhat involuntarily. If Pope had attempted to make a stand at Centreville, with defeated and utterly disheartened troops, against the exulting graybacks flushed with victory, it is possible, and even probable, that his army would have been destroyed. The pet commander of the War Department—little more than a man of straw—would have had small chance against Lee and Jackson. It was because McClellan's advice was taken that the army was saved for further battles.

McClellan has been severely censured for the above message to his wife, especially by Nicolay and Hay, who reflect Stanton's prejudices. And that McClellan was again too outspoken is true; but the man who had been so cruelly accused of incapacity by Stanton may be forgiven for remarking on the dangerous incompetence of Stanton's favorite. It was indeed no time for mincing terms.

On September 1, McClellan saw Halleck at headquarters. The latter gave him verbal instructions to take charge of the Washington defenses, limiting him strictly to the garrisons and forbidding him from giving orders to the troops under Pope. In the afternoon of the same day, Halleck requested McClellan to come to his house and confer with Lincoln.

The President told McClellan he had reason to believe that the Army of the Potomac was not supporting Pope properly,

[3] *O.R.*, Ser. I, Vol. XII, Pt. 1, p. 103.

that he had "always been a friend of mine," and asked McClellan to use his influence to correct matters. McClellan answered that Lincoln was misinformed, that the Army of the Potomac would do its full duty. Lincoln, a good deal affected, then suggested that McClellan telegraph "Fitz John Porter or some other of my friends," trying to do away with the feeling against Pope.[4]

McClellan responded generously, though not crediting in the least Pope's accusations against his friends. "I ask you for my sake," he wrote Porter, "that of the country, and of the old Army of the Potomac, that you and all my friends will lend the fullest and most cordial coöperation to General Pope in all the operations now going on.... This week is the crisis of our fate. Say the same thing to my friends in the Army of the Potomac, and that the last request I have to make of them is that, for their country's sake, they will extend to General Pope the same support they ever have to me."

In this way Lincoln sought to save Pope, but Pope was past saving. He had failed, and his failure jeopardized the government.

In the evening of September 1, the authorities gained full knowledge of the extent of the disaster, which, of course, had been known before to the people of Washington, who were exhibiting great uneasiness—except Southern sympathizers. There was a vision of gaunt, hairy beings riding into Washington like centaurs (or circus-riders, as the Confederate cavalrymen were described) and perhaps gleefully setting fire to the Capitol and White House, to be followed by the terrible Jackson and his disreputable-appearing men, all ready for slaughter and rapine. People slept badly that night.

Pope was now about to be thrown overboard and McClellan brought back to authority. In the morning of September 2, Lincoln, who had wisely taken the ordering of affairs into his own hands, went to McClellan's house in company with Halleck. The President was greatly depressed, stating that the situation was bad with the army in full retreat on Washington. "He instructed me," wrote McClellan, "to take steps at once to stop and collect the stragglers, to place the works in a proper state of defense,

[4] *Ibid.*, p. 104.

SAVES THE UNION AGAIN 157

and to go out to meet and take command of the army when it approached the vicinity of the works; then to place the troops in the best position—committing everything to my hands." [5]

In his last account, written shortly before his death, McClellan says that Halleck had sent his adjutant general, Colonel Kelton, to the front to learn the condition of affairs. On September 2, shortly after breakfast, Lincoln called on McClellan in company with Halleck.

"The President informed me that Colonel Kelton had returned and represented the condition of affairs as much worse than I had stated to Halleck on the previous day; that there were thirty thousand stragglers on the roads; that the army was entirely defeated and falling back to Washington in confusion. He then said that he regarded Washington as lost, and asked me if I would under the circumstances, consent to accept command of all the forces. Without one moment's hesitation and without making any conditions whatever, I at once said that I would accept the command and would stake my life that I would save the city. Both the President and Halleck again asserted that it was impossible to save the city, and I repeated my firm conviction that I could and would save it. Then they left, the President verbally placing me in entire command of the city and of the troops falling back upon it from the front." [6]

This statement of McClellan's, which is substantially the same as that in his book, has been called in question by historians; they accuse him of drawing the long bow. It may be true that, seeing events through the veil of years and frustrated ambition, he exaggerated somewhat, but not very much. What appears to be true is that Halleck, who was more alarmed than Lincoln, gave the color to the interview. Of Halleck's demoralization at this moment there can be no doubt, because he gave preliminary orders for the evacuation of Washington—orders that were canceled by McClellan. It was Halleck's panic that McClellan remembered when he wrote.

McClellan, again in the saddle, at once set to work, dispatching his staff officers with orders for the various commands and

[5] *Ibid.*, p. 105.
[6] *B. and L.*, Vol. II, p. 149.

to further supplies and ammunition to the retreating troops. Having made all preparations, he was about to proceed to the front and take command in person when he was halted by a message from Halleck conveying an order from Lincoln not to do so until the troops had reached the vicinity of the Washington defenses. This was a last attempt to save Pope. Waiting until the afternoon, McClellan rode to Upton's Hill, the most advanced of the forts protecting the city.

There he met Pope and McDowell. Firing was going on in the direction of Chantilly; Pope thought a serious engagement was in progress. He, however, had no intention of remaining longer with the troops and asked McClellan if he objected to his proceeding to Washington. McClellan replied that he did not, but that he himself was going to the firing line. With one aide and three orderlies he rode across country to reach the retiring column by the shortest way. When he was recognized by the weary, disheartened, and disillusioned men, he was received with a cheer that roared up and down the line for miles. It was the greatest moment of his life. It was vindication. There have been few more dramatic moments in American history than McClellan's reception by the army that was still his, soul and body.

The cabinet members, even in the midst of appalling disaster, had not abandoned the fight against McClellan, which seemed as important to them as the defense of the capital against the Confederates. Chase exclaimed bitterly over McClellan's report that there were 20,000 stragglers from the beaten army, declaring it to be "infamously false and sent in for infamous purposes." Then the listening Welles was shown a petition to the President, much modified from the former one, requesting him not to put McClellan in command. This paper, according to Welles, was in the writing of Attorney General Bates—the more violent petition had been written by Stanton—and was signed by Stanton, Chase, Smith, and Bates.[7] Welles goes on to say that Seward was out of town, "if I am not mistaken, is purposely absent to be relieved from participation in this movement, which originated with Stanton, who was mad—perhaps with reason—and

[7] *Op. cit.*, Vol. I, p. 101.

determined to destroy McClellan. Seward and Stanton act in concert, but Seward has opposed or declined being a party to the removal of McClellan, until since Halleck was brought here, when Stanton became more fierce and determined. Seward then gave way and went away. Chase, who has become hostile to McClellan, is credulous and sometimes the victim of intrigue, was taken into Stanton's confidence, made to believe that the opportunity of Seward's absence should be improved to shake off McClellan, whom they both disliked, by a combined Cabinet movement to control the President, who, until recently, has clung to that officer. It was difficult, under the prevailing feeling of indignation against McClellan, to enlist Smith. I am a little surprised that they got Mr. Bates, though he has for some time openly urged the removal of McClellan. Chase took upon himself to get my name, and then, if possible, Blair was to be brought in. In all this, Chase flatters himself that he is attaching Stanton to his interest; not but that he is himself sincere in his opposition to McClellan, who was once his favorite, but whom he considers a deserter from his faction and whom he now detests." So Welles continues to give the history of the conspiracy, which might indeed have injured Lincoln as well as McClellan.

Welles held out against joining in a cabinet attack on the general, though he favored his removal. He declined to "enter into combinations to control" Lincoln, which he considered not only disrespectful but dangerous. Chase, thus rebuked, disclaimed any intention to be disrespectful to the President.

Welles declares, "It was evident there was a fixed determination to remove and, if possible, disgrace McClellan." Chase, in his dislike for McClellan, went so far as to say that if he were president the general would be shot. This rather shocked Welles, who, however, took occasion to express his own unfavorable opinion of McClellan, principally because of the latter's failure to coöperate with the navy to the satisfaction of Welles. It makes his testimony all the more valuable that he himself disliked McClellan but was too honest to engage in a reprehensible intrigue to ruin an officer of high reputation and standing.

Lincoln seems never to have been aware of Stanton's treacherous conduct in this affair, for the conspirators were underhanded. The President continued to place confidence in McClellan in spite of Stanton's and Chase's unrelenting misrepresentations. It seems certain that they would have succeeded in ruining McClellan at this time if the course of events had not frustrated their plot.

The cabinet met on September 2. It was like a meeting of a defeated government, and it was a government facing defeat. While awaiting Lincoln's arrival the cabinet officers discussed the situation, grumbling over the fact that Pope "without consultation or advice" was retreating to the Washington defenses. Pope's friends were hard put to defend him. Welles, eagerly listening to the talk, states that "Blair, who has known him [Pope] intimately, says he is a braggart and a liar, with some courage perhaps, but not much capacity." Pope's friends then attempted to frame an alibi for the unhappy general, declaring that McClellan, Franklin, and Porter were really responsible for the defeat. The feeling was bitter.

Stanton was almost beside himself for a time. He announced to the cabinet that he had heard that McClellan was assigned to command the forces in Washington. A murmur of surprise ran around the table; the conspirators looked at each other. A fine end to the cabinet protest from which so much had been expected!

Just then the President entered the room and was at once assailed with questions about McClellan. Was he really back in the saddle after all? Voices rose angrily.

Lincoln answered, in quiet but firm tones, that he had done what seemed to him best and that he was responsible to the country. Halleck, who was present, agreed. McClellan, he said, was excellent on defense, a good engineer, an admirable organizer, "good for nothing for an onward movement."

At this a confused clamor arose. Men spoke, despondently and angrily. "The President was greatly distressed." McClellan's enemies vented their various objections, but Lincoln and Blair insisted that he, beyond any other officer, enjoyed the confidence of the army and so was the man of the hour.

Most reluctantly the cabinet concurred in the President's decision, except Chase, who protested emphatically against Mc-

Clellan's reappointment to command.[8] He attacked the general in the bitterest terms, rehearsing the whole Peninsular and Second Manassas Campaigns and accusing McClellan of being responsible for Pope's defeat. Lincoln was much disturbed to find the cabinet lined up against McClellan but remained firm, declaring that he knew no one who could handle the situation as well. Chase heatedly suggested Hooker, Sumner, Burnside, but the President was unshaken in his determination. And by his resolution in this matter he saved the Union, for it was the most important decision he made in the whole war.

Stanton appears to have let off most of his steam before Lincoln came, as he was much less obstructive than Chase, probably for the reason that he was thoroughly scared and not unwilling to have the situation saved even by McClellan. Washington was seething with rumors, more excited than it had been at any time since the battle of Bull Run in July of the year before. It was a rather wretched small town just beginning, under the stimulus of war, to be of importance. Badly built, with a vast, unpaved Pennsylvania Avenue on which horses stalled in winter and from which dust storms blew in summer, it had no business except politics and barrooms. It grew greatly in the war and, after the war, was immensely improved by the famous Boss Shepherd, whose absurd statue crowned his labors.

At that moment there was no head of the army. Welles says, "Halleck is here in the Department, a military director, not a general, a man of some scholastic attainments, but without soldierly capacity." He did not think that McClellan was a fighting general, a curious commentary on the man who had fought the fiercest battles of the war. Welles expresses an opinion for which Stanton was largely, but not entirely, responsible that the defeat of Second Manassas was mainly due to McClellan. No doubt McClellan and his friends were deeply affronted by the slights put on him, says Welles, but they should have placed duty before resentment. "Stanton, in his hate of McClellan, has aggrieved other officers.... The introduction of Pope here, followed by Halleck, is an intrigue of Stanton's and Chase's to get

[8] Chase's Diary, *American Historical Association Report*, 1902, Vol. II, p. 63.

rid of McClellan. A part of this intrigue has been the withdrawal of McClellan and the Army of the Potomac from before Richmond and turning it into the Army of Washington under Pope."

The attack on McClellan had been maturing for some time. Welles states that, long before, he had overheard Chase telling the President that the whole movement against Richmond by the Peninsula was wrong, that Washington should be made the base of operations for an overland campaign. "What would you do?" Lincoln asked. "Order McClellan to return and start again," replied Chase. Pope said, "If Halleck were here, you would have, Mr. President, a competent adviser who would put this matter right." Lincoln then went to West Point to consult Winfield Scott; shortly afterward Halleck was called from the West and put in command. The army, on Halleck's recommendation, was then withdrawn from the James. Thus Welles gives the origin and various steps in the plot against McClellan. His evidence has been largely overlooked by historians. He was in no sense a partisan of McClellan's; in fact, he had small confidence in the general, but what he did have was an unconquerable desire to set down in writing his observations and experiences.

On September 4, Welles was with Lincoln when Pope, seeking to vindicate himself, read an account of his operations beginning with Cedar Mountain. It was a narrative tinged with wounded pride and a keen sense of injustice. Seward came in while the reading was in progress but immediately left. Pope, walking out with Welles, maintained that his misfortunes were entirely due to McClellan, Franklin, and Porter. If they had not been blamed, somebody else would have been; Pope earlier had opened on Sigel, whom he wished removed. He was of the type that has an alibi for everything. He was not outgeneraled, oh no! His dispositions had been perfect but the traitorous officers of the Army of the Potomac had ruined them. They were to blame, not he. His complaints would have had no effect on the public, which had judged him and found him wanting, but it did confirm Lincoln in the belief, incorrect though it was, that McClellan had deliberately left Pope to his fate. All that can be reasonably charged against McClellan was that, being the victim of a wretched intrigue, he did not lend altogether wholehearted support to a general whom he knew well to be one of the conspirators. After all, human beings are human.

Meanwhile, Washington was quieting down. If McClellan had not been there, it is possible that Lee would have attempted something against the capital; but he learned quickly that McClellan was in command at Washington. Consequently, he steered clear of the city, moving to the fords of the Potomac many miles upstream. He would seek to detach Maryland from the Union cause and perhaps carry the war into Pennsylvania.

It was the darkest hour of the whole war for the Union. Everything at headquarters was recrimination and depression. Halleck's incompetence was plainly evident; in a crisis he was just a fumbling, ox-faced old man. Pope was doing nothing but storm and rage against McClellan and Porter, making the most ridiculous accusations against the latter, whose troops, as a matter of fact, had saved the army from ruin.

On September 2, Halleck informed McClellan that he was in command of the defenses and that orders coming from him should be considered as coming from Halleck himself.[9] On the same day McClellan stopped a movement of Halleck's to ship everything in the arsenal at Washington to New York. McClellan was never better than in a great emergency like this. His courage rose with the need for it. He declared, "I do not despair of saving the capital." It is evident that the authorities were preparing to abandon Washington if Lee advanced against it. McClellan appears to have stopped the panic. Halleck replied that there were 50,000 or 60,000 small arms in the arsenal as well as many pieces of artillery. If he had carried out his first intention these would have been sent away, leaving Washington largely defenseless. A subordinate told McClellan of Halleck's order, whereupon McClellan countermanded it. This day, September 2, saw the height of the panic. McClellan's assignment to the command of the Washington defenses now became known and almost immediately had a calming effect.

On September 3, Pope was in the same position in which McClellan had been a few days earlier, that is, he was inquiring what his status was. "Does McClellan command in chief on this

[9] *O.R.*, Ser. I, Vol. XII, Pt. 1, p. 797.

side of the river [north] or do his functions only extend to designating the positions to be occupied by the troops arriving from Centreville?" McClellan would have liked an answer to the same question. Everything was in the air, and what he did he did with the vaguest authority.

Pope reported that he was ready "to advance again to the front with the fresh troops now here.... Let us not sit down quietly but push forward again." [10] No comfort came to him from Halleck, who directed him to report in Washington as soon as his troops came to the vicinity of the defenses. "General McClellan commands all troops in the fortifications. A reorganization of the army for the field will be immediately made. Till then General McClellan, as senior and as commanding the defenses of Washington, must exercise general authority." This showed Pope that the game was almost up, and he went to Washington to see Lincoln.

He still held out, sending Halleck a plan for reorganization. The next day Halleck informed McClellan that Pope had been relieved of command and that Reynolds, Porter, and Franklin were also relieved from duty until the charges against them could be examined. Pope hoped on, asking Halleck if he was to take the field under McClellan's directions. He protested that the latter was giving orders to the troops without consulting him. Pope then demanded a vindication of his course from Halleck, which, as a matter of fact, he had a right to ask since he had acted under Halleck's direction. The latter answered that the Army of Virginia and the Army of the Potomac were consolidated. "The troops at present are under McClellan's orders, and it is evident that you cannot serve under him willingly." Besides, Pope's testimony was needed at the proposed court of inquiry. A report on his recent operations had best not be given out at that time. No blame attached to Pope. "On the contrary, we think you did your best with the material you had.... The differences and ill-feeling among the generals are very embarrassing to the administration, and unless checked will ruin the country. It must

---

[10] *Ibid.*, Pt. 3, p. 808. McClellan wrote, on September 5: "Again I have been called upon to save the country. The case is desperate, but with God's help I will try unselfishly to do my best."

cease." On the same day Halleck directed Pope to report to the Secretary of War.

Pope was sent West, disappearing from the theatre of the war. He was a party to the attempt to ruin McClellan, seeking to have the command of the army himself. If he had received lukewarm support from McClellan's friends, it was only a fitting recompense for his own treacherous course. He had plotted with Chase, Stanton, and Halleck to bring the Army of the Potomac from the James River and consolidate it with his Army of Virginia, thus depriving McClellan of his command. The two armies were consolidated, but it was Pope, not McClellan, who had been thrown out. He was hoist by his own petard; there can be no regret that this plotting and incompetent general was relegated to the backwoods. He had had his chance and failed.

Seward came to McClellan, expressing uneasiness about the garrison at Harper's Ferry. McClellan answered that Harper's Ferry should be evacuated. Halleck angrily refused to remove the troops, declaring the garrison to be safe. Thus McClellan and Halleck were still at odds.

For some days McClellan's status was vague, and it never became very definite again. He says, "I was afterwards accused of assuming command without authority, for nefarious purposes, and in fact I fought the battles of South Mountain and Antietam with a halter around my neck, for if the Army of the Potomac had been defeated and I had survived, I would, no doubt, have been tried for assuming authority without orders, and, in the state of feeling which so unjustly condemned the innocent and most meritorious General F. J. Porter, I would probably have been condemned to death." [11]

It would seem that McClellan was put in command of the field army by Halleck, though the latter denied it just as Lincoln denied doing it. McClellan would hardly have gone as far as he did go—could not have done so, in fact—without the assent of his superiors. What is probable is that Halleck, as general in chief, gave McClellan verbal directions to take command of the army while the crisis lasted. It was an indefinite and most unsatisfactory commission, but it was a commission.

[11] *B. and L.*, Vol. II, p. 552.

At this moment the chances favored the Confederates. By their genius and daring, Lee and Jackson had transformed the war. Owing to the plot against McClellan, Richmond had been saved and Washington endangered. If the chief, if Lincoln, had not kept his head at this juncture, Chase and Stanton would have been willing to do once more what they had so disastrously just done: trust the army to another inferior general, in the very face of the greatest military combination of modern history—Lee and Jackson.

Such a course might well have been fatal. The Union forces were so disorganized, the generals so disgruntled, the troops so disheartened that anything might have happened. The evidence is cumulative and convincing.

Welles wrote on September 5, "There is a good deal of demoralization in the army; officers and soldiers are infected." On the next day he added, "The War Department is bewildered, knows but little, does nothing, proposes nothing."

In this crisis one man remained cool, and that was Lincoln. He did not like McClellan, for McClellan's manner, which was probably a little precious at times, annoyed him, as it had the cabinet members; but he was much too intelligent to let personal prejudice stand in the way of public service in a moment of peril. Against the wishes of everybody around him except Halleck, who in his panic leaned on McClellan, Lincoln reappointed the general of the Army of the Potomac to the command of the troops around Washington, although in an indefinite and impermanent way. Evidently he did not expect McClellan to remain at the head of the army, but as long as the Confederates were in Maryland and threatening Washington, he intended to keep the one general who had the confidence of the troops. Lincoln categorically denied that he ever did anything more than appoint McClellan to command the Washington defenses.

McClellan immediately went to work, and from chaos order began to emerge. The disorganized masses were falling in line; the thousands of runaways and stragglers who filled Washington rejoined their commands. Welles notes, on September 6, with a jab at McClellan, "Our army is passing north. This evening some twenty or thirty thousand passed my house within three hours. There was design in having them come up from Pennsylvania Avenue to H Street, and pass by McClellan's house, which is at the corner of H and 15th. They cheered the General lustily, instead of passing by the White House and honoring the President." But McClellan had earned the cheers, for nobody else in Washington could have rallied those demoralized fugitives in a day or two as he had done. Welles added, "McClellan and his partisans have ascendancy in the army, but he has lost ground in the confidence of the country, chiefly from delays, or what the President aptly terms as 'slows'."

The conspirators were in a bitter mood at McClellan's recovery of power. Chase, on September 7, walking with Welles, disburdened his heart. He said, almost in tears, that everything was going wrong. He was afraid that the country was ruined. McClellan was having everything his own way, as he, Chase, had expected if he was not dismissed. "It was a reward for perfidy." Welles, while agreeing with Chase in much of his estimate of McClellan, answered, "But I did not believe he was unfaithful and destitute of patriotism."

Welles went on to say, "From what I have seen and heard within the last few days, the more highly do I appreciate the President's judgment and sagacity in the stand he has made, and the course he took. Stanton has carried his dislike or hatred of McClellan to great lengths, and from free intercourse with Chase has enlisted him, and to some extent influenced all of us against that officer, who has failings enough of his own to bear without the addition of Stanton's enmity to his own infirmities. Seward, in whom McClellan has confided more than any member of the Administration ... yielded to Stanton's malignant feelings, and yet, not willing to encounter that officer, he went off to Auburn, expecting the General would be disposed of whilst he was away. Most of this originated, and has been matured, in the War Department, Stanton and Chase being the pioneers, Halleck assenting, the President and Seward under the stress of McClellan's disease, 'the slows.' ...." The recall of the army from Richmond was opposed by some of the best military men. "Placing Pope over them roused the indignation of many. But in this Stanton had a purpose to accomplish, and in bringing first Pope here, then by Pope's assistance and General Scott's advice bringing Halleck, and concerting measures which followed, he succeeded in breaking down and displacing McClellan, but not in dismissing and disgracing him." That Lincoln would not permit.[12]

Thus it will be seen that Stanton and Chase had been able to undermine McClellan in the President's estimate without securing all that they expected. There is no evidence to show that McClellan in any way betrayed Pope. All the testimony (including that of Longstreet) indicates that Porter did the right thing at the Second Manassas, and his troops, being more or less intact, prevented the ruin of the army. Franklin, at Centreville, rallied the routed and fleeing men and, beyond doubt, helped to frustrate the Confederate pursuit. He was of more value at Centreville than he would have been on the battlefield, because his 10,000 men could not have staved off defeat. If all of McClellan's army could have been incorporated in Pope's army in time to form an integral part of it, the result might have been different; Pope should have fallen back to the Occoquan in order to accomplish this. But he elected to attack Jackson instead of withdrawing and so was responsible for the disaster that befell him. Against the weight of the Chase-Stanton prejudice, McClellan has been helpless to secure justice. He was perfectly right in protesting against the withdrawal from James River, where he could hold Lee; and if he showed no vast enthusiasm to assist men who were plotting to ruin him he cannot be blamed. The self-made martyr is comparatively rare. Welles makes no bones about the matter, and no man knew more about it than he did. He states over and over again that Stanton was out to destroy McClellan.

On September 7, Welles, walking with his son, met McClellan and his staff. McClellan stopped, rode up to the sidewalk and shook hands with Welles, stating that he was going to take command of the "onward movement." "Then you go up the river," said Welles. McClellan answered that he had just started to take command of the army. "Well onward, General, is now the word. The country will expect you to go forward." "That,"

[12] Welles, *op. cit.*, Vol. I, p. 113.

he answered, "is my intention." "Success to you, then, General, with all my heart."

Welles went on to say that he would not have given the command to McClellan, but that it might be for the best. "The army is, I fear, much demoralized, and its demoralization is much of it to be attributed to the officers whose highest duty it was to prevent it. To have placed any other general than McClellan, or one of his circle, in command would be to risk disaster."

It is singular, in light of what had gone before, that Chase at this time confessed to Welles that it might have been hazardous to dismiss McClellan. In fact, the evidence indicates that it would have taken any other officer than McClellan weeks to reorganize troops thoroughly disorganized and disheartened. There is no doubt that thousands of men had left the ranks and gone home. The situation parallels that of Lee's army in the winter of 1864-65, when men deserted in squads. Other thousands of men were loafing in Washington or near it; these were quickly rounded up by the magic of McClellan's name but could not have been rallied for some time by anybody else.

"Admiral Foote used to laugh at the gasconade and bluster of Pope. Halleck, Foote insisted, was a military imbecile, though he might make a good clerk. Stanton and Pope took occasion to praise Halleck's superlative merits to Lincoln. . . . How far Halleck was assenting to or committed to Stanton's implacable hostility to McClellan or whether he was aware of its extent before he came here, I cannot say. Shortly after he arrived I saw that he partook of the views of Stanton and Chase. By the direction of the President he visited the army on the James and became a partner to the scheme for the recall of the troops. This recall or withdrawal he pronounced one of the most difficult things to achieve successfully that an accomplished commander could execute." Welles also states that he could not see that Halleck himself did anything in the withdrawal.

The story told by Welles in his diary is borne out by Chase's diary. As early as August 3, Chase was pressing for McClellan's removal from command, but Halleck at that time opposed it.[13]

[13] Chase's Diary, *American Historical Association Report, 1902*, Vol. II, p. 57.

Halleck, however, was soon won over to anti-McClellan views, for Chase states: "Stanton and Halleck had sent Burnside to James River, to act as second in command—or as adviser of McClellan, in reality to control him."[14] On August 19, Chase and Stanton had a conference on the military situation. Stanton was much dissatisfied with "the President's lack of decision," as Chase calls it in regard to McClellan, whom Stanton was then actively attempting to get removed. Stanton thought that Burnside was too partial to McClellan "to be safe."[15] The fact was that Burnside was too scrupulous to engage in the intrigue. While the fighting was going on at Manassas, Stanton and Chase approached Bates, who signed Stanton's petition. Welles, however, could not be constrained to sign it. Bates suggested a modification of the first, rather violent, petition, and the second paper was then prepared. Bates in his diary fully corroborates Welles and gives the key to the whole matter.

Why, it may be asked, was the cabinet so prejudiced against McClellan, so determined to have him removed from command? For two reasons: because McClellan was hopelessly conservative in politics, opposed to the abolition of slavery, against turning the war into a crusade instead of a defense of the Union. Bates states, "scheming ultras at the north are now working to force the President to deprive him [McClellan] of all command."[16] The second reason was that McClellan did not communicate his plans to the cabinet, which was ambitious of conducting the war itself. Stanton especially complained that McClellan did not report to him. Bates goes on to say: "I think Stanton believes, as I do, that McClellan has no plans but is fumbling and plunging in confusion and darkness."

Bates himself, though a moderate politically, had always been against McClellan and had persuaded Lincoln to remove him from the position of general in chief.[17] The feeling of the radicals was so strong against McClellan that Senator Zachariah

---

[14] *Ibid.*, p. 59.

[15] *Ibid.*, p. 62.

[16] Bates's Diary, *American Historical Association Report, 1930*, Vol. IV, p. 240.

[17] *Ibid.*, p. 239.

Chandler, drunk, denounced the general in the lobby of Willard's Hotel as a liar and coward. Whereupon General Sturgis applied the same terms to Chandler, who immediately retreated.[18] Bitter attacks were also made on other officers, Halleck being pictured as an "opium-eater."

The implications of the anti-McClellan cabinet conspiracy have never been fully realized by historians. McClellan was the occasion rather than the cause. The real purpose of Chase's petition was to present Lincoln with a cabinet ultimatum: either McClellan would have to go or the cabinet. If the plan had worked Lincoln would have become a puppet in the hands of Chase and Stanton, both of whom were not well disposed toward him. The cabinet was very nearly lined up: Chase, Stanton, Bates, Blair, and Smith all endorsed the paper, and Seward, wavering and closely watching events, would have signed if all the other members had done so. But Welles's loyalty to Lincoln (for which he cannot be too highly commended) prevented his joining, though as much opposed to McClellan as the others. This defection, and Pope's rout, with the resulting situation, frustrated the plot. The fact remains that on August 30, 1862, when his main army was being defeated by Lee, Lincoln was faced by a cabinet rebellion, which might have had far-reaching consequences. It was the supreme moment of his career. He never showed greater insight and adroitness than he did in retaining McClellan in command in the crisis while practically disclaiming responsibility for doing so. It is true, however, that Lincoln never knew of the extent of the conspiracy and the imminence of his danger. Had Chase and Stanton's plot succeeded, he would have been forced to yield to cabinet dictation or would have appeared before the world as unable to control his government. Either course would have been disastrous. He retained McClellan in command long enough to save the Union cause from impending ruin and then relieved him when the crisis was past, and he could bend to the pressure put on him, claiming "dilatoriness" as the cause of the removal. It was a political masterpiece.

Chase, more than Stanton, was behind this particular phase

[18] *Ibid.*, p. 260. (January 4, 1863).

of the plot, and ambition was his motive. He wished to be president and was thinking of the election of 1864 or 1868. Unable to get a nomination from the Republican party, he flirted warmly with the Democrats in 1868. It was not the chief justiceship he wanted, but the presidency.

Welles gives a vivid sketch of Stanton: "Stanton is no favorite of mine. He has energy and application, is industrious and driving, but devises nothing, shuns responsibility, and I doubt his sincerity always. He wants no general to overtop him, is jealous of others in any position who have influence and popular regard; but he has cunning and skill, dissembles his feelings, in short is a hypocrite, a moral coward, while affecting to be, and to a certain extent being brusque, overvaliant in words."[19]

At the next cabinet meeting Lincoln stated that Halleck had offered the command to Burnside, who declined, declaring himself unequal to the position. There was no alternative but McClellan. Lincoln went on to explain that he had put him in command of the Washington defenses but not of the field army. That had been done by Halleck in his capacity of general in chief.

On September 3, Halleck directed McClellan to report on the extent of the forces in the vicinity of Washington, as it was necessary to organize an army for field service. On the same day Burnside reported to McClellan as in command. The former was still at Aquia. On September 4, McClellan sent a flag of truce to Lee for the burial of the dead on the battlefield. He signed himself, "Major-General, commanding."

McClellan was putting the army in shape in a marvelously short time, though he was criticized for not doing it by magic and advancing against the Confederates the next day. Seemingly the authorities were still so ignorant of military affairs that they thought it easy to organize a new army out of the shattered remnants of two armies, restoring discipline and confidence to men who had lost respect for their superiors, as was the case with the Union troops at that moment. The privates in the ranks were too intelligent not to see the vast superiority of the generalship of Lee and Jackson to that of Pope, and they

---

[19] Welles, *op. cit.*, Vol. I, p. 127.

welcomed the return of McClellan with an enthusiasm that was half the battle of recovered morale.

There were two stages in McClellan's restoration to command. Lincoln, in the panic that followed the battle of August 30, had wisely put in his hands the defenses of Washington; by that very move he checkmated any design that Lee might have had on the capital. Then it was that Halleck, realizing his own inadequacy, took the step of putting the field army under McClellan. This was destined to frustrate Lee's invasion of Maryland, entered on so hopefully by the Southerners.

Reports came in fast from the upper Potomac of the Confederate movement into Maryland. As always before, their numbers were greatly overrated, A. P. Hill being credited with 30,000 men. Harper's Ferry, where there was a large garrison, was, quaintly enough, left under Wool, commanding at Baltimore. Halleck suggested the advisability of removing the troops there to Maryland Heights, across the Potomac from Harper's Ferry, a suggestion that Wool did not follow. The garrison was left at Harper's Ferry and proved (most unexpectedly) an important factor in the failure of Lee's Maryland campaign.

Meanwhile McClellan, whose headquarters were at Rockville, had to find out what was going on in front. On September 6, Lee was reported to be moving east and was supposed to be about to threaten Washington. In that case the Union army would take position at Rockville to defend the city. Then came news that the Confederates were moving on Frederick, which proved accurate. Halleck was opposed to stripping the forts on the Virginia side of the Potomac, fearing an attack from that direction. McClellan requested that Porter be placed in charge of the defense of Harrisburg, Pennsylvania, supposed to be threatened by Lee's advance. An accurate dispatch came from Governor A. G. Curtin, who gave the Confederate force at Frederick at 3,500: "Were shoeless, unclad, taking possession of all stores having shoes, army goods, or other supplies, paying for the same Confederate scrip."

In the afternoon of September 5, Lincoln telegraphed McClellan, who was at Rockville bringing up troops, "How does it look now?" With what an anxious heart the President put that brief question, realizing that the fate of the Union depended on McClellan! McClellan reported that if the Confederates were in Maryland in force they were west of the Monocacy. Later he wired Halleck that Jackson was at Frederick. He thought he could now prevent an attempt on Baltimore while covering Washington. He was prepared to attack any force crossing the Potomac east of the Monocacy. "Our information is still entirely too indefinite to justify definite action. I am ready to push in any direction, and hope very soon to have the supplies and transportation so regulated that we can safely move farther from Washington and clear Maryland of the rebels. . . . As soon as I find out where to strike, I will be after them without an hour's delay." [20]

McClellan was blamed at the time, and has been since, for not moving instantly against Lee and driving him from Maryland soil. Such criticisms are what might be expected from laymen, who do not understand the fog of war. One reading the reports coming in to McClellan at this time will realize the puzzle of such a situation. Reports at first indicated that the Confederates were moving on Baltimore. The estimates of their strength varied widely. Their exact positions could not be determined by the Union cavalry scouting the roads. All this goes to show that McClellan was alive to the situation and on the alert. The fog had to clear a little before he could move far from Washington, which, for all he knew, might be the real objective of the Confederates; it had to be taken into consideration that they might be feinting in western Maryland, only to double back toward Washington if McClellan should be drawn too far west. Such generals as Lee and Jackson might attempt anything. Late at night on September 8, McClellan telegraphed Halleck that he would move his whole army the next morning. The same night he wired Wool at Baltimore: "The army is now massed between Rockville and Brookville, in position to move on the enemy, should he attempt to go toward Baltimore from any point above here, to advance into Pennsylvania, or attack Washington. Our information regarding the enemy's movements is very vague and conflicting."

[20] O.R., Ser. I, Vol. XIX, Pt. 2, p. 211.

In these days the tone of the army was being rapidly restored. The confidence and affection felt for McClellan by all the rank and file and most of the higher officers was lifting the depression following the Second Manassas. Burnside reported that his men were in better condition than they were when they left Washington. Other reports reveal that this was the universal experience.

It is a commentary on the situation that the Pennsylvania authorities at this moment were wildly calling for troops to protect that state; Wool actually granted permission to Governor Curtin to stop at Harrisburg troops bound for Washington. Lincoln and Stanton restrained him, stating, what was true enough, that the army was Pennsylvania's best defense. McClellan wired Curtin that if the Confederates advanced northward he would move against them, but that he did not think they menaced Pennsylvania. On September 8, all that was actually certain was that the Confederates were in force in or near Frederick. On September 9, McClellan at Rockville sent word to Halleck that Jackson and Longstreet, according to reports, had about 110,000 men near Frederick. To the very last McClellan exaggerated the size of the Confederate army, which at this time hardly numbered 50,000 men.

McClellan had his troops arranged in the vicinity of Rockville on September 9: Burnside, Sumner, Banks, Franklin, Couch, and Sigel commanding the various detachments. Porter was in command of the defenses at Arlington. Later he was sent to McClellan.

That night McClellan received word that Jackson was at New Market and Stuart at Urbanna, indicating that the enemy intended moving on Baltimore. Burnside was instructed to push a reconnaissance toward Westminster. At the same time, in answer to a requisition, Quartermaster General Meigs informed McClellan that he had 6,000 wagons drawn by 30,000 animals and yet that, owing to the prevailing confusion, he could not send McClellan what he asked. Officers' wagons should be emptied and the officers required to move without extra baggage. Banks was now in command of the Washington defenses, and Heintzelman was put under him. In such manner officers, out of favor or considered incompetent, were got out of the way.

On September 9, Wool informed McClellan that Lee, Jackson, and D. H. Hill were at Frederick, in a position to take roads to Chambersburg, Hagerstown, Gettysburg, Baltimore, or across the Potomac.

On September 10, Lincoln again telegraphed McClellan, "How does it look now?" McClellan answered that Pleasanton reported a movement of the Confederates to the south side of the Potomac. Pleasanton was watching all the fords. The main enemy force under Jackson was declared to be still at Frederick.

Pleasonton had come in contact with Stuart's cavalry at Catoctin Mountain and had attempted to drive it back from the mountain top, but unsuccessfully. At the same time Burnside and Hooker were moving slowly westward, reaching for a contact with the Confederates.

Several things were now becoming evident. First, that the Confederates seemed to be moving westward, since a portion of them were at Hagerstown. Second, they apparently were not veering toward Baltimore. Their movements rather indicated an intention to invade Pennsylvania behind South Mountain. "Men ragged and filthy, but full of fight" was the description of the Confederate troops. Pennsylvania, especially Philadelphia, was desperately uneasy, and a demand came for Reynolds to head the defenses there. McClellan answered that he could not spare Reynolds; there was quite a controversy over this, as the War Department was willing to let him go.

McClellan, on September 11, sent word to Halleck that he was no longer uncertain as to the movements of the enemy. He had left Washington strongly garrisoned since Lee's maneuver might have been a feint preceding an attack on the city. However, all the evidence went to show that the entire Confederate army, amounting to 120,000 men, was in the vicinity of Frederick. There would probably be a great battle soon. "The momentous consequences involved in the struggle of the next few days impels me, at the risk of being considered slow and overcautious, to most earnestly recommend that every available man be at once added to this army." He asked that the garrison at Harper's Ferry be ordered to join him.[21]

These troops were not sent to McClellan and were captured by Jackson a few days later. In the morning of September 12, McClellan received information that the Confederates had evacuated Frederick. Halleck the same day heard from Wool that the Confederates had left Frederick, moving toward Hagerstown, with Jackson leading. The tension in Washington was higher than it had been before and higher than it ever was to be again.

Lincoln now authorized the governor of Pennsylvania to call out the militia of that state to help repel the Confederate invasion; the uneasiness in Philadelphia at this juncture was intense—greater even than in 1863 before the battle of Gettysburg.

On September 11, McClellan wired Governor Curtin that he would learn that day whether the Confederates were still massed at Frederick, whether they had any force east of the Monocacy, or whether they had moved on Hagerstown in force. He thought their army was now on the north side of the Potomac, being ignorant of the movement against Harper's Ferry. The next evening (September 12) the signals from Sugar Loaf Mountain informed McClellan, then at Urbanna, that Union troops were entering Frederick. The remainder of Burnside was approaching that town; Sumner was near Urbanna, with his advance guard thrown out to the Monocacy. McClellan wired Halleck that if the Confederates moved into Pennsylvania he would follow, and if they attempted to recross the Potomac he would endeavor to cut off their retreat. "My movements tomorrow will be dependent upon information to be received during the night." The same evening he wired Lincoln that he occupied Frederick and was trying to communicate with Harper's Ferry, to send relief if necessary. He thought he could save the garrison there if it was yet in Union possession.

The panic still continued. Hooker protested against losing Reynolds, requisitioned by the governor of Pennsylvania. "A scared governor ought not to be permitted to destroy the usefulness of an entire division of the army on the eve of important

[21] O.R., Ser. I, Vol. XIX, Pt. 2, p. 254.

operations." On September 12, Curtin requested Lincoln to send 80,000 troops to defend Pennsylvania. Lincoln replied that he could not comply, that all available troops were in the rear of the enemy, supposed to be invading Pennsylvania. That McClellan was not alone in overestimating the Confederate numbers is evidenced by a panic-stricken dispatch from Curtin, on September 12, quoting some informant who asserted that the Confederates had in Maryland about 190,000 men and 250,000 in Virginia menacing Washington. "The gentleman who gives me this information is vouched for as reliable and truthful by the best citizens of the place where he lives." (Liars are often vouched for by best citizens.) Lincoln was still plagued by panicky demands from Pennsylvania. Pennsylvania, he replied, was in no danger. "At all events Philadelphia is more than 150 miles from Hagerstown, and could not be reached by the rebel army in ten days, if no hindrance was interposed." Still Curtin called out 50,000 men to defend the state.

On September 13, Halleck wired McClellan that he thought Lee would feint toward Pennsylvania, to draw McClellan in that direction, and would then move on Washington. "The capture of this place will throw us back six months, if it should not destroy us."

However, the period of uncertainty, by an abrupt interposition of Fate, ended suddenly. The importance of chance in human events has never been fully determined by philosophers, but it is certainly very great. At this moment McClellan received definite information of Confederate movements, for the information came from Lee himself.

At noon of September 13 McClellan sent an exulting telegram to Lincoln from Frederick, which he had reached. "I have all the plans of the rebels, and will catch them in their own trap if my men are equal to the emergency. . . . My respects to Mrs. Lincoln. Received most enthusiastically by the ladies. Will send you trophies. All well, and with God's blessing will accomplish it." At the same time he wired Halleck, more specifically, that an order from Lee had fallen into his hands. Troops had been ordered to march on September 10 and capture Union forces at Harper's Ferry and Martinsburg by surrounding them, to take possession of the railroad and concentrate at Boonsboro or Hagerstown. The plan was confirmed by heavy firing from the direction of Harper's Ferry. The Confederate army, 120,000 strong and commanded by Lee, intended to invade Pennsylvania. McClellan pushed forward that day and had several skirmishes with the enemy, forcing them to destroy a train of 150 wagons. The army would move by forced marches to relieve Harper's Ferry, but McClellan feared he would be too late. "Unless General Lee has changed his plans I expect a severe general engagement to-morrow. I feel confident that there is now no rebel force immediately threatening Washington or Baltimore."

The order from Lee was the famous "Lost Dispatch," addressed to D. H. Hill and picked up in a deserted Confederate camp at Frederick, wrapped around two cigars. Evidently some careless soul of an officer or courier had used the paper as a cigar case in lieu of anything else. Hill declared he had in his possession his copy of the order (there were two copies), but his insistence that it afforded McClellan no essential information rather shows a guilty conscience.

It was of considerable value to McClellan, for it clarified the situation, if only for the moment. He learned, for one thing, that Lee had divided his army, sending a part to Harper's Ferry and the other portion to Hagerstown. What was more important was the assurance that neither Washington nor Baltimore was immediately threatened, that the movement towards Hagerstown was not a feint but the beginning of a march to Pennsylvania. Knowing just where Lee's troops were and what they were doing, McClellan was able to advance with an assurance that would not otherwise have been possible. If the order had not been found, it is almost certain that Jackson could have completed his operation at Harper's Ferry and rejoined Lee before McClellan obtained definite information of the movement. There would have been all the difference in the world if Jackson had been at South Mountain when McClellan advanced instead of a small force under D. H. Hill and Longstreet. The battle on the mountaintop would have been bitterly contested, with the chances favoring the Confederates.

It is true, however, that accurate information of Confederate movements was reaching headquarters from other sources. On September 13, Curtin informed McClellan that Longstreet was said to have reached Hagerstown and Jackson to have crossed the Potomac at Williamsport to capture Martinsburg and Harper's Ferry, all of which was true.

McClellan was advancing but has been blamed for not advancing more rapidly. On September 14, he wired Halleck, "We occupy Middletown and Jefferson. The whole force of the enemy is in front. They are not returning to Virginia.... Will soon have a decisive battle." On the same day Halleck wired McClellan that a large force of the enemy was south of the Potomac. "If so, I fear you are exposing your left flank, and that the enemy can cross in your rear." Halleck was holding back, not McClellan.

The picture was now entirely altered, and all in two weeks. McClellan had taken a broken, disheartened, and disorganized army, reorganized it, largely on the march, restored confidence and made ready for battle. The army still bore traces of its recent disorganization; it still was not firmly knit, still loosely held together, and these facts were to have an important bearing on the battle of Sharpsburg; but it was a very different army from the one that had fled from the field of Manassas, disgruntled, cursing its officers, unwilling in many cases to face the enemy. It was now confident, enthusiastically prepared for battle, determined to drive the Southerners from Maryland.

Indeed the facts were strangely reversed. Two weeks before, Washington had been in danger, for so great was the demoralization there that the Confederates could have taken the city but for McClellan's restoration to command. And it is not impossible that Lee would have attempted to take it if he had not heard of McClellan's return; he wanted to attack no more fortified positions held by such an opponent. Doubtless that had something to do with his decision to invade Maryland west of the capital and threaten Pennsylvania.

Now it was Lee who was in peril. With his army divided in front of McClellan's concentrated host, he might be attacked and beaten in detail. McClellan was advancing and Jackson was still at Harper's Ferry, Longstreet at Hagerstown, the rest of the army scattered. Stuart was in front heroically holding back the Union cavalry, but the situation was the most dangerous that Lee had faced. Counting on more time than McClellan allowed him, calculating naturally enough on a lengthy reorganization of the Union army, he had ventured to disperse, and was caught dispersed. In fact, his campaign of invasion was ruined. He could not dream of Pennsylvania now; he would have to fight for life in Maryland or else fall back into Virginia and admit failure.

What is certain is that no other officer available could have done what McClellan did in the time elapsed. No deed of the whole war exceeds his restoration of the Union army after its terrific defeat at Manassas and its disorderly retreat. More than the battles McClellan fought were his two masterly accomplishments: the taking of the Army of the Potomac across Lee's front to Harrison's Landing in the Seven Days and the restoration of organization and morale to the army after the Second Manassas. These two feats should give McClellan place among the masters of war, and they would but for the prejudice against him which has inspired nearly all writers on the War between the States.

CHAPTER THIRTEEN

SHARPSBURG

OR, IF YOU PREFER IT, ANTIETAM CREEK

WHILE MCCLELLAN was reorganizing the Union army and doing all the work necessary for transporting, feeding, and camping an army on the move, Lee had not been idle. Seeing that Harper's Ferry was a trap containing 13,000 troops, he determined to take it. This decision was one of the mistakes of his life. Feeling that he had a week or so at least for moving, he broached the Harper's Ferry plan to Longstreet, but met with a blunt refusal from the none-too-polite subordinate. Longstreet thought that he had squelched Lee completely, for Longstreet had a positive way about him, and the idea was indeed dangerous. But when Longstreet entered Lee's tent at Frederick he heard the tones of Stonewall Jackson and realized that Lee was asking that soldier who quailed at nothing to undertake the venture. So Jackson went in place of Longstreet.

Lee now, in contempt of the Washington government and all that it could do, divided his army most perilously; his audacity sometimes outran his discretion. Instead of keeping the rest of his army where it could reach Jackson speedily in case of need, Lee sent Longstreet to Hagerstown, possibly preparatory to a movement into Pennsylvania, while the important passes in Catoctin Mountain and South Mountain were held by D. H. Hill with a small force. But on September 13, McClellan had read the Lost Dispatch and was pressing forward. Almost in a moment Lee passed from relative safety into grave danger.

In order to promote his strategy, Lee retired from Frederick, which was exposed to attack from the east, sending Jackson to

Harper's Ferry and remaining with Longstreet himself or nearby. Longstreet was at Hagerstown, thirteen miles from Boonsboro, just west of South Mountain, the passes of which were occupied by D. H. Hill with his small command.

East of South Mountain runs the Catoctin Ridge, which was held by Stuart with his cavalry. In the morning of September 13, Hill received a dispatch from Stuart, then at a gap in the Catoctin, stating that he was being followed by two brigades of Union infantry and asking Hill to check the pursuit at South Mountain. Hill responded by sending two brigades and several batteries.

In the evening of September 13, Longstreet urged Lee to evacuate Hagerstown and Boonsboro and concentrate at Sharpsburg, which he declared was a better position for a battle. Lee, however, demurred. The loss of the South Mountain passes was a serious matter; Sharpsburg was only two miles from the Potomac River, wide and difficult to ford. He determined to hold South Mountain and directed Longstreet to join D. H. Hill, then in the passes of the range. Longstreet, sullen and reluctant, did not move quickly, with the result that his weary troops failed to reach Boonsboro and the battleground until the afternoon of September 14. In sending Longstreet to Hagerstown Lee made a serious strategic error; it divided his army to the point that invited destruction.

Harper's Ferry had not yet surrendered, and Lee was worried about the situation, for McClellan was showing much more energy than he had expected from a recently routed army. He sent word to Hill to go to Turner's Gap and help Stuart defend it. But when Hill reached that point he found that Stuart had gone to Crampton's Gap, some miles south. The force at the Mountain House (Turner's Gap) where the National Road crossed South Mountain was perilously small. Only one brigade was at the Mountain House and another at the eastern base of the mountain. And at that moment Jacob D. Cox with two divisions was approaching the Mountain House while Franklin was in the vicinity of Crampton's Gap. Between these two points was Fox's Gap, held by a small Confederate command. The scanty force under Hill was now threatened on both sides by much larger numbers of infantry supported by heavy batteries.

Cox, beginning what was intended for a reconnaissance, went ahead, turning the movement into a battle. The situation was serious, for the Confederate wagon trains were on the roads just west of South Mountain and might be taken if the passes were forced. It is difficult to describe the confused conflict known as the battle of South Mountain or Boonsboro. The main Confederate position was at the Mountain House on the National Road, held by Garland's brigade. The Unionists attacked at Fox's Gap, a mile to the south, at the Mountain House itself and north of it.

In the largeness of that glorious landscape troops and wagon trains looked small. Soldiers on the mountaintop gazed for miles back toward Frederick and saw the wagons strung out like white beads and the columns of infantry like dark blue snakes winding along as far as the eye could reach. It was evident to the Confederates on the mountain that the whole of McClellan's army was coming up, and rapidly. Lee was in imminent danger. If South Mountain should be forced, McClellan might get between Lee and Jackson, still at Harper's Ferry.

The situation was saved, but at great cost. The Confederate batteries were outranged and overwhelmed by the heavier Union guns. The blue troops, clambering up the mountainside with impressive valor, came to grips with the defenders, and the two lines—the one on the top, the other ascending—began blazing away at each other with furious volleys. Cox was successful at Fox's Gap driving the Confederates away. Colquitt (Confederate) at the foot of the mountain was used up, while Hooker, coming from north of the National Road, made progress on that side. Garland's brigade held out heroically at the Mountain House, even after the death of its commander. In the afternoon Longstreet arrived and put several of his brigades into action, but by that time the Confederates were being pushed back almost everywhere.

McClellan, Burnside, and Reno had come up while the fighting was in progress; orders were issued for the whole line to advance and sweep the Confederates from their stubborn hold

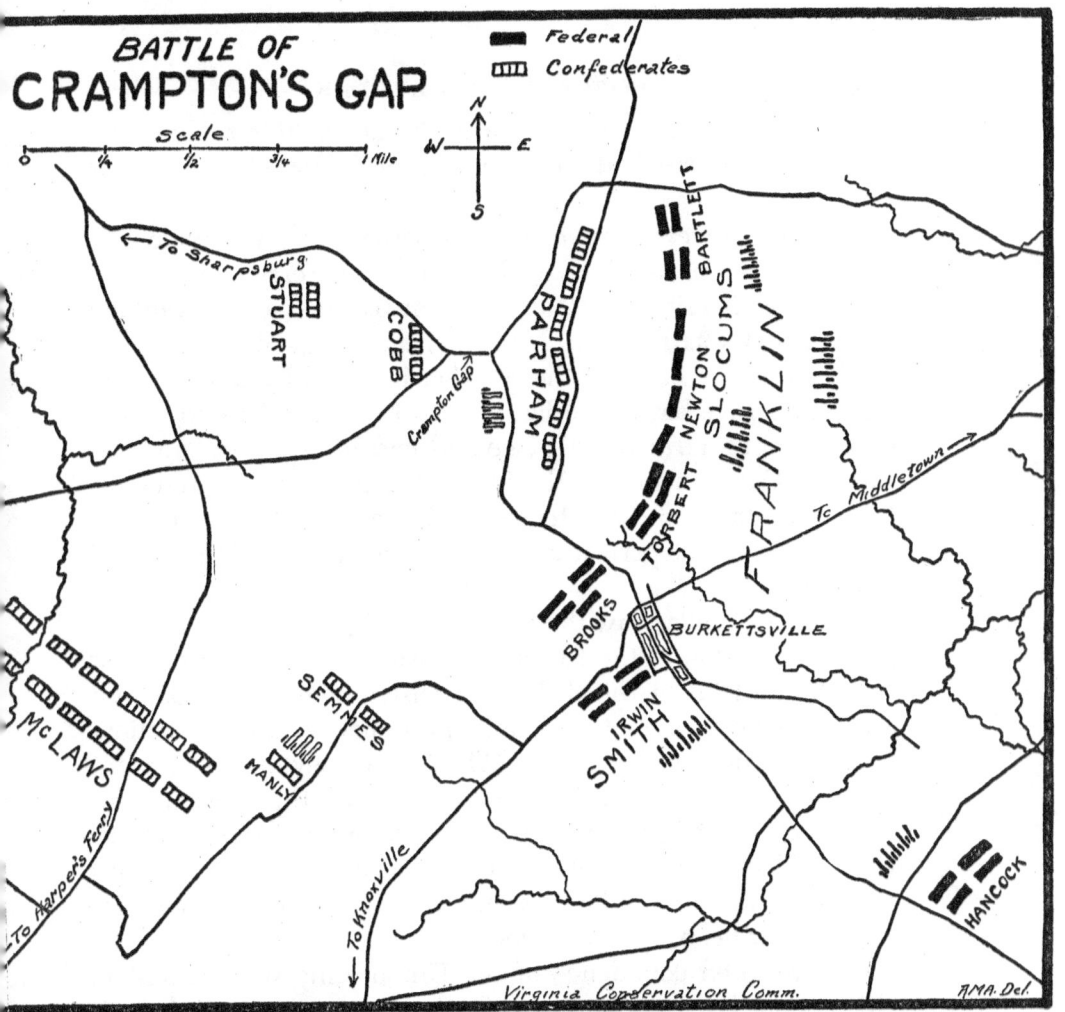

at the Mountain House. The line went forward, and with general success; at this moment Reno was killed. Hooker's men were well up the mountain on the Confederate left, which was in grave danger. It is not impossible that the coming of nightfall saved this portion of the Confederate army from destruction.

Longstreet had decided that the day could not be retrieved at South Mountain and possibly, owing to the circumstances, he was right. At all events the wagon trains had been saved. After nightfall orders came from Lee to fall back to Sharpsburg. Thus Longstreet realized his first objective, which was to get the troops from Hagerstown and South Mountain to Sharpsburg. He was disheartened and did not wish to fight but to retreat into Virginia. But when he broached this to Lee, the chief refused. He had no intention of being kicked out of Maryland.

Already, however, his campaign was ruined. His wide dispersion of troops and his attack on Harper's Ferry had brought him into such a situation that retreat or battle at a disadvantage was all that was left him. McClellan's strategy was brilliantly vindicated. Lee had lost the position he should have occupied for the decisive battle and had retired to an inferior one, where defeat would mean ruin. If Lee had had his army in hand behind the Catoctin and South Mountain the situation would have been different, and the outcome might have been different, too. It was a place of peril into which his matchless audacity had led him.

When McClellan saw the gray-brown figures melt away from the mountaintop in the twilight, he was exultant. For the first time he had taken the definite offensive against the Confederates holding a strong position, and he had won that position. He wired Halleck that night: "After a very severe engagement the corps of Hooker and Reno have carried the heights commanding the Hagerstown road. The troops behaved magnificently. They never fought better. . . . The action continued until after dark, and terminated leaving us in possession of the entire crest. It has been a glorious victory."[1]

The restored confidence of the Union army was evident in this action. It is true that the Confederates were greatly outnumbered, as only a few of Longstreet's brigades were engaged, but it was no mean feat for men to clamber over the rocks on the mountainside and ascend the slope in the face of the Confederate fire. They felt that night that they had won an important victory. Important it was, though in a strategic, not tactical, sense. D. H. Hill had done well to hold out against a large part of McClellan's army. With Longstreet's tardy support, he could not have been expected to win a victory. South Mountain was really a delaying action, but it should not have been; it should have been the main battle. Lee succeeded in saving his wagon trains and in carrying the half of his army to a

[1] *O.R.*, Ser. I, Vol. XIX, Pt. 2, p. 289.

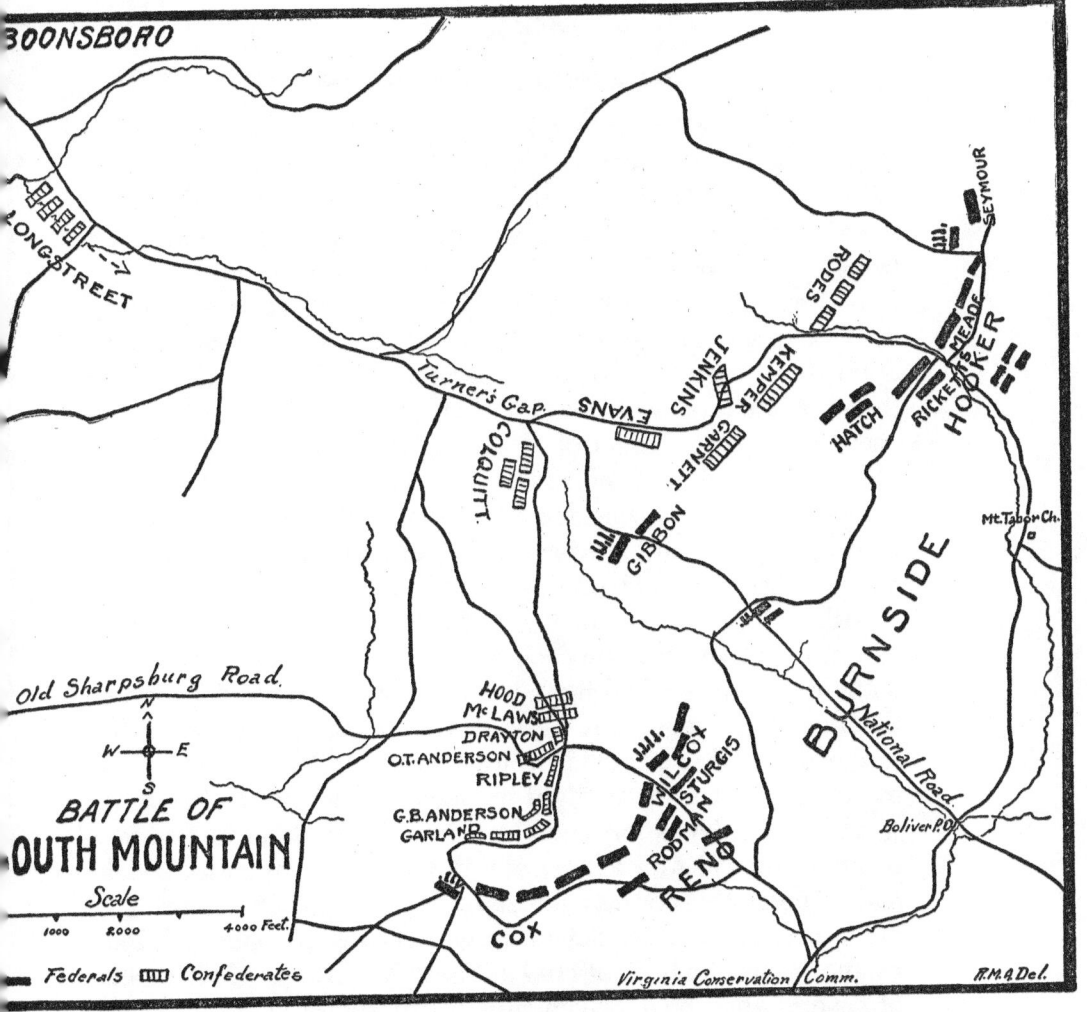

point where union with Jackson would be easy, and so far he had been successful; but he had lost the best position for a defensive battle in all that region. With his troops in line and his batteries established on the slopes of South Mountain, he would have been a hard nut for McClellan to crack, perhaps too hard a nut. As it was, he was being beaten in detail. At last he would either have to retreat across the Potomac or fight in a bad position, where a decisive victory was practically impossible. So far McClellan had outmaneuvered him. The invasion of Maryland was breaking down, just when it promised success. The gray-brown army would not go into Pennsylvania this year.

The Confederates fell back from South Mountain to Sharpsburg, which Longstreet had described to Lee as being a much better position. It appears that Lee would have retired across the river without a battle if, at this time, word had not come from Jackson that Harper's Ferry had surrendered, leaving him free. Lee then, knowing that Jackson would soon join him, decided to stand his ground behind Antietam Creek. Longstreet, upon this, urged Lee to retreat across the Potomac, declaring that the situation was now materially changed, since Jackson was no longer in danger of attack at Harper's Ferry. But Lee's blood was up and he refused to retire. Historians think he was moved by political considerations, that he had entered Maryland hoping to bring it over to the South and felt that he could not withdraw without serious loss of prestige.

Although he did not realize it, he had already lost the campaign. By having his army too widely dispersed to concentrate on South Mountain and fight McClellan there, he had forfeited the advantages gained by his vigorous and skillful strategy; the lure of Harper's Ferry had been his undoing. But it is only fair to say that he had every right to calculate that the Union army would be paralyzed for several weeks at least. What he had not reckoned on was McClellan's amazing organizing genius, which had turned bodies of demoralized troops into what was becoming a disciplined and efficient army. Lee was disconcerted, too, by the reverse he had suffered at South Mountain, where a part of his army had been driven from a strong position.

McClellan, crossing South Mountain, followed on the footsteps of the retiring Confederates to the vicinity of Antietam Creek. Lee had taken position along the west side of the creek and immediately in front of the little town of Sharpsburg, from which Southerners derive the name of the battle that followed. On September 15, after reading McClellan's enthusiastic dispatches, Lincoln wired to Illinois, "I now consider it safe to say that General McClellan has gained a great victory over the great rebel army in Maryland, between Fredericktown and Hagerstown. He is now pursuing the flying foe." [2]

In the morning of September 16, McClellan telegraphed

---

[2] *Ibid.*, p. 295.

Halleck, "The enemy yesterday held a position just in front of Sharpsburg. When our troops arrived in sufficient force it was too late in the day to attack. This morning a heavy fog has thus far prevented us doing more than to ascertain that some of the enemy are still there. Do not know in what force. Will attack as soon as situation of enemy is developed. . . . The time lost on account of the fog is being occupied in getting up supplies, for the want of which many of our men are suffering." [3]

In the afternoon of September 15, the various units of the Union army came to the vicinity of Antietam Creek. Jacob D. Cox, arriving with his command about three o'clock, found McClellan surrounded by a group of officers. Cox and Burnside with him were cordially greeted by McClellan, who was evidently in an excellent humor since the campaign was going well.

Walking up the slope of the ridge, the Union commanders looked westward over what was to be the battlefield. In front was the Antietam between the hills that lined both sides. Off to the left was Sharpsburg, behind fields fenced with stone. Off to the right was a wood and the white of the Dunker Church, sharply outlined against the green trees. Farther off both to the right and left were timbered ridges and cultivated fields. It was a smiling landscape of prosperous farms, little obscured by the forest nearly everywhere present in Virginia, the most open battleground of the war so far.

The officers, peering through their glasses, attracted the attention of the graybacks on the other side of the stream. Presently smoke puffed out from the direction of Sharpsburg and a shell went shrieking over the group. McClellan, who never feared for himself, directed all of the officers but one or two to retire behind the ridge while he continued to make his examination, walking slowly. Cox says, "I noted with satisfaction the cool and business-like air with which he made his examination under fire. The Confederate artillery was answered by a battery, and a lively cannonade ensued on both sides, though without any noticeable effect. The enemy's position was revealed, and he was evidently in force on both sides of the turnpike in

[3] *Ibid.*, p. 308.

front of Sharpsburg, covered by the undulations of the rolling ground which hid his infantry from our sight."[4]

The reconnaissance occupied the remainder of September 15, as the various commands of the Union army, one by one, reached the field. September 16 passed without any serious collision, though there was more or less constant artillery firing and picket fighting. Whenever the blue soldiers showed themselves on the ridge east of the creek the Confederate batteries opened on them, whereupon the Union batteries would respond, and a lively cannonade would follow and finally die out. In the afternoon McClellan and Burnside conducted a careful reconnaissance of the Confederate position, with the result that the general made changes in his dispositions. With his usual care, he sent a staff officer to guide each command to its new bivouac. All this time the engineers were testing Antietam Creek, which is a deep stream, for fording places for infantry. Hooker, on the extreme right, apparently at his own solicitation, was permitted to make a reconnaissance that might develop into an attack. Late in the afternoon the officers on the left wing of the Union position heard Hooker's guns, way off to the right, followed by the crackling of musketry, but Hooker was only feeling out the Confederate position preparatory to the real attack, which was to come on the morrow.

Jackson had reached the field early on September 16, and Lee now had his whole army with him, except A. P. Hill's division, left at Harper's Ferry to complete the surrender. Lee and Jackson together surveyed the situation and examined with their glasses the Union position east of the Antietam from which puffs of cannon smoke were constantly rising. Longstreet was with them, cool but disturbed; he had advised against fighting here, and his advice was sound. Jackson seems not to have ventured any opinion; he usually trusted Lee's judgment unreservedly.

The Confederate position, instead of being good as it has been described, was in reality bad because it was too shallow. The moment the Confederate infantry appeared above the ridges they were fully exposed to the whole weight of the

[4] *B. and L.*, Vol. II, p. 631.

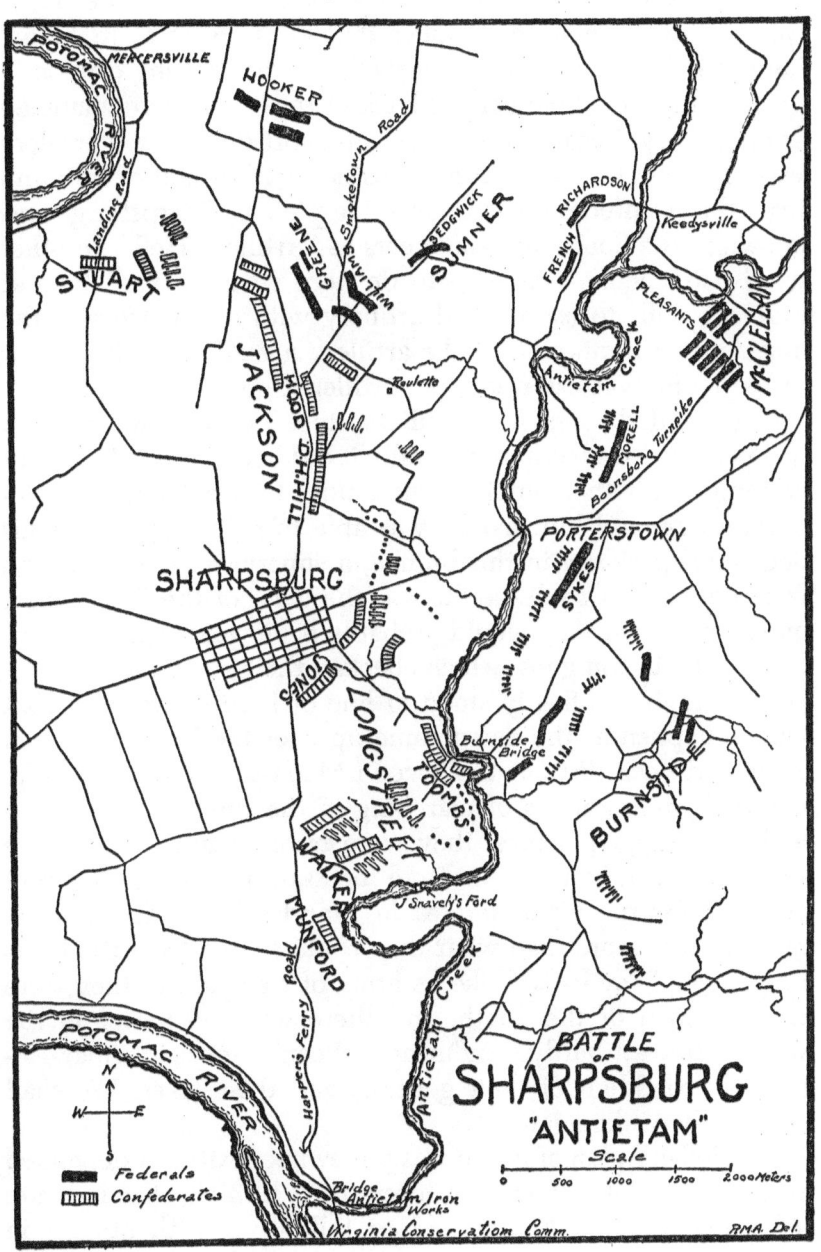

endless rows of guns, of long range for those days. The ridges east of the Antietam are higher than those west of it; before long busy figures in blue along the hills were getting cannon in place, until the whole heights back of the creek were crammed with artillery. Because the range was short this massed artillery was to sweep the Confederate position with a hail of iron and tear the Confederate ordnance to pieces. Sharpsburg was known to the Southern cannoneers as "Artillery Hell." In other words, McClellan was able to do here what he had done at Malvern Hill: to use massed artillery with effect. He was the first American officer to make artillery a really decisive factor in battle; he was essentially an artillerist and a great one.

The Confederates had artillery, too, but the ammunition was poor and scanty, and generally it did not compare in weight or range with that on the Union side. It is a tribute to McClellan's generalship that he was able to make full use of his decided superiority in this branch, a superiority that kept him from defeat. For so desperate was the valor of the Southerners on this field that they would probably have won a great victory but for the Union guns, which checked their every move.

The graybacks finally stood in line of battle, awaiting what was to happen as the dawn came up over the Union position. They had been dirty at the Second Manassas; they were filthy now from many miles of marching in the sun and rain. They had been ragged before; they were tattered now. They were sun-blackened, hairy, gaunt from incessant marching and want of food, for the Confederates in Maryland had few regular rations, little more than what they could snatch from the fields in passing. They looked like an army of tramps, but they were the best men of the South, and there were no better in the world: brave, hardy, enduring, cheerful—even jocular—supremely confident of their generals and themselves. We shall not see their like again.

McClellan's plan of battle was somewhat flexible; it depended on developments. It was an attempt to turn the Confederate left flank and break that and to follow up with attacks in echelon, from the left to the extreme right, where another main assault was to be tried. If either the Confederate left flank or

SHARPSBURG

right flank gave way, McClellan planned to throw his reserves at the center and sweep the field. It was not a bad plan, but it was not carried out completely and, partly for this reason, McClellan failed to sweep the field.

Hooker had been ordered to cross the Antietam early in the afternoon of September 16 by a bridge near Keedysville and a ford nearby. After his troops were over, he rode to McClellan, who told him he might call for reinforcements at need. Later the commander went forward to observe what was going on; Hooker again urged reinforcements for his turning movement. Mansfield, commanding a corps, was ordered to join Hooker and camped that night about a mile and a half from the latter's position. Sumner was also ordered to support the movement, but the order did not reach him until 7:30 A. M., when the battle was well under way.

Crossing the Antietam without any notable resistance, Hooker moved westward, hoping to reach the ridge on which the Hagerstown road runs, a dominant feature in the landscape. This ridge is some distance from the Antietam; for a mile he met with no resistance.

Meanwhile the Confederates had not been standing still. Hood's two brigades, troops second to none, were shifted from the center to the extreme left of the line. These soldiers occupied an open wooded space, known as the East Wood, not far from the Dunker Church. Skirmishing followed and sharp artillery practice, but no general action. Hooker did not wish to engage until he had passed quite beyond the Confederate left flank and was in a position to turn it. He bivouacked on the ridge along the turnpike and not far from the Potomac River. It was a good position from which to launch an attack, and the attack would probably prove successful if followed up. But it was not followed up promptly, owing to the lateness with which Sumner received his order. Hood's division, which had suffered some loss in the afternoon of the sixteenth, was replaced by Jackson's division (J. R. Jones) and by Ewell's. These troops were formed on the left of D. H. Hill (the center) and almost at right angles with his line.

At dawn on September 17, Hooker, looking eastward, saw

before him a rolling country, the principal features of which were the white walls of the little Dunker Church standing out against the foliage of the West Wood. Beyond was a large cornfield and then the East Wood, with dips here and there. On a ridge near the church and extending across the Hagerstown turnpike and into the East Wood were the graybacks in battle line, meagerly sheltered by piles of fence rails and, here and there, by outcropping bowlders. The high ground about the church was the key to the position; if Hooker could take it the battle would be won. But Jackson was there and Jackson's men.

When a Confederate battery fired on the Unionists, Hooker ordered an advance. Doubleday's division was leading. The line moved swiftly forward, breaking through a picket fence and coming into the cornfield, where the corn was higher than their heads. Meanwhile the Confederates had opened on the advancing bluecoats with a terrible fire of artillery and musketry. The Union line, leaping a fence at the south side of the cornfield, charged across an open space in front of the Confederate position. Here the fire at close range of musketry and guns was beyond endurance; men fell by scores and hundreds. The Unionists broke, falling back into the cover of the corn, where they rallied. When the Confederates tried a countercharge, they in turn were driven back by infantry fire and the canister from the cannon that had accompanied the movement. Other charges were made by the Unionists and countercharges by the Confederates; the fighting was close and furious. Whenever the bluecoats came out into the open they were decimated by infantry fire, and whenever the Confederates followed the retiring Unionists they were in turn driven back, chiefly by the Union artillery. Ricketts' division did gain the edge of the East Wood, where the Confederate left wing adjoined D. H. Hill and the center; but the Confederate line, though strained and suffering heavy losses, was unbroken. It was now eight o'clock, and Hooker's main effort had failed, possibly for want of support, possibly not.

Mansfield, at the head of the Twelfth Corps, was coming up behind Hooker; earlier he might have been of more use. The corps consisted of two divisions under Williams and Greene.

As these troops were new and largely untrained, it took some time to deploy them in line, and in doing so Mansfield was mortally wounded. Almost at the same moment Hooker was wounded, leaving the direction of affairs in Williams' hands. Williams now attacked, obliquely to the direction taken by Hooker and more to the westward. He relieved Doubleday, who had been under severe pressure, but Williams came under the full infantry and artillery fire and seems to have been partly enfiladed. "Our officers in part were deceived," says Cox, "as to the extent and direction of the enemy's line by the fact that the Confederate cavalry commander, Stuart, had occupied a commanding hill west of the pike and beyond our right flank and from this position, which, in fact, was considerably detached from the Confederate line, he used his batteries with such effect as to produce the belief that a continuous line extended from this point to the Dunker church."[5] Stuart grabbed batteries wherever he found them and massed them against the advancing Unionists.

When Mansfield's troops came on the field, Meade, who had just been assigned to Hooker's command, withdrew the First Corps to the ridge where it had camped the night before. It was quite unfit for further immediate action, having lost 2,500 killed and wounded, and even more by straggling. Indeed the corps had gone to pieces. It showed that McClellan, in the short space of time allowed him, had not been able thoroughly to integrate his army; the seams were still there. That evening less than 7,000 men were with the colors of the First Corps.

Greene's division, on the left flank of the Twelfth Corps, was able to drive the Confederates, much reduced by their losses, out of the East Wood and across the open fields up to the Dunker Church. Greene succeeded in getting a foothold on the ridge around the church. The Confederates had suffered so severely from the artillery fire (both of guns carried with the infantry and of guns across the Antietam) that the famous Stonewall brigade was disorganized, only a handful of men remaining. Early's brigade, posted among the rocks of the West Wood and supported by Stuart's artillery, was all that held the

[5] *B. and L.*, Vol. II, p. 640.

left flank of Lee's army at that moment. About half of the Confederates engaged here had been killed or wounded. The survivors were still resisting, for these were picked men of the Anglo-Saxon race. Shortly thereafter Hood came up, but for a time the Confederate left was in a most precarious condition. Could Hooker and Mansfield have attacked together, the result would have been serious for Lee, perhaps even decisive defeat.

McClellan has been censured for this lack of coördination. It does not appear, however, that he was to blame. He had ordered Mansfield to Hooker's support and, if Mansfield camped at some distance from the latter, it would seem to have been that officer's fault. However, it appears that McClellan was slow in sending Sumner orders to support Hooker, since the order did not reach the former until Hooker's main battle was almost over.

Sumner, hastening up to support Mansfield, met Hooker being carried off on a stretcher and was hurried by the latter's words. Two of his divisions were up—Sedgwick's and French's—Richardson's being left behind until Porter came up in reserve. The new arrivals crossed the Antietam where Hooker had passed but did not verge as far to the west. Arriving opposite the Dunker Church, they changed direction; the Union line charged down on the Confederates still holding the battered left. The troops advanced in three lines, sixty yards apart. When they reached the position held by Greene of the Twelfth Corps at the Dunker Church, French formed on Greene's left while Sedgwick, under Sumner's direction, moved to the right, crossed the turnpike, and entered the West Wood. Here there were no Confederate troops at all. Early was farther to the east, opposing Williams of the Twelfth Corps. He now hastened to get around in front of Sedgwick and halt his progress, but without success.

This was a moment of crisis, for a few brigades of Confederate troops were opposing two corps of the Union army. But Lee and Jackson had not lost control of events. At this very moment, when defeat loomed large, Lee threw Walker's and McLaws' divisions, fresh from Harper's Ferry, on the Union right in front of the Dunker Church. Walker, charging headlong into Sedgwick's flank, rolled him up, while McLaws, passing Walker, hurled his men on Sumner's already retiring troops. Taken at a disadvantage and fired on from several sides, the Union line dissolved in spite of the efforts of Sumner and of Sedgwick, who was severely wounded. Sumner's corps and the Twelfth Corps, mixed up in the rout, retreated to the ridge where Hooker's corps had camped and which was now again held by Hooker's troops. Here were thirty guns and many thousands of men. When Jackson, seeking to enlarge his success, advanced toward this position he was met by such an infernal fire of infantry and artillery that he was in turn repulsed with loss. But the Confederates, decimated as they were, were still organized while the right wing of the Union army had partly broken up. Stragglers by thousands deserted the firing line and got into shelter of some kind. Sumner signaled to McClellan, "Reënforcements are badly wanted. Our troops are giving way." It was now about ten o'clock.

The Confederates were at length free to concentrate against Greene, who still held stubbornly to his position at the Dunker Church. He was driven across the open fields to the edge of the East Wood, where, with the aid of a number of batteries, he continued to hold on. French's troops had come up on Greene's left; with the help of many batteries here and on the ridge held by Hooker, the Unionists maintained themselves, although utterly unable to advance. The battle on the Confederate left flank thus ended; there was no more serious fighting at this end of the line. The Confederates had met with terrible losses, but they had repulsed all attacks, and two Union corps had more or less disintegrated.

McClellan had failed here. The fault was partly his, but also partly that of his subordinates. If Hooker, Mansfield, and Sumner could have attacked in unison, success would possibly have crowned their efforts. But to get the coördination of several commands is difficult enough with highly trained troops, almost impossible with volunteers. The three corps, thrown in together, would probably have got in each other's way unless the battle line had been greatly extended; and, if the line had been extended, many Confederate commands would have been involved. If the three corps could have deployed, one behind the other, and have gone forward in successive waves, the battle might have been won, but such a maneuver would have been difficult of accomplishment. What seems to be the truth is that the Southern resistance was too strong for troops recently defeated and in process of reorganization. It appears that there would have been a complete rout of the right wing of the Union army but for the many batteries behind the infantry or firing across the creek. It was the artillery that saved McClellan at Sharpsburg.

McClellan was not through, even if his first thrust had failed. About one o'clock he telegraphed Halleck, "We are in the midst of the most terrible battle of the war—perhaps of history. Thus far it looks well, but I have great odds against me. Hurry up all the troops possible. Our loss has been terrific, but we have gained much ground. I have thrown the mass of the army on the left flank. Burnside is now attacking the right, and I hold my small reserve, consisting of Porter's (Fifth) corps, ready to attack the center as soon as the flank movements are developed. I hope that God will give us a glorious victory." [6]

Thus it will be seen that McClellan was still clinging to his plan of assailing first one flank and then the other, to follow up any break by an assault on the center. At that very moment the Confederate center, just beyond the right flank, was being furiously assailed. There D. H. Hill was in position, almost in front of Sharpsburg, with a very small force, as the situation was so threatening on both flanks that Lee could not spare many men for the middle.

French advanced on Greene's left over the open fields near the town, driving Hill's thin line before him. Richardson, who had not been engaged before, now came up on French's left, and the heavy Union line, far outflanking Hill, moved forward. The Confederates resisted desperately. "Foot by foot, field by field, from hill to hill and from fence to fence, the enemy was pressed back, till after several hours of fighting the sunken road, since known as 'Bloody Lane,' was in our hands, piled full of the Confederate dead who had defended it with their lives.... On the

[6] *O.R.*, Ser. I, Vol. XIX, Pt. 2, p. 312.

Confederate side equal courage had been shown and a magnificent tenacity exhibited."[7]

For a time the Confederate center was so denuded of troops that only a single North Carolina regiment remained. D. H. Hill, seizing a musket like Ney in Napoleon's retreat from Moscow, rallied the fragments of broken regiments and maintained resistance. Longstreet put his staff officers to work on a battery, holding their horses for them.

All the while McClellan was witnessing the battle from his headquarters near the center of the line at the Pry house, which stood on a commanding eminence. From this point the view ranged for miles in either direction. McClellan sat in an armchair in front of the house surrounded by the staff, whose horses were hitched near-by. Stakes driven in the earth held telescopes through which officers constantly peered at the changing battle scenes. Porter was with McClellan, watching the progress of the conflict.

The very thin gray line would have been broken by the desperate assaults made by the best troops of the Union army if Lee had not hurried detachments to the center from the left wing, where Jackson commanded, and the right wing, held by Longstreet. So serious were these drafts that Longstreet was left with a force inadequate for the next phase of the battle.

About ten o'clock Franklin's (Sixth) corps arrived at the Sharpsburg bridge, where Sumner held position. A part of Franklin was ordered to Sumner's aid and, advancing, relieved Greene's and French's divisions, which were holding the line from Bloody Lane to the East Wood. The Unionists held this position until Lee retreated.

The main crisis of the battle had come at ten o'clock when, for a moment, the Union chances for decisive victory seemed bright. But Lee, by throwing in McLaw's and Walker's divisions at the zero moment, had changed the whole outlook of the battle. Sedgwick was routed, and for a while it appeared that the Union right wing would dissolve. Sumner indeed informed McClellan that Hooker's corps had dispersed; McClellan accepted this report as true and limited his action in this quarter to holding the

[7] B. and L., Vol. II, p. 645.

East Wood and the adjoining hill, where Sedgwick's batteries were massed. Franklin's corps, coming up, was held in support of the hard-pressed right wing.

In order to create a diversion and also to carry out his plan of attacking both the Confederate flanks, McClellan ordered Burnside to cross the Antietam at the lower bridge and try to turn Lee's right flank. The time of the order has been disputed; McClellan states that it was issued at eight o'clock, Burnside that he received it at ten o'clock. The difference is important because the attack, if made earlier, might have been entirely successful owing to the pressure put on Lee's left flank by the corps massed there. The officer who carried the order said he received it at nine o'clock.

Cox was with Burnside when the order came. For several hours the two had watched the raging conflict as far as their sight extended, which was the Dunker Church. "As the morning wore on we saw lines of troops advancing from our right upon the other side of the Antietam and engaging the enemy between us and the East Wood. The Confederate lines facing them now rose into view. From our position we looked, as it were, down between the opposing lines as if they had been the sides of a street, and as the fire opened we saw wounded men carried to the rear and stragglers making off. Our lines halted, and we were tortured with anxiety as we speculated whether our men would charge or retreat. The enemy occupied lines of houses and stone walls and their batteries made gaps in the National ranks. Our long-range guns were immediately turned in that direction, and we cheered every well-aimed shot.... The contest was going on, and it was yet uncertain which would succeed when one of McClellan's staff rode up with an order to Burnside." Burnside and Cox then began to make preparations for forcing a passage of the bridge.

This was a difficult task because, owing to the curve of the Antietam valley, the bridge was not commanded by the guns on the east side of the creek while it was enfiladed by the Confederate batteries just in front of Sharpsburg. The only Confederates on this end of the line were the four skeleton brigades making up the division of D. R. Jones. The brigade commanded by Senator

Robert Toombs was immediately in front of the bridge and was supported by the other brigades.

The Unionists were handicapped by having to move in column instead of deploying into line and were much exposed to the Confederate batteries. Burnside, viewing the attempt to force the bridge as hazardous, was determined to cross also by a ford below the bridge. Walker's division earlier in the morning had been in position in front of the ford but had been called away to support the Confederate left wing. Consequently the chance of forcing the passage of the Antietam was probably better in the afternoon than it had been in the morning, for the force holding the Confederate right was now extremely small. The troops, however, were of first-rate quality.

Sturgis' division advanced toward the bridge, with Crook's brigade in front. When Crook's troops reached the bank of the stream above the bridge they at once came under the Confederate fire. Putting his men under such cover as was possible, Crook returned the fire; the two lines opposed each other across the Antietam, firing in each other's faces. Batteries were brought up by the Unionists, and the fight waxed furious, but the Unionists were repulsed every time they approached the strategic bridge.

McClellan was now almost beside himself in the determination to push home the attack here and force the Confederates to recall troops from the Union right, which was generally believed to have gone to smash. He sent repeated orders to Burnside, who, going over Cox's head, ordered Sturgis to force the passage of the stream at all hazards.

Several regiments not yet engaged were formed in column, a howitzer was brought up and double-shotted with canister. The regiments advanced, the howitzer swept the bridge, and in a few moments the Unionists were across. Toombs's brigade, which had defended it heroically for hours, retired over the hill back of the stream. The Unionists advanced to this ridge, and at the same time the troops that had gone to the ford below the bridge crossed the stream and joined their comrades on the hill. It was now about one o'clock, and three hours had been spent in a bitter conflict across the narrow stream. The Unionists suffered heavy casualties, but they seemed to have won a decided advantage at last.

The bluecoats presently brought batteries across the creek to enable them to hold their position and to advance. The men were made to lie down in ranks in order to escape the storm of canister and shell turned on them by the Confederate batteries at Sharpsburg. Troops were needed to replace Sturgis' shattered command, and ammunition as well. Cox sent these requests to Burnside, who complied, but the narrow bridge impeded crossings. It was three o'clock before the Unionists on the extreme left were ready to advance again. Burnside in person did his best to hasten the arrangements, which could not be completed briefly. It might have been best if the bluecoats had relied on the bayonet and gone ahead without ammunition, but they did not. Willcox was placed in line to relieve Sturgis, who was kept in reserve.

Willcox's division formed the right of the line; Crook's brigade supported Willcox. Rodman's division, which had crossed by the ford, formed the left wing, Scammon's brigade being on the extreme left. Many batteries accompanied the infantry; other batteries on the east side of the Antietam took part in the attack.

The Unionists had an excellent chance of success, as at this end of the battlefield they were in vastly superior strength; the greater part of Lee's army was holding the left and the shattered center. The blue line moved toward Sharpsburg, furiously resisted by Jones's small brigades. Deployed diagonally across the Union front, the graybacks held the stone fences and cross ridges, aided by their artillery firing at close range, but they were pressed back by superior weight. The conflict was here as bitter as in other portions of the battlefield. Jones made a final stand in an orchard but Willcox's batteries blasted the Confederates out, and Willcox's infantry, charging, occupied a part of Sharpsburg. Rodman on the left had advanced but had not made the progress of Willcox owing to the resistance encountered.

Lee was looking anxiously on, surrounded by his officers. He had no other troops in reserve, as his left wing was opposing the masses of three Union corps and his center was shattered. It appeared that he was doomed to defeat.

At this moment the Unionists in line of battle at Sharpsburg saw troops approaching through the high corn and thought them to be friends because many of them wore blue uniforms. But the newcomers were A. P. Hill's division, just arrived from Harper's Ferry and clad in captured uniforms, for which the Southerners had discarded their rags. The Union left, exposed to a heavy fire, now broke. Cox, riding forward, saw that a further advance was impossible, and ordered Sturgis up to fill the gap. The Unionists withdrew from Sharpsburg and formed a new line some distance to the rear of their former position. The Confederates, pushing forward, were repulsed with loss and fell back to a line running from Sharpsburg to the mouth of the Antietam at the Potomac River.

It was now growing on toward evening and both armies were utterly worn out. No other movement of importance was made on either side, and the September sun sank behind the Confederate position. Gradually the batteries ceased firing and nothing was heard but the cracking of rifles as the opposing sharpshooters sniped at each other. And then this noise, too, died away, and silence fell on the vast and bloody stage.

"The close of the battle presented a magnificent spectacle as the artillery of both armies came into play.... Far up on the Union right, as well as in the center, the Union batteries were pounding. I recall a remarkable scene. The sun was going down—its disk red and large as seen through the murky battle cloud. One of Sumner's batteries was directly in line toward the sun ... and there was one piece, of which the gunners, as they rammed home the cartridges, seemed to be standing in the sun. Beyond, hid from view by the distance and the low-hanging branches of the oaks by the Dunker Church, the Confederate guns were flashing. Immediately north of Sharpsburg, and along the hill in front ... Longstreet's cannon were in play.... All the country was flaming and smoking; shells were bursting along the contending lines.... The sun went down; the thunder died away, the musketry ceased, bivouac fires gleamed out as if a great city had lighted its lamps." [8]

For a whole day it had been a hell of men in blue or gray-brown charging through the tall corn with ringing cheers that

[8] *B. and L.*, Vol. II, p. 684.

were swallowed up in the rattle of musketry and the roar of cannon. Ever the ground thundered with detonations as the massed artillery east of the Antietam swept the ridges behind which the Confederates lay, mowing them down in rows when they appeared on the crests. Ever the blue men, coming closer through the powder smoke, saw the bowlders and stone fences spouting flame and heard the canister go ripping through their lines. Sweating, powder-begrimed, almost too weary to load and fire, the two gallant opponents had faced each other through the long day and had taken such punishment as no troops in America had ever endured before. All honor to both sides! The stand of the Confederates is forever memorable, for the gray-brown men were almost in the last stages of exhaustion from incessant marching and lack of proper food. Lee had driven them to the uttermost limit of human endurance in the effort to gain a decisive victory, and he had failed.

The idea, however, that Lee was defeated and driven back across the Potomac, circulated after his retreat, is erroneous. What frustrated Lee was the bad position he occupied. So far from thinking of retreat, Lee and Jackson were considering a counteroffensive. Lee sent one of his artillerists to see if massed batteries could crush the guns on McClellan's right and give the Confederates a chance to turn that end of the Union line. The artilleryman reported adversely and Jackson confirmed his judgment. Lee reluctantly abandoned the idea of a counteroffensive. But he determined to continue standing on the defensive, despite the objections of his subordinates, who wished to retreat. Consequently, the Southerners remained in position all day of September 18, picking up their dead and rescuing their wounded.

McClellan has been censured for not putting his reserve, Porter, into the battle. As a matter of fact, Sykes and Griffin were engaged, though the remainder of the corps remained inactive. McClellan's reply to this criticism was that he did not think it prudent to strip his center of all reserves. Apparently he did not, at this time, believe he had won a victory. He was so impressed by the disintegration of Hooker's corps and the rout of Sedgwick that he supposed his right wing had dissolved, as Sumner reported. Consequently, it would appear that he made the attack on the Confederate right partly in an effort to relieve his own endangered right, which, as a matter of fact, did nothing all through the afternoon while the battle was raging at Burnside's Bridge. It was too exhausted to try again. McClellan, going there, attempted to rally that wing.

When the sun went down behind murky smoke clouds on September 17, McClellan sighed a breath of relief, for all this time he had expected a counterattack by Lee and had held back the greater part of Porter's corps, his single reserve, to meet such an emergency. Nor was he satisfied that the attack would not come as the sun dawned on September 18. At eight o'clock he wired Halleck, "The battle of yesterday continued for fourteen hours, and until after dark. We held all we gained, except a portion of the extreme left; that was obliged to abandon a part of what it had gained. Our losses were heavy, especially in general officers. The battle will probably be renewed to-day. Send all the troops you can by the most expeditious route." [9]

Thus it is evident that on the morning of September 18, McClellan still expected Lee to attack and had no intention of renewing the offensive himself. But as the hours wore away without any activity on the other side of Antietam Creek than the occasional firing of pickets, McClellan regained confidence. It was evident that the Confederates were as badly hurt as he was and in no condition to advance.

Great blame has been attached to McClellan for not renewing the attack on September 18. The criticism is unjust in light of the facts as reported. McClellan believed that Hooker's corps had gone completely to pieces and he put Meade in command of it with the object of reorganizing it for conflict as quickly as possible. The corps commanded by Mansfield and Sumner were in little better case. The troops on the left wing had also lost heavily in forcing the passage of the creek. Every command was in bad shape except Porter, and Porter was the only reserve.

If McClellan had attacked on September 18, he would have done just what Lee wanted him to do. He would have given Lee a chance to win a great victory, for though the Confederate losses had been terrible, the army was better coördinated and even

[9] *O.R.*, Ser. I, Vol. XIX, Pt. 2, p. 322.

yet more confident than its opponent. While ammunition was running low, there was still some in the caissons and cartridge boxes, and the men could be depended on to use the bayonet if need be. The long-range artillery east of the Antietam made it impossible for Lee to win a victory except in one way: a rout of the opposing infantry that would enable his men to mix with fugitives and so escape cannon fire. And that such a rout would have been possible everything goes to show.

In the first place, the reorganized Union army had given signs that it had been hastily put together and had not entirely recovered from the Second Manassas in the short space of time intervening. If nothing else indicated this, the extraordinary number of casualties among the higher officers testifies that the men had to be led rather than directed, that the generals in that terrible battle on the Union right exposed themselves recklessly in the effort to carry the Confederate position. In fact, no such fighting had ever taken place on the American continent; the open country, affording little cover, and the numerous batteries on both sides made it bloody beyond anything that had gone before. The battle was epochal.

McClellan was wise in not attacking on September 18, just as Meade was wise in not counterattacking on July 3, 1863. In both cases the Union gained a great advantage without running the risk of a serious reverse. Lee's Maryland Campaign was ruined, and there was nothing left for him to do but to recross the Potomac and admit frustration. A renewal of the battle would have given him a last chance to snatch victory out of failure. It is hard to estimate the actual number of troops McClellan had present for duty on the morning of September 18, but it could not have been much more than 50,000, if that many. He had lost 15,000 men in the battle. Lee had nearly 30,000 men left, and they were veterans of the first water, the best troops on earth fighting on the defensive. Another day's battle would have been touch and go. All accounts tell of the thousands of stragglers behind the Union lines; probably 10,000 men had left the colors and sought cover.

McClellan has also been criticized for not putting more troops into the battle at the same time. It is true that he could have made an attack on both flanks simultaneously and this might have embarrassed Lee, but General Cox points out that in the morning Walker's division was at the Burnside Bridge and would have repelled any attempt there. The attacks made successively by Hooker, Mansfield, and Sumner brought about as many troops to the scene of action as could be advantageously deployed. In fact, these attacks, made one after the other, tried the Confederates greatly, endangering them more than a general attack all along the line might have done. McClellan's arrangements were judicious and had been carried out with reasonable efficiency. What chiefly frustrated the attack on the Confederate left had been the extraordinary resisting power of the Confederate soldiery, expert marksmen that they were, and the fact that Lee had been able to throw McLaws and Walker into the conflict at the psychological moment. He had fought the battle skillfully, using every man in his army at one point or the other, doing everything that could be done to retrieve the initial error of fighting on a field that gave the long-range Union artillery a great advantage over the short-range Confederate ordnance.

Much to the astonishment of McClellan, who still vastly overrated Lee's forces, September 18 passed without incident. Lee did not attack, did not show any belligerent tendency. Even the picket firing was not brisk. Both armies were worn out and something like a truce was on the lines.

In the night of September 18-19, Lee retreated across the Potomac without the movement being observed by the Union pickets, or, at least, without its being disturbed in any way by the bluecoats. Nothing was left on the north side of the river except some damaged equipment and a few stragglers who were picked up by the Unionists in the morning. Lee's ammunition was nearly out; he had little or no food, and he knew that large reinforcements were coming up to McClellan but none to him. Retreat was the only course open to him, and he retreated with his usual skill. The Union pickets, observing a silence in front of them in the early morning light, advanced into Sharpsburg, finding nothing but dead and wounded and the *disjecta membra* of a bitter battle. Lee had disappeared.

When McClellan learned of this he felt that the victory was

his; Lee had retreated, leaving the field to him. At 8:30 A.M. he wired Halleck, "Last night the enemy abandoned his position, leaving his dead and wounded on the field. We are again in pursuit. I do not yet know whether he is falling back to an interior position or crossing the river. We may safely claim a complete victory." [10]

Shortly afterward McClellan was informed that Lee had crossed the Potomac, and at 10:30 he dispatched Halleck, "Pleasonton is driving the enemy across the river. Our victory is complete. The enemy is driven back into Virginia. Maryland and Pennsylvania are now safe."

Before he learned of Lee's retreat, McClellan was anything but confident that he had won the battle; he had feared a counterattack until then. As soon as he was assured of Lee's withdrawal across the Potomac, he assumed that he had gained a great victory. He had won a success in frustrating Lee's invasion of Maryland—the most important success won for the Union in the war—but he had not gained a tactical victory in front of Sharpsburg. He had fought what was a drawn battle and, despite all criticism to the contrary, he had shown considerable initiative and skill. The blows he struck were the most intense delivered in the war up to that time. He made little use of the cavalry, it is true, but he coördinated infantry and artillery to a degree never before known on an American battlefield. Lee's losses had been staggering in consequence, too great to enable him to take the counteroffensive under the circumstances, even if his position had been better.

Lee may have fought at Sharpsburg for political purposes, though it is doubtful. It is more likely that he fought because his blood was up and he had confidence in his army. Longstreet credited him with "headlong combativeness," but the phrase is inaccurate. Lee was not headlong but he was combative. He was a lion, and the lion is usually ready for a fight. Lee fought at Sharpsburg because the enemy was there, hoping that some happening would throw the chance of victory his way. That chance never came; indeed, he was rather glad to get his battered army out of a bad position with the deep Potomac at his back.

[10] *O.R.*, Ser I, Vol. XIX, Pt. 2, p. 330.

SHARPSBURG

It is possible that he fought because of the difficulty of crossing the river in front of the enemy.

Jackson was also always ready for a fight; but Jackson, left to himself, would probably have preferred not to fight at Sharpsburg, for he fought to win and always wished to fight at an advantage. The difference between Lee and Jackson is well illustrated by an incident of Sharpsburg. Lee, the Christian warrior always taking care for private property, issued an order forbidding looting. Just before the battle he came on a private who was trying to make off with a stolen pig (the poor fellow was doubtless hungry, as the Confederates had no rations) and became enraged at this flagrant disobedience. He sent the offender to Jackson with directions to have him shot. Jackson obeyed the order in the most jesuitical way; he put the fellow in the forefront of the battle where he would probably be shot by the enemy while shooting at the enemy; Jackson could see no utility whatever in executing an able-bodied soldier when every musket was needed. The man fought gallantly and went through the battle without a scratch, whereupon Jackson dropped the matter. The difference between the ideal and the practical.

McClellan's claim of a "complete victory" was unfortunate. He should have said, instead, that he had foiled the invasion in a battle desperate and uncertain until the end, that he had been fortunate indeed to hold the field and force the Southerners to recross the river. If he had said that, the magnitude of his achievement would have been recognized. But by claiming such a decisive victory he at once raised the question why he had not followed up that victory—why, if so successful on September 17, he had not destroyed Lee on September 18. And that view of the battle has obtained ever since. The truth is that, in spite of his superiority in numbers—which he never believed—he was fortunate in escaping defeat at the hands of two such generals as Lee and Jackson commanding the Confederate army at its best.

McClellan had saved the Union but he had not performed the well-nigh impossible feat of destroying Lee. The next year Meade, on the defensive, managed to repulse Lee, but he was entirely unable to destroy Lee, though the latter had a long retreat to make instead of the two miles to the Potomac at Sharpsburg. The next year Grant set out to destroy Lee, but all that he could do was to work Lee around to the position that McClellan had occupied two years before. Destroying Lee was much like going into a lion's den with a spear for a weapon; nobody accomplished his defeat until his army was worn out. But the civilians, who were about to abandon Washington in panic when Lee was near, lost fear of Lee when he was distant. "Why didn't McClellan destroy Lee?" everybody said. And they still say it. But McClellan was largely to blame with his "complete victory." Once more he said too much.

CHAPTER FOURTEEN

COMEDY AFTER TRAGEDY, BUT COMEDY WITH A BAD ENDING

OUR ANCESTORS in their desire for relief from somber emotions liked to see a farce comedy follow a tragedy; thus, in those days, a performance of *Hamlet* concluded with *Box and Cox*. In the same way the great tragedy of Sharpsburg (Antietam) was followed by the comedy of the unseating of McClellan after a curious series of maneuvers.

The last shots along the Antietam had hardly died out before a storm of criticism broke over McClellan's devoted head. There was immense relief in Washington when the news came that Lee was back across the Potomac, but the relief was immediately followed by chagrin that McClellan had not destroyed the Southerner and his leonine army. As we have noted, McClellan was not a little responsible for this criticism by announcing a "complete victory," when, as a matter of fact, he had fought for life and had not known the outcome of the battle on the morning of September 18. It was not until Lee retreated across the river that the realization swept over him that he had won a victory. Lee had appeared extremely formidable to the authorities in those first two weeks of September, 1862; but Lee, on Virginia soil again with a shattered army, seemed to be easy pickings to the armchair strategists in the War Department.

How near the Union had been to complete demoralization is evident from many things, among them the panic of the authorities in Pennsylvania. On September 19, Brigadier General John F. Reynolds reported to Halleck from Hagerstown that he had expected to bring into the field 14,000 men but that, to his surprise, all the regiments refused to march.[1] "What will be done, or can be done, with the force here I cannot say, though I do not think much can be expected of them." On September 20, Brigadier General George Stoneman, at Point of Rocks, reported to Halleck, "The whole country is covered with stragglers from General McClellan's army. . . . I am trying to collect them together."

Confirming the demoralization of the army, in September, 1862, Meade reported: "The development here made of straggling and abandoning their commands on the part of officers and men is so startling, and so important in its bearing on the reliance to to be placed on the command with which I have been honored, that I deem it due to myself and the general commanding to make this communication.

"How this serious and terrible evil can be cured is a difficult question to solve inasmuch as the disease seems to pervade the whole body. Nothing, in my judgment, short of taking life will have any effect."[2]

McClellan made an explanation to Halleck on September 22, for he was already aware of the criticism. He said that when he was assigned to the command of the army it was disheartened by defeat and its efficiency was much impaired. In the battles recently fought he had lost ten general officers and many regimental and company officers in addition to large numbers of enlisted men. "The army corps have been badly cut up and scattered by the overwhelming numbers brought against them in the battle of the 17th instant, and the entire army has been greatly exhausted by unavoidable overwork, hunger and want of sleep and rest. When the enemy recrossed the Potomac the means of transportation at my disposal was inadequate to furnish a single day's supply of subsistence in advance. Under these circumstances I did not feel authorized to cross the river in pursuit of the retreating enemy, and thereby place that stream . . . between this army and its base of supply." It was necessary to reorganize the army; the skeleton regiments should be filled at once. As soon as pontoon bridges could be laid he expected to

[1] *O.R.*, Ser. I, Vol. XIX, Pt. 2, p. 332.
[2] *Ibid.*, p. 348.

occupy Harper's Ferry with a view of advancing into the Shenandoah Valley.[3]

It is strange that the authorities in Washington did not recognize the necessity of making adequate preparations for the campaign in Virginia. Apparently they expected McClellan, commanding a half-organized army, without any supply base south of the Potomac, and with nothing but wagons for transportation to open an active campaign in the desert of northern Virginia. Such a movement against such a foe as Lee and Jackson would have been to invite disaster, as McClellan well knew; but, as noted before, the authorities had lost their fear of Lee and Jackson, now that they were in retreat. They thought that McClellan could go ahead and finish the war at a blow. Consequently, his frustration of the invasion of Maryland and the great battle of Sharpsburg had done him little good. He had not nailed the lion's hide to the door as the civilians expected. Nor was Meade, under much more favorable circumstances, able to do it the next year. In the one case McClellan was entirely superseded; in the other case Meade was made to play second fiddle to Grant.

Food stores were inadequate. Rufus Ingalls, chief quartermaster of the army, wired Meigs from Sharpsburg that the army must have its supply depot for a time at Harper's Ferry, as it was some distance both from the Hagerstown and Frederick depots. "The country here on both sides of the Potomac is exhausted of all supplies. It would be found impracticable to supply so large an army beyond the river with wagons." McClellan desired the Chesapeake and Ohio canal to be repaired for the purpose of conveying supplies. He also asked that the railroad bridge at Harper's Ferry be repaired, as he expected to occupy that town.

McClellan was pushing preparations for an advance, but he had no intention of penetrating Virginia without proper supply connections. He asked Halleck for twenty new regiments to fill up the army and for bridges to be built over the Potomac and over the Shenandoah at Harper's Ferry on existing piers. "I cannot too strongly urge the importance of expedition in this matter. Until this or the railroad bridge is finished, it is scarcely possible

[3] *Ibid.*, p. 342.

to advance from Harper's Ferry in force, and as that is clearly our true line of operations, I need not urge upon you the necessity of completing our communications there."

Instead of complying with McClellan's reasonable request, Halleck demanded to know his plans and suggested that he cross the river lower down in order to cover Washington. "It seems to me that Washington is the real basis of operations, and that it should not under any circumstances be exposed." Thus it will be seen that McClellan was being forced into a campaign in the terrain immediately south of Washington, devastated as it had been in the Second Manassas campaign. McClellan, who was determined to make Harper's Ferry his supply base, went to that place and decided to fortify Maryland Heights on the north side of the river. It is thus evident that his plans and those of the authorities were once more not in agreement.

Some days passed while McClellan was busy attempting to get ready to move across the river. At his suggestion a force from Washington pushed southward, reconnoitering and capturing some prisoners at Warrenton. Of the main Confederate army McClellan received only confusing reports. That it was in the vicinity of Winchester was all that he could learn for some time. Halleck, on October 4, wired him that Cavalryman Bayard reported Longstreet to be moving to Leesburg while Jackson confronted him at Harper's Ferry.

At this time McClellan again spoke unwisely—without regard for his own situation and that of the country. On September 22, Lincoln, presuming that Sharpsburg was a Union victory, issued the long-contemplated Emancipation Proclamation. It was communicated to the army on September 24. McClellan, with his usual openness, did not fail to show his lack of sympathy with a revolutionary measure, which, if carried into effect, meant the confiscation of a billion dollars worth of private property. Strongly conservative, unaffected by the abolition hysteria then sweeping the North, the commander of the Army of the Potomac was now in a really impossible position. On October 7, he referred to the proclamation in a general order, warning the soldiers not to indulge in heated political discussions and assuring them that the "remedy for political errors, if they are committed, is to be found only in the action of the people at the polls," which was a gentle reminder that Lincoln's action might be repudiated in the approaching election.

Not that McClellan wished to take any part in political controversies. In a letter to his wife, on October 5, he wrote, "Mr. Aspinwall is decidedly of the opinion that it is my duty to submit to the President's proclamation and quietly continue doing my duty as a soldier. I presume he is right, and am at least sure that he is honest in his opinion. I shall surely give his views full consideration." [4] Evidently McClellan did not understand the political situation.

Lincoln was far from satisfied with McClellan, being much under the influence of Stanton, who was protesting against the delay in crossing the river in pursuit of Lee. The authorities either did not understand the unprepared state of the army or they deliberately ignored facts in order to make out a case against McClellan.

Lincoln, on October 1, visited McClellan in his camp on the Potomac. He wished to learn the condition of the army and determine why McClellan was tardy in following up what had been pronounced as a signal victory of the Northern forces. For several days the tall President, crowned with the absurd top hat of the period, was to be seen strolling through the camps, looking about and stopping to make inquiries. McClellan says that Lincoln expressed satisfaction with his course, only criticizing him mildly for wishing to be fully prepared before moving. He gave Lincoln a detailed account of his operations and of his reasons for not crossing the Potomac immediately. In fact, he was actually handicapped by his scientific outlook. A general of political inclinations, seeing how the wind blew, would have gone ahead and taken a chance of being decisively defeated or having his troops starve for lack of adequate supplies, but McClellan had that idea of thorough preliminary preparation that in the present age is associated with the German army. Unwisely McClellan ventured on the step of giving Lincoln political advice.[5] This, no doubt, had its effect.

[4] *McClellan's Own Story,* p. 655
[5] *Ibid.,* p. 627.

Lincoln spent five days at army headquarters. He visited the battlefields and inspected the different corps. McClellan, who was not lacking in intuition, said that he felt that the real purpose of Lincoln's visit was to push him into a "premature advance" into Virgina, but as the days went by and the President remained friendly, and was even congratulatory, McClellan's distrust lessened. On one occasion Lincoln said to him, "General, you have saved the country. You must remain in command and carry us through to the end." [6]

The President departed, leaving McClellan in a happy humor. Everything was going well; the needed supplies were at last beginning to arrive. What was the general's consternation when, on October 6, this order came from Halleck: "The President directs that you cross the Potomac and give battle to the enemy or drive him south. Your army must move now while the road is good!" McClellan then understood that the explanations that he had made Lincoln in regard to the army and its needs had fallen on deaf ears; the November elections were at hand and the Washington authorities wanted a military success to put before the country following the Emancipation Proclamation.

McClellan could not immediately comply with the order, for, on October 4, the Confederates had started on a raid, and consternation reigned once more in Maryland. In the night the gray cavalry burned Little Cacapon Bridge twenty miles from Cumberland and captured a company of Pennsylvania troops. It was not Stuart who was raiding but Imboden; Averell was at once sent in pursuit. This movement was unfortunate because, by drawing off Union cavalry, it gave Stuart the opportunity for which he had been looking.

The raid was important because it had much to do with the overthrow of McClellan and the ruin of the Confederate cavalry. When Averell, with his cavalry, had been drawn off in pursuit

---

[6] Clarence Edward Macartney, *Little Mac* (New York, Dorrence and Co., 1940), p. 284. McClellan says: "At the time I received the order of Oct. 6 . . . the army was wholly deficient in cavalry, and a large part of the troops were in want of shoes, blankets and other indispensable articles of clothing."

of Imboden, Stuart rode with 1,800 horsemen to McCoy's Ferry, where on the morning of October 10, 1862, he crossed the Potomac. The cavalry column, soon after reaching the National Road, was observed. Union forces picketed the crossings of the river for miles, and by 10 A.M. Hagerstown was informed of the raid. This is noted because McClellan was accused of not being on the alert; it is difficult to see how any officer could have been more alert.

McClellan's signal system was so efficient that by noon of the same day signals were being flashed from a dozen stations asking for information of the gray raiders. Rain fell on October 11, obscuring vision, but on the next day the signal station on Sugar Loaf near the Monocacy observed every stage of the raid until the recrossing of the river.

The Army of the Potomac, concentrated for the advance into Virginia, had headquarters at Knoxville, where Pleasonton's cavalry happened to be. McClellan held this cavalry, the only force on hand for the pursuit, until he had some inkling of Stuart's movements. Owing, however, to the lack of telegraph lines in that part of Maryland, McClellan for some hours received no news as he anxiously waited at headquarters preparatory to launching the horse after Stuart.

At 9:30 P.M. Halleck telegraphed him: "A rebel raid has been made into Pennsylvania today and Chambersburg captured. Not a man should be permitted to return to Virginia. Use any troops in Maryland or Pennsylvania against them." McClellan answered: "Every disposition has been made to cut off the retreat of the enemy's cavalry that today made a raid into Pennsylvania."

McClellan had made a wise disposal of his forces in the attempt to bag the daring Stuart. The latter could not have been headed off from Chambersburg because he had too good a start, but he would have to recross the river at one of many fords, and McClellan sought to cut him off from all of them. Averell was ordered to follow Stuart's route. Troops were rushed to McConnelsville and Hancock, where a road crossed the Potomac. Kelley, at Cumberland, picketed the Potomac between Cumberland and Hancock. Between Hancock and Harper's Ferry pickets were reinforced. Troops were sent from Baltimore to Frederick and Harrisburg. McClellan put troops on trains and held them, prepared to send them in any direction at short notice. By midnight of October 11 the west and south were blocked for Stuart. When McClellan had some definite idea of his movements he launched Pleasonton in pursuit. Here was the rub, however. Pleasonton had only 700 cavalry with him, far too small a force to do anything but hold Stuart until infantry could come up. Stoneman had a mixed force of infantry and cavalry, but it was needed for picketing duty. Averell was far to the west and never came near Stuart. All of the Union cavalry was in bad shape, owing to the oot-and-mouth disease, which was raging in the army and the adjacent country. McClellan was never able to make the Washington authorities understand how debilitating this horse epidemic was, how reduced his cavalry was on account of it. The government's failure to supply him with needed mounts was one of the principal factors in delaying his forward movement into Virginia.

Meanwhile the gray riders had been having a high old time. Singing, flourishing their plumed hats at stolid Pennsylvania women, they took possession of Chambersburg, where they charmed all they met by their urbanity and respect for private property. The Confederates, in grimmer mood, burned Chambersburg in 1864, in retaliation for the devastation of Virginia, but in 1862 they were all smiles and flourishes—gay cavaliers that they were.

Stuart calculated his return with great acumen. Knowing that all the short routes to the Potomac would be heavily guarded, he turned eastward toward the fords in the vicinity of Leesburg. Pleasonton, after much misinformation and some mishaps, finally got on Stuart's trail and made for the same crossing of the river, arriving there ahead of the raiders with only 400 men. The Confederates brushed him aside, rode through other bodies of troops and crossed the river at White's Ford, escaping from the whole cordon of foes.

It was a feat that made the South re-echo with prideful laughter while it enraged the Washington authorities. Lincoln is said to have remarked that it reminded him of a game in which a person who was three times encircled was out. McClellan had been encircled twice; the third time he would be out. It was an ominous pleasantry.

The raid could not have been prevented with the cavalry at McClellan's command. It did the North no injury except to its vanity; it almost wrecked the Confederate cavalry. Stuart's men in October were not quite what they had been in June, for many of the race horses were gone, but many of them remained. Stuart brought with him some hundreds of horses captured in Pennsylvania; these brought with them the foot-and-mouth disease. The result was that at Gettysburg some months later Confederate cavalrymen were riding mules and plow-horses. The gain was all on the Union side of the balance sheet—except that McClellan was further in the bad graces of his masters in Washington.

These spectacular raids that aroused gleeful laughter in the South were productive of much more harm to the Confederate cause than to the Union. Stuart's ride around McClellan in June, 1862, warned the Union commander of the danger to his communications and hastened, if it did not cause, the change of base to James River. A year later, in June, 1863, Stuart was to ride around the Army of the Potomac once more, and with disastrous results, for his separation from Lee left the latter without information as to the movements of the Union army, prejudicing his operations in Pennsylvania. But to civilians these daring rides seemed important, and they did have some effect in bolstering the morale of the South.

The tendency of civilians to pass from extreme depression to over-confidence is something against which professional soldiers have no guard. It was assumed in Washington that all that McClellan needed to do was to follow Lee into Virginia to destroy the Confederate army and win the war. McClellan might have taken the risk, but what a risk it would have been against Lee and Jackson on their own ground! McClellan did not take the risk, and that is probably one reason why the Union finally triumphed. To have assumed the offensive against Lee in October, 1862, would have been to play into Lee's hands.

People did not know this then, and historians have not learned it since. It was largely a question of equipment and supply. McClellan conducted the Maryland campaign with an army lacking nearly everything for a protracted season. He naturally and properly did not wish to move into the devastated region of northern Virginia with an army in such a condition, but he has been denounced ever since for not doing so.

The supply system of American armies has invariably been bad from the Revolution down; it was notably so in 1861-65 and 1898. Definite organization has nearly always been lacking; the methods followed have been haphazard and hand-to-mouth. The result has ever been that American armies have suffered unnecessarily.

The Confederate troops almost always were in need of proper rations, clothing, and equipment. This was partly due to a real lack of materials and partly to poor organization and the handling of the railroads, which were permitted to run passenger trains on schedule even in times of military crisis. Moreover, the railroads became inefficient for want of rolling stock and rails. If the railroads had been in good condition and had been properly utilized, the progress of the war would have been much different.

The Confederate government made great strides in overcoming its early deficiencies. It established clothing and shoe factories, which, even without machinery, turned out large quantities of products. It made excellent munitions and good artillery. It had more food in its depots in April, 1865, than at any previous time. In short, the Confederacy collapsed at the very moment that it was coming on a war footing.

The North suffered from no such lack of mechanical agencies; it was filled with the small factories of the day, and the government might have obtained any amount of equipment in a short time; by 1862 the Union armies should have been admirably equipped; and, thanks to McClellan, the Army of the Potomac began the Peninsular Campaign well outfitted in most respects. However, much of the equipment was left behind on the James and returned slowly, and much was lost in Pope's ill-fated campaign. Moreover, while the fighting was going on in August and September, 1862, the Union government was not preparing for future needs. The quartermaster general of the United States army, Meigs, was not much more competent than his rival, Northrop, of the Confederate service.

When, after the Maryland campaign, McClellan for the first time had an opportunity to check up on equipment, he found it lamentably lacking. He had only two regiments of horse in condition to oppose the larger and better cavalry force of Lee's army. He needed draught horses for artillery and wagons and obtained them only after constant applications.

Tents were lacking, and medical supplies; there were not sufficient rations on hand for a forward movement into Virginia. Another important deficiency was clothing; the men's uniforms were wearing out and the nights were becoming cool; overcoats were required, and overcoats were not forthcoming. A large part of the army was barefooted or nearly so. Such needs should have been foreseen and provided for, but they were not. The inevitable result was delay, for which McClellan has been censured ever since; the blame should rest on the supply system, not on the commander who exerted himself to the utmost to secure the necessary equipment for his army.

McClellan, with every effort, could not have moved for several weeks after Sharpsburg. His army, hastily coördinated in September, had been shattered; the loss in officers had been especially heavy, both at Second Manassas and Sharpsburg. Many of the commands were mixed up; thousands of stragglers had to be brought back to the colors. And yet the civilians in Washington could not see why McClellan did not cross the Potomac on the morrow of Sharpsburg and win the war at a single stroke.

By the first date at which McClellan could possibly have moved, with an army still in need of clothing and supplies, Lee had recovered from the Maryland Campaign. The 10,000 barefooted men who had been unable to keep up with the army in Maryland had, by this time, come in; Lee was stronger than he had been at Sharpsburg. Consequently, there would have been no apparent gain if McClellan had immediately entered Virginia, as he was desired by his government to do.

It is necessary to go into the matter of supply in some detail, for the records revealing the needs of the army form McClellan's best defense against the criticism to which he was subjected then and with which his memory is still weighted. While it is true that the Union supply service was not the carnival of graft it had been at an earlier period, when contractors bribed officers and furnished paper shoes and cotton blankets, it was still piecemeal, unorganized, and inefficient to the last degree.

The raid of October, 1862, was exactly what Stanton and McClellan's other enemies in Washington desired. It enabled them to picture McClellan as an unenterprising commander unable to prevent the enemy cavalry from encircling him at will. There can be little doubt that Stuart's raid hastened McClellan's fall, though it did not occasion it. After the Emancipation Proclamation it was impossible for a political conservative to remain at the head of the main Union army.

On October 7, Halleck informed McClellan that the army must move, as the country was becoming impatient at its inactivity. (Apparently McClellan's strenuous efforts to equip and provision the army was regarded as inactivity.) "I am satisfied that the enemy are falling back toward Richmond. We must follow them and seek to punish them. There is a decided want of legs in our troops. They have too much immobility, and we must try to remedy the defect." [7]

Halleck was once more indulging in his fatuous reflections. Even he, professional soldier, did not see the need of better preparations for a campaign in northern Virginia in the cold season just coming in.

Meanwhile McClellan was attempting to secure the many things direly needed by an efficient army. Tents. He was asking for thousands of them and getting no assurances. Ingalls, on October 7, was complaining to Washington that clothing and other supplies ordered had not arrived at Harper's Ferry. He requested 5,000 suits sent to the latter place. Horses were needed, many horses, and they were not reaching the army. And there were other things.

On October 8, McClellan wired Halleck that his headquarters were at Knoxville, Maryland, near Harper's Ferry. "I am push-

[7] *O.R.*, Ser. I, Vol. XIX, Pt. 2, p. 394.

ing everything as rapidly as possible to get ready for the advance."

Meigs was informed that McClellan's requisitions for 4,000 blankets, 5,000 shelter tents and 5,000 additional blankets had not been filled. Some days later the clothing and shelter tents as well as a few horses began to reach McClellan. At this time it seems that the Union troops were in want of uniforms (particularly overcoats) and shoes; yet the authorities could not understand why they were not ready for a winter campaign in Virginia.

Ingalls, in vexation, wired Washington on October 10, "There is no clothing at Hagerstown, and an entire corps is waiting for it. What is the matter? The operation is becoming painful. The railroad to Hagerstown is disgustingly slow.... In mercy's name, get after this clothing."[8] On the same day Ingalls wired the depot quartermaster at Hagerstown, "Clothing for Porter's, Franklin's, and Reynolds' troops—say, at least 10,000 suits—was ordered to you on the 7th. It should be now at your place.... When it arrives issue it rapidly and, if possible, simultaneously, to each corps. Do you hear where the clothing is? Telegraph Harrisburg and answer me."

At the same time Rufus Ingalls asked for the railway to Winchester to be repaired, only to be informed by H. Haupt, chief of transportation, that it was the worst railroad in the country and incapable of being put in condition for satisfactory transportation. Ingalls was wiring desperately to Washington that 100 cars were needed to carry supplies to Hagerstown, the sending of which would prevent the dispatch of forage to Frederick and Harper's Ferry. "What is the matter? I supposed the clothing was already sent to Hagerstown.... It looks as though there has been fatal misunderstanding somewhere." Presently Ingalls was requesting 1,500 cavalry horses at once, and Stanton was writing to Meigs directing him to supply the need. On October 14, Halleck wired McClellan that every effort was being made to increase the cavalry force, then at low ebb. He added, "The President has read your telegram, and directs me to suggest that, if the enemy had more occupation south of the river, his cavalry

[8] *Ibid.*, p. 408.

would not be so likely to make raids north of it." [9] Apparently Lincoln, too, had little idea of the preparations needed.

Halleck wired McClellan that news had come that the Confederates were concentrating 7,000 to 10,000 cavalry at Leesburg preparatory to another raid into Maryland and asked him to prevent it. Almost in depair McClellan replied that at that time he had only one cavalry regiment available in addition to one under Stoneman at Harper's Ferry. "With my small cavalry force it is impossible for me to watch the line of the Potomac properly, or even make the reconnaissances that are necessary for our movements. This makes it necessary for me to weaken my line very much by extending the infantry to guard the innumerable fords."

Meigs now came back tartly at McClellan, declaring that he had supplied the army with 10,000 horses since the first of September; in the six weeks preceding, an average of 1,500 horses weekly. The wastage in the campaign had been very great. There were 3,300 broken-down horses in the depot, which indicated "a fault in the management of horses in the army."

There was a fault but it was not McClellan's. The trouble was that the Union cavalrymen were seldom horsemen and did not understand the care of beasts. They rode them too hard and did not handle them properly. In addition, the foot-and-mouth disease, destined later to ruin the Southern cavalry, was rife at this time in the Union army. Poor McClellan, trying desperately to get a sufficient number of horsemen to cope with Stuart, had to listen to lectures on the wastage of horses, and the expense of buying them, from a quartermaster general who was hostile to him and only too glad to get material to use against him. At this time the fear of Stuart was so great that McClellan apprehended a dash into Washington by the Southern raider. The anticipated raid did not come; Stuart's horses were also broken down. As late as October 15, Halleck wired McClellan that it was believed the enemy were preparing for another raid in order to cut McClellan's communications or attack Washington. "The inactivity of our army encourages these depredations."

[9] *Ibid.*, p. 421.

COMEDY WITH A BAD ENDING 225

The situation was maddening. Here was McClellan trying desperately to get enough cavalry and tents and uniforms and blankets and shoes and other things needed by an army for a winter campaign and, instead of receiving prompt help, he was being lectured on the "inactivity of the army." As a matter of fact, a case was being made against him; at least, the circumstances suggest it. The soldier who had foiled the invasion of Maryland could not be dismissed at once; but, by tardiness in complying with his requisitions, he could be made to seem criminally slow in following Lee into Virginia. And then the charge of slowness would serve as a good excuse to relieve him. It was simply the old conspiracy under a new form. The conspirators could no longer say that McClellan would not attack the Confederates, for he had attacked them ferociously at Sharpsburg; but they could make it appear that by "inactivity" he had thrown away the opportunity of winning a decisive advantage and ending the war. "Inactivity!" At that very moment, while fat old Halleck sat at his desk like a Buddha, doing nothing but criticize, McClellan was laboring to secure the equipment needed by his army for the projected campaign. He answered Halleck, it must be said, with good temper, "I am using every possible exertion to get this army ready to move. It was only yesterday that a part of our supplies and clothing arrived at Hagerstown. It is being issued to the troops as rapidly as possible."[10]

On October 15, Reynolds wrote to Chief of Staff Marcy, "My quartermaster has just returned from Hagerstown, where he went to procure clothing for this corps. He was able to procure only a complete supply of overcoats and pants, with a few socks, drawers and coats. He reports that there are no shoes, tents, blankets, knapsacks, or other clothing there. This leaves many of the men yet without a shoe. My requisitions call for 5,251 pairs of shoes."[11]

"*This leaves many of the men yet without a shoe.*" In other words, many of the Union soldiers a month after Sharpsburg were barefooted or nearly so. It is true that thousands of Lee's

[10] *Ibid.*, p. 429.
[11] *Ibid.*, p. 430.

men were also barefooted, but that was because few shoes were made in the South. In the North hundreds of shoe factories hummed; there seems to be no reason why the Pennsylvania factories could not have supplied this want. The trouble was with the supply system of the Union army. Supplies were poor and deliveries tardy. McClellan had to pay for it.

The politicians in Washington were denouncing McClellan for not following Lee into Virginia in a winter campaign, when some of his men were actually barefooted. This criticism of McClellan's slowness has continued and has been perpetuated in history. As a matter of fact, all the evidence goes to show that McClellan, in the face of slack efforts to supply him, equipped in a surprisingly short time an army that had been in want of nearly everything when he took charge.

On October 16, A. S. Williams, commanding a division of the Twelfth Corps, reported that his requisitions for clothing had not been filled. A limited supply of clothing had just reached his command. The division had lost most of its best officers in Pope's campaign and was in bad condition generally. At the same time Chief of Staff Marcy notified Porter that 10,000 uniforms, 10,000 shelter tents, and 20,000 blankets should soon reach him at Harper's Ferry. Shoes would be sent that day. Meanwhile McClellan was urging that the skeleton regiments be filled up from the draft and asking for regiments from Washington to complete brigade organization, badly needed.

On October 22, Meigs wrote indignantly to Ingalls that Porter had told him the day before that his troops were in want of clothing and tents, that McClellan reported a lack of clothing, and that one of his corps commanders needed 5,000 pairs of shoes. Meigs declared that all requisitions had been promptly met and that the supplies must have reached the army but had not been distributed. He had sent a special wagon train carrying 10,000 pairs of shoes that day; 10,000 horses had been bought on McClellan's requisitions. "General McClellan blames the Quartermaster's Department for want of proper action in forwarding supplies. Leave no ground for such accusations to be justly made." At the same time Halleck wired McClellan that all

COMEDY WITH A BAD ENDING 227

requisitions for shoes had been filled and that the supplies must be at army depots.[12]

Lincoln continued to be dissatisfied with McClellan's progress, less probably because of Stanton's misrepresentations than those of Halleck. Stanton was, at least, an open enemy and an able and energetic administrator. Halleck, on the other hand, was a soldier of no ability, consumed with jealousy of McClellan, to whom he still pretended friendship. Indeed Halleck's mismanagement of Pope's campaign had done much to bring about the disaster of Second Manassas. Possibly he was trying to cover his own deficiencies at McClellan's expense.

McClellan was fully aware that he was under the shadow of the ax. It is a testimonial to his integrity as well as to his thoroughness that he refused to plunge into Virginia until the army was properly equipped. He would not be governed by political expediency.

On October 15, Major General Darius N. Couch, commanding the Second Corps, at McClellan's order sent Hancock's division out from Harper's Ferry on a reconnaissance toward Charlestown. The next morning McClellan visited Couch and proposed that the two go out and see what Hancock was doing. Artillery was firing when McClellan and Couch arrived near the troops. McClellan, sending for a map of Virginia, spread it out before Couch and indicated the movements he wished to make, which would compel Lee to concentrate at Gordonsville or Charlottesville. Then he added, "But I may not have command of the army much longer. Lincoln is down on me."[13]

So saying, he showed Couch a paper, reading it to him. This was a letter from Lincoln. Couch said he thought it showed no

---

[12] On October 22, McClellan sent a circular to the various commanders stating that there were at Harper's Ferry: 24,000 bootees, 1,800 blankets, 3,000 stockings, 4,000 infantry trousers, 4,000 infantry overcoats, 7,500 knit jackets, 1,500 cavalry trousers, 3,000 cavalry overcoats. At Hagerstown: 2,000 hats, 1,800 knit jackets, 7,000 flannel shirts, 4,000 infantry overcoats, 4,000 artillery overcoats, 200 cavalry jackets, 250 artillery jackets, 2,000 shelter tents. Division commanders were required to send wagon trains for clothing that night in order to be supplied next day.

[13] B. and L., Vol. III, p. 105.

ill-feeling toward the general. McClellan answered, "Yes, Couch, I expect to be relieved from the Army of the Potomac, and to have a command in the West; and I am going to take three or four with me," naming several officers. Lincoln's letter, dated October 13, was as follows:

"My dear sir: You remember my speaking to you of what I called your over-cautiousness. Are you not over-cautious when you assume that you cannot do what the enemy is constantly doing? Should you not claim to be at least his equal in prowess and act upon the claim? . . . Change positions with the enemy, and think you not he would break your communication with Richmond within the next twenty-four hours? You dread his going into Pennsylvania; but if he does so in full force, he gives up his communication to you absolutely, and you have nothing to do but to follow and ruin him. . . . Exclusive of the water line, you are now nearer Richmond than the enemy is, by the route you *can* and *must* take. . . . It is all easy if our troops march as well as the enemy, and it is unmanly to say they cannot do it. This letter is in no sense an order."

The letter showed McClellan the hopelessness of the situation, the uselessness of attempting to convince Lincoln that the army was in need of many things before taking the field. It lacked many things, for the records show this to be true; but Lincoln was convinced by Halleck, who was now actively trying to ruin McClellan, that the army was properly equipped and was in want of no essentials. Thus Halleck at the same time betrayed McClellan and ill served Lincoln.

On October 21, McClellan wired Halleck that since the receipt of the President's order he had made every exertion to get the army equipped with clothing and now had it nearly accomplished. What he needed most was horses for the cavalry, in order to cope with the large Confederate cavalry force. "Under the following circumstances, I beg to ask whether the President desired me to march on the enemy at once or to await the reception of the new horses, every possible step having been taken to insure their prompt arrival."[14] Halleck answered that the President had no change to make in the order of October 6, that he

[14] *O.R.*, Ser. I, Vol. XIX, Pt. 1, p. 81.

did not expect impossibilities but also did not wish to lose the good weather in inactivity.

To his report McClellan stated that his cavalry was still far below requirements. However, he pitched on November 1 as the date for the advance into Virginia. On October 28, Halleck, now very hostile to McClellan, wrote Stanton, "In my opinion there has been no such want of supplies in the army under General McClellan as to prevent his compliance with the orders to advance against the enemy." Yet the order to advance was issued on October 6, a time when, according to all evidence, the army was in great need of clothing and shoes as well as other things. McClellan says, "An advance under the existing circumstances would, in my judgment, have been attended with the highest degree of peril, with great suffering and sickness among the men, and with imminent danger of being cut off from our supplies by the superior cavalry force of the enemy, and with no reasonable prospect of gaining any advantage over him." [15]

This statement illustrates one of McClellan's most amiable qualities: his care for the welfare of private soldiers. No American general has been more deeply concerned for the health and comfort of the rank and file than McClellan, a humane man who viewed suffering and the necessary horrors of war with almost too great a sensibility. He would have been more successful if he had been less considerate. If he had had the indifference to suffering of Jackson, who cared too much for success to think of its price, and of Grant, whose egoism made him callous to others, he would have gone into Virginia unprepared, at the urgings of the politicians, wild as they were for some decisive success before the November elections. He would have lost many men from exposure and sickness, but he might have succeeded in keeping the command of the army and of attaining the victory so much needed and so ardently desired. McClellan, then as always, was too conscientious for his own good. Yet he had his reward in the feeling of his men, for probably no other American general has ever gained the affection of private soldiers to the same extent as McClellan. They knew that he looked out for them and they loved him for it.

[15] *Ibid.*, p. 82.

As late as October 22, Ingalls informed Washington that there was a great deficiency of clothing at Harper's Ferry. On October 24, Ingalls wired, "The clothing arrives slowly. Can it not be hurried along faster." [16] The troops were not only in need of outer clothing but also of underclothing, which had worn out in the summer campaign. Food supplies were moreover behindhand.

McClellan's troubles were not in the least realized in Washington. Lincoln, who otherwise would have understood, was too much occupied with many matters to take care for detail and was also influenced by Halleck. When McClellan reported to Halleck on the prevalence of foot-and-mouth disease among the horses of the army—which had indeed caused the loss of many beasts—Lincoln sent the following telegram, often quoted as a reflection on McClellan: "I have just received your dispatch about sore-tongued and fatigued horses. Will you pardon me for asking what the horses of your army have done since the battle of Antietam that fatigues anything?" If Lincoln, with his large understanding, could not understand the situation, smaller-minded men may perhaps be forgiven for doing McClellan similar injustice.

McClellan answered the taunt with good temper. He said that his cavalry had been constantly engaged in picket duty and scouting, that since the battle of September 17 some regiments had traveled 200 miles—55 miles in one day. Pleasonton in following Stuart moved 78 miles in a day. "If any instance can be found where overworked cavalry has performed more labor than mine since the battle of Antietam, I am not conscious of it."

Lincoln replied but less humorously, stating, "Stuart's cavalry outmarched ours, having certainly done more marked service on the Peninsula and everywhere since. Secondly, will not a move-

---

[16] *Ibid.*, Pt. 2, p. 467. Ingalls asked for 5,000 forage caps, 7,500 blouses, 7,500 knit jackets, 15,000 infantry dress coats, 10,000 pairs of infantry trousers, 10,000 flannel shirts, 10,000 pairs of drawers, 2,000 pairs of cavalry and artillery boots, 10,000 pairs of bootees, 15,000 pairs of stockings, 5,000 infantry overcoats, 5,000 knapsacks, 5,000 haversacks, 5,000 canteens, 5,000 gum blankets, 500 artillery jackets, 1,000 cavalry jackets, 5,000 shelter tents, 500 camp kettles, 1,000 mess pans, 5,000 ax slings, and some other articles.

ment of our army be a relief to the cavalry, compelling the enemy to concentrate instead of foraying everywhere?"

McClellan came back the same day with another communication, for he was hurt by Lincoln's statement that the Confederate cavalry had done better service than the Union. He thought that some one (presumably Stanton) had given Lincoln an erroneous idea of the Union horse. On September 8, 9, and on many subsequent days Pleasonton's cavalry had engaged the Confederate horsemen, winning many small engagements. "Up to the 19th of September our cavalry was for thirteen consecutive days in close contact with the enemy, and each day engagements of some kind took place, in every one of which our cavalry was successful and steadily advanced." It was true that Stuart had outmarched the Union cavalry in his two raids, McClellan admitted, but he had fresh relays with him and had captured 1,000 horses in Pennsylvania, giving him another relay while Pleasonton had no change of horses in his pursuit.

It is characteristic of Lincoln that, feeling he might have been hard on the cavalry, he apologized the next day, October 27: "Most certainly I intend no injustice to any, and if I have done any I deeply regret it. To be told, after more than five weeks' total inaction of the army, and during which we have sent to the army every fresh horse we possibly could, amounting in the whole to 7,918, that the cavalry horses were too much fatigued to move, presents a very cheerless, almost hopeless, prospect for the future, and it may have forced something of impatience in my dispatch. If not recruited and rested then, when could they ever be?"

McClellan, now moving, wired a request to Lincoln to fill up the skeleton regiments in the army "before taking them again into action." Lincoln returned, "Is it your purpose not to go into action again until the men now being drafted in the States are incorporated in the old regiments?" [17]

McClellan could not fail to read the menace in this question. He answered apologetically that he had heard that authority was required to transfer conscripted men to the old regiments and that he requested this authority. He had asked an aide to

[17] *O.R.*, Ser. I, Vol. XIX, Pt. 2, p. 497.

draft a telegram to the President; the aide had sent it without letting him see it. "He unfortunately added, 'before taking them into action again.' This phrase was not authorized or intended by me. It has conveyed altogether an erroneous impression as to my plans and intentions. To Your Excellency's question I answer distinctly that I have not had any idea of postponing the advance until the old regiments are filled by drafted men. I commenced crossing the army into Virginia yesterday, and shall push forward as rapidly as possible to endeavor to meet the enemy."

On October 29, Lincoln wired McClellan, "I am much pleased with the movement of the army. When you get entirely across the river, let me know. What do you know of the enemy?"

In the last days of October, McClellan began to make preparations for his advance after a careful consideration of the factors in the situation. His statement in his report is testimony to his strategic ability. He first thought to move into the Shenandoah Valley. The reason was that the railroad and the various turnpikes furnished facilities for bringing up supplies. Furthermore, as his cavalry was weak, communications could be better protected by this route. Moreover, in this autumn season the Potomac was very low and fordable, and McClellan apprehended that if he crossed the river east of Harper's Ferry the Confederates would cross above and renew the invasion of Maryland. As a result of the course proposed, Lee would either be brought to battle in the vicinity of Winchester or fall back on his railway communications.

The army was not ready to move until late October, and circumstances had changed. The Potomac was rising and the season of floods was approaching. The bad roads would deter the enemy from bold movements and cause them to fall back toward their supplies. McClellan determined to move east of the Blue Ridge, disregarding the threat of an invasion of Maryland. In regard to the defense of the upper Potomac, he said he was never able to make Halleck see the necessity of fortifying Harper's Ferry adequately and protecting the Baltimore and Ohio Railroad.

On October 25, McClellan asked Halleck once more for means to protect the upper Potomac and concluded, "I commence crossing the river at Berlin in the morning, and must ask a prompt decision of the questions proposed herein." [18] Halleck answered, "Since you left Washington I have advised and suggested in relation to your movements, but I have given you no orders. I do not give you any now. The Government has entrusted you with defeating and driving back the rebel army in your front. I shall not attempt to control you in the measures you may adopt for that purpose. You are informed of my views but the President has left you at liberty to adopt them or not, as you may deem best."

McClellan, on October 29, told Halleck of the dispositions he desired for the upper Potomac, adding, "I repeat that I do not look upon the forces I have been able to leave from this army as sufficient to prevent cavalry raids into Maryland and Pennsylvania, as cavalry is the only description of troops adequate to this service, and I am, as you know, deficient in this arm."

On October 25, the pontoon bridge at Berlin was constructed. The next day two divisions of the Ninth Corps and Pleasonton's cavalry crossed and occupied the south side of the river. The First, Sixth and Ninth Corps, the cavalry, and the reserve artillery all crossed between October 26 and November 2. The Second and Fifth Corps crossed at Harper's Ferry between October 29 and November 1. The movement was somewhat delayed by heavy rains.

McClellan tells us in his report of his plan of campaign that he intended to advance along the east side of the Blue Ridge, holding the passes and making Warrenton his immediate objective. He would depend on Harper's Ferry and Berlin for supplies until the Manassas Gap Railroad was reached, when supplies could be brought from Washington. He hoped that, by striking between Culpeper and Little Washington, he would either beat the Confederates in detail or force them to concentrate at Gordonsville. That would enable the Army of the Potomac to move on Richmond by way of Fredericksburg or else proceed to the Peninsula again.

The various units of the army advanced. On November 2, the Second Corps occupied the important pass of Snicker's Gap. The Confederates offered no serious opposition. The Second Corps

[18] *Ibid.*, Pt. 1, p. 84.

moved up to Upperville, as did the Ninth Corps. The other commands were near-by. Pleasonton drove the Confederate cavalry out of Upperville after a severe brush. On November 4, the Second Corps took Ashby's Gap. On November 5, the First Corps reached the Plains. On November 6, the First Corps advanced to Warrenton, the Second Corps to Rectortown, the Eleventh Corps to New Baltimore. Other commands were going ahead. The movement continued on November 7, 8, and 9. It is believed a study will show that these dispositions were skillfully made and that Lee would probably have been forced to give ground before accepting battle on favorable terms. Longstreet says, what is true, that McClellan was developing every day. Sharpsburg had given him a degree of confidence he had never had before, and he seemed at last on the way to decisive victory.

But on November 7, the long-impending blow fell. McClellan was to make no more campaigns to prevent the division of the Union. Late in the night of the seventh he received an order from Lincoln relieving him of the command of the army and directing him to turn it over to Burnside. McClellan at once complied. His day of glory was over. A new group had come in. Would it give the Union the success that Stanton and the President thought McClellan had failed to bring? That the future was to show. The order was issued on November 5. It ran:

"By order of the President, it is ordered that Major-General McClellan be relieved from the command of the Army of the Potomac, and that Major-General Burnside take the command of that army. Also that Major-General Hunter take command of the corps in said army which is now commanded by General Burnside. That Major-General Fitz John Porter be relieved from the command of the corps he now commands in said army, and that Major-General Hooker take command of said corps....

A. LINCOLN."

"HEADQUARTERS OF THE ARMY,
WASHINGTON, November 5, 1862.
"MAJOR-GENERAL MCCLELLAN, COMMANDING, etc.
GENERAL: On receipt of the order of the President, sent herewith, you will immediately turn over your command to Major-General Burnside, and repair to Trenton, N. J., reporting, on your arrival at that place, by telegram, for further orders."

COMEDY WITH A BAD ENDING

But there never were further orders.

In the evening of November 8, Couch was standing in the snow supervising some arrangements when McClellan rode up with Burnside and the staff.

"Couch," he said, "I am relieved from command of the army, and Burnside is my successor."

"General McClellan, I am sorry for it," Couch said. "General Burnside, I congratulate you."

"Couch, don't say a word about it," Burnside replied. [19]

Later, Burnside told Couch he did not wish the command but took it to prevent its going to some one unfit for it, presumably Hooker.

Wild words were cried out by the grief-stricken staff when the news of McClellan's removal came thunderbolting to them; Custer was especially outspoken. It is to McClellan's credit that he had at once stopped this criticism of the government and urged the officers to continue to do their duty to the country.

In this season there began a vast propaganda against McClellan, launched by his enemies and by all those who thought that the war should have been won in quick time; in 1864 Grant's victory at Vicksburg kept him from suffering such censure. Moreover, by 1864 the public had awakened to the large proportions of such an undertaking as the destruction of Lee's army. The stories brought out about McClellan were mostly absurd on the face of them but were devoutly believed by a large part of the public, just as the public believed inconceivable tales in the World War. The most grotesque of the rumors about McClellan was one to the effect that he had made a proposal to Lee to join armies and march on Washington together, apparently with the idea that McClellan was to be dictator. The people who propagated this report would stop at nothing, and the people who accepted it would swallow any yarn ever concocted in an idiotic brain. That McClellan was more or less a traitor was believed by many people as a result of all the propaganda put forth about him. Beyond doubt this feeling has had something to do with the attitude of historians toward this most ill-judged man in American history.

[19] *B. and L.*, Vol. III, p. 106.

There were other stories to the effect that McClellan did not wish to crush Lee completely but to continue the war until a compromise settlement might be made that would preserve the Union but save slavery. A staff officer was dismissed from the army by Lincoln for repeating some such tale. There is not the slightest evidence to show that McClellan did not do everything in his power to destroy Lee's army, and only failed because the task was impossible. Meade did not destroy Lee's army, and tales were circulated about Meade. Grant utterly failed in his first efforts against Lee and only succeeded in the end when the Confederacy had completely broken down in the West and Lee's army had been reduced to half its former size. But civilians, ignorant of military matters and prone to suspicion, could not understand that it was the Southern army, commanded by one of the foremost generals of modern history, that frustrated the efforts of McDowell, McClellan, Pope, Burnside, Hooker, and Meade and that stood Grant off for nearly a year.

CHAPTER FIFTEEN

EXCHANGE OF PRESIDENTIAL COURTESIES

Policies pursued by governments in wartime often seem inexplicable to those who fail to understand that politics enter into war as much as military operations. In fact, war is merely a phase of politics, even if an unfortunate one.

Historians generally explain the dismissal of McClellan from command of the Army of the Potomac in November, 1862, on the ground that he was not satisfactory to the government from a military point of view. The reverse is true: he was too efficient, too scientific, too successful to be continued in command. The government had long wished to get rid of him but it had used him to frustrate the invasion of Maryland and to put a disorganized and more or less demoralized army in fighting trim. Then it decided it might dispense with his services and sent him an order, with no complimentary phrases, relieving him of his command and turning it over to a subordinate.

On the surface it would seem that the government acted in a short-sighted and mistaken way, but such is not the case. Lincoln was moved in the matter by political considerations of great importance; in fact, he could not have acted otherwise. He could have done nothing but dismiss McClellan after he had decided on the radical policy of emancipation, for McClellan was too conservative to be in sympathy with the overthrow of institutions and the confiscation of private property.

There was danger that McClellan would win the war and thereby gain such prestige as to imperil Lincoln's whole policy. It was recognized as early as the summer of 1862 that he might become a presidential candidate in the election of 1864. And with the glory of ending the war enveloping him, he would in all probability be a successful candidate, for at that time Lincoln had not gained the supreme place in the affections of the Northern people to which he subsequently attained. McClellan as president might mean the balking of emancipation, the return of the South to power, which would carry with it the hampering of that industrial development of the North which was by far the most important result of the War between the States. In other words, Lincoln could not afford to let McClellan win the war, knowing what the political consequences might be. The possibility is so great as to approach probability that the war would have ended in 1863 if McClellan had remained in command. Southern resources were already wearing out in the autumn of 1862; the Confederacy had passed its peak at the beginning of September, 1862, and was now on the downgrade. It is almost certain that the Union army, if McClellan had remained at its head, would not have suffered the two disastrous defeats of Fredericksburg and Chancellorsville, which endangered the North again. McClellan would have found his way to the James River once more and the siege of Richmond; he would himself have carried out the policy that Grant, his successor, brought to fruition.

In relieving McClellan and replacing him with Burnside, Lincoln took a step that might well have resulted in the success of the Confederacy if its government had had the wisdom to make the most of the opportunity. Fortunately for the North, it answered Lincoln's blunder by a mistake equally great, and thus the cause of the Union was saved.

The blunder lay in replacing McClellan, the ablest Union commander, with a man utterly unfit for the place, and largely for political reasons. Burnside had been groomed as McClellan's successor for some time; he would have been put in command after Pope's failure but for the fact that Lincoln needed McClellan in that hour of crisis. The politicians favored Burnside, particularly the influential Senator Sprague. He came from the good state of Rhode Island, not the bad state of New York. He was all right on political questions and would make no trouble over radical policies; furthermore, he was too dull and unmagnetic to be a formidable presidential candidate.

The trouble was that the government fancied it could pick a general out of a slot—any general—and win the war. And, in fact, McClellan had so improved the army in morale and had equipped it so well that it was in better condition than it had ever been before. Thus McClellan's successor profited by all that McClellan had done, accomplishments for which McClellan was damned then and has been damned ever since. It was a supreme mistake of the government, however, to imagine that it could put any general in command of the army and beat such antagonists as Lee and Jackson. But Lee and Jackson were far from Washington, and the panic created by their nearness had been replaced by confidence.

The mistake of the government was not in getting rid of McClellan—it had to do that—but in appointing a successor before any competent officer had come to the front. Porter, the best lieutenant, was in disgrace because of Pope's charges and also because he was McClellan's intimate friend. Hooker was angling for high command but had done nothing to deserve it; his corps had been so badly beaten at Sharpsburg as to dissolve in part. Meade and Reynolds had done well but in subordinate capacities. Thus the government, already almost committed to Burnside, gave him the place.

Burnside, with good opportunities, had not accomplished much. At the head of a formidable expedition, he had beaten a handful of Confederates in North Carolina and had done little else. In command of a large force at Falmouth in Pope's campaign he had shown no initiative, contenting himself with watching the fords of the Rappahannock. At Sharpsburg he had incurred the serious criticism of McClellan, who thought he let a small Confederate brigade hold him off from crossing the Antietam for hours. Ambrose E. Burnside was honest, brave, and loyal—excellent qualities in themselves—but he lacked driving power, had no plans, and was generally regarded as a routine officer of small ability. It was with the utmost consternation that the Army of the Potomac, officers and men, heard that McClellan had been superseded by him. Its high morale at once began to subside; it had a premonition of disaster. Burnside, much to his credit, had indulged in no intrigue to gain command. Indeed, he did not want the place, urging, with commendable modesty, his unfitness for it. He would have preferred to go on serving under McClellan, whom he regarded as a warm friend and his master in the art of war. But the government, thinking that he under-rated himself, patted him on the back and urged him on. It felt sure that modesty covered merit.

This advance southward with winter coming on was a dangerous adventure. In the cold season the roads in Virginia then, and for ages afterward, were impassable, as Burnside was destined to learn to his cost. Little in the way of supplies could be found in a country turned to wilderness by contending armies. If Burnside moved south of the Rappahannock River he would be obliged to rely on wagons for conveyance, and his communications would be in grave peril. The army would have to stumble forward through bottomless roads, exposed to rain and snow and in danger of being cut off from supplies. But criticism had made the government sensitive, and it was doing again what it had done in the summer of 1861: sending an army into the interior of Virginia without any plans, staking everything on the gamble of beating the Confederates and ending the war before spring opened. Against Lee and Jackson there was almost no possibility of success and every chance of disastrous failure.

Lee heard of McClellan's removal with a certain regret mingled with satisfaction. He knew of the order within twenty-four hours of McClellan's reception of it. "We always understood each other so well," he sighed. "I fear they may continue to make changes till they find some one I don't understand."[1] He had always respected McClellan as a man and as a soldier, approving particularly of his refusal to make war on noncombatants. Lee's opinion of McClellan as a general had risen in the Maryland Campaign, and he had faced the Union commander again, not without misgivings, noting McClellan's skillful dispositions. He was well aware that Burnside was not McClellan's equal, and consequently that a new opportunity was offered him; but even Lee,

[1] B. and L., Vol. III, p. 80.

with his astute judgment of character, did not fully appreciate the uniqueness of the opening.

Burnside, assuming command on November 9, sent a rapidly conceived scheme to Washington, since he was compelled to have some plan. He discarded McClellan's dispositions, which were so made as to leave Lee and Jackson in doubt as to the point threatened. Jackson was in the Shenandoah Valley, watching the mountain gaps, while Longstreet, with the other half of the Southern army, was in the vicinity of Culpeper. Lee hoped to be able to envelop the Union army between his two wings and crush it.

Burnside reported that he would feint toward Culpeper and Gordonsville and then move to Fredericksburg, with the design of advancing southward on Richmond. This would mean that Washington would be well covered, the same old idea that had led to the defeat of McDowell and Pope and that had brought McClellan into disfavor for opposing it. Another advantage Burnside claimed for Fredericksburg—and it was a real one— was that he could have a supply base at Aquia Creek or Belle Plain on the Potomac River, greatly lessening the length of the communication lines.

But the disadvantages overweighed the assets. This was the worst line for a movement on Richmond because it gave the Confederates too many defensive positions. Lee, instead of having to seek the enemy, would enjoy the luxury of having the Unionists invade his lion's den. The Rappahannock River at Fredericksburg offered a formidable obstacle in a deep stream backed by a line of hills. If the Rappahannock were successfully passed, the North Anna and South Anna had to be surmounted, while beyond them and immediately in front of Richmond lay the Chickahominy and its swamp.

On November 14, Halleck wired Burnside, "The President has just assented to your plan. He thinks that it will succeed, if you move very rapidly; otherwise not." [2]

Lincoln's commentary was astute; the only possible chance of success of such a plan lay in surprise. But the chance of surprising Lee in his own country, with his excellent intelligence

[2] O.R., Ser. I, Vol. XIX, Pt. 2, p. 579.

service, was small indeed. Thus Burnside's plan of campaign, if it may be called a plan, was foredoomed to failure. Furthermore, he introduced an element of confusion by reorganizing the army into three Grand Divisions under Sumner, Hooker, and Franklin. The two former were no particular friends of McClellan, but Franklin was. Hooker was not well disposed toward Burnside, desiring his place. Neither officers nor soldiers had any confidence in him and awaited events with gloomy forebodings.

While Lee with Longstreet watched at Culpeper, and Jackson remained in the Shenandoah Valley, ready to come down on the Union flank as that army advanced southward, Burnside was moving on Fredericksburg with very little in the way of concealment. On November 15, Sumner's Grand Division, in advance, left Warrenton (modern horse-show town), reaching Falmouth opposite Fredericksburg in the afternoon of November 17, a rapid march. Sumner, perceiving that there was nothing in Fredericksburg but a small observation force, wished to cross the Rappahannock and take position on the southern bank. Burnside refused, as the bridges were broken and he feared a Confederate attack on the detachment. Nor was he without reason: Lee had already read his design and was himself moving to Fredericksburg. On November 18, Lee directed Longstreet to concentrate behind Fredericksburg and he sent for Jackson from the Shenandoah Valley. In this season Jackson had advanced to Winchester, producing another panic in Pennsylvania, which expected to see his ragged men on the road to Harrisburg.

Any chance of surprise was lost; the only possibility of success had lain in pushing across the Rappahannock before Lee could come up in force. But Burnside was as badly served in Washington as McClellan had been. For weeks the Unionists lay on the north side of the Rappahannock waiting for pontoons to bridge the stream. Meanwhile Hooker's and Franklin's Grand Divisions arrived, holding with Sumner the north side of the river from Falmouth to a point some distance below Fredericksburg. Sumner's headquarters were at the colonial house, Chatham, where Lee years before had courted his wife.

Jackson, obeying, came with speed from the west side of the mountains and reached Fredericksburg at the last of November.

PRESIDENTIAL COURTESIES 243

When informed by Lee that he expected to fight in this position, Stonewall demurred. The Confederates occupied a range of low hills that ran from some distance west of Fredericksburg several miles to the southeast of the town. The position could be turned by fords above Falmouth, of which there were several. Much more important was the fact that the Unionists would occupy the higher range of hills on the north side of the river with their numerous and powerful artillery while the river would protect their flanks. A counterattack would be difficult and risky. At a glance Jackson took in the situation and pronounced against the battle, declaring that the Confederates would win but would not be able to follow up the victory. However, he was destined to offer his advice and seldom have it accepted. A more powerful person had intervened in this case.

President Davis wished Lee to fight at Fredericksburg, though Lee himself did not like to do so. Thirty miles south of Fredericksburg flows the North Anna River, a small but difficult stream offering fine facilities for defense. It was there that Lee wished to fight, and Jackson would have been content with that position. But Davis, averring that the Unionists would find supplies in the Rappahannock Valley, desired Lee to fight on that stream instead of the North Anna. Davis's real reason for this decision was that he did not wish the enemy to approach Richmond. A short time before, his army had been in Maryland; now the Unionists seemed, on the other hand, about to threaten the Southern capital.

The strategical possibilities were quite lost on him; he was thinking only of the political. Jefferson Davis was a man of strong character, brave, determined, and patriotic. But he had had a military education preceding a career in politics, with the result that he had become a military politician and a political soldier. He could not see what Lee saw so clearly but lacked the self-assertion to present forcibly: that the thing to do was to lure the incompetent Burnside away from his strong position at Fredericksburg to the North Anna River, where his communications would be in danger in case of defeat and where his artillery could not save him. It was Lee's hour of opportunity; the supreme mistake of his life lay in not asserting himself and fighting where he thought best instead of allowing the government to overrule him. He paid for the error in the final defeat of his army, after incredible campaigns and the downfall of his cause. At one time he thought seriously of falling back to the North Anna; if Jackson had come up earlier he might have done so, but by the time the redoubtable Stonewall arrived the decision had been made to fight on the Rappahannock.

Burnside was by no means eager to attack the Confederates at Fredericksburg. He knew that Longstreet was behind the town but was not aware of Jackson's position for some days. He was not happy either, for Halleck was sticking his finger in the pie. The general in chief with Lincoln visited Burnside in his headquarters opposite Fredericksburg and attempted to plan his campaign for him. By a curious coincidence, Davis was interfering with Lee, and Lincoln and Halleck with Burnside. The two Union chiefs suggested to Burnside that it might be well to cross the Rappahannock at Hooppole Ferry, about thirty miles below Fredericksburg. Jackson, perceiving that something was going on in that direction, stretched his force out for miles along the river. Burnside attempted to find crossings somewhere, but all the passages below Fredericksburg were bad in one way or another; everywhere the Confederates were found to be on the alert. Burnside came to the conclusion that the only practical place was Fredericksburg and made preparations to try there. Noting that the southern extremity of the range of hills on the other side of the Rappahannock, four miles below Fredericksburg, had not been occupied, he hoped to seize this point and turn Lee's flank. It was fatuous to suppose that Lee, with full warning, would leave his right exposed, but Burnside's wish was father to the thought.

The weather had turned bitterly cold, with deep snow. Confederate pickets, few of whom had overcoats, sometimes froze to death; but the Union soldiers were warmly clad, thanks to McClellan and to him alone. The government would have been willing for them to go into Virginia without the overcoats for which he had delayed his movement.

In the Union camps on the north side of the Rappahannock all was dejection and lack of confidence. On the southern side the only person out of harmony with Lee's plans was Jackson; he was still unreconciled to fighting at Fredericksburg but loyally supported Lee in the decision. Since Lee, bowing to the will of his government, had elected to make battle there, Jackson did not oppose. But he realized the greatness of the mistake.

In the evening of December 9, Sumner in Burnside's absence called a council of the corps, division, and brigade generals. The conversation was free and quickly drifted into a condemnation of Burnside's arrangements. To officers accustomed to McClellan's methods, Burnside's plan, or rather lack of plan, seemed inexplicable. On them it had been gradually borne that Burnside had no clear ideas at all, that he was letting the campaign shape itself, waiting for something to turn up.

Sumner, the soul of loyalty, was grieved when he learned that practically all the officers united in condemning Burnside's proposed head-on assault on Lee's strong position south of the town. Burnside, hearing of the council of war, was annoyed. Calling a council himself at Chatham, he announced to the assembled generals that he understood they were opposed to his plan of attack, dwelling especially on Hancock, who had expressed no stronger views than others. Burnside declared he had formed his plan and that all he required was the loyal service of his lieutenants. Hancock answered that he had intended no discourtesy to the commanding general, but he knew that the opposite heights were fortified and would be hard to take. Couch, rising, declared he would do his best. French, coming in just then, asked, "Is this a Methodist camp meeting?" [3] The generals attempted a show of confidence.

Lee made no effort to hold the town; indeed, he welcomed the attack on his position. However, to impede and delay the Union movement while Jackson came up, he occupied Fredericksburg with a brigade of Mississippi troops, used as skirmishers. The fire of these snipers greatly annoyed the Unionists in laying pontoon bridges on the river. In order to drive them out, the Union artillery on the hills north of the river opened a terrific bombardment of the town, destroying many houses but signally failing to dislodge the Mississippians. Hunt, best of American

[3] *B. and L.*, Vol. III, p. 108.

artillery officers, had put into position 150 guns, destined to play an important part in the events that followed, for it was these guns that prevented Lee from making a counterattack and so limited his victory. Finally, however, the bridges were laid and the Union troops, crossing, drove the skirmishers out of the place.

The Union army crossed at two points, at the town and several miles down the river from it. At the latter point Burnside expected to make his main effort, hoping to occupy the ridge there before Lee could prevent it. Here, for almost the first time in America, war was on a panoramic scale. The two armies gazed at each other from opposite heights across an open river valley. The outlook was wide and little obscured by forest.

Snow covered the ground and a heavy fog lay on the land in the morning of December 13, when Burnside began his attack. There was now not the least chance of occupying the ridge, for Jackson had come up in force and held the right wing of Lee's army from the point where his command joined Longstreet, who was on the left.

The mist rose, showing the Confederates on the ridge the massed columns of bluecoats, decorated with the flashing colors of many flags; across the intervening space the blaring music of brass bands came clearly to their ears. It was a fine spectacle.

The battle on the Union left was warmly contested for some time. Advancing gallantly across the open fields from their position on the turnpike parallel to the river, the Unionists breasted the slope held by Jackson and actually penetrated his position at one point. Jackson, calling up his reserves, hurled them back; they stumbled down the slope, leaving many men prone on the earth. The Confederates, rashly following them into the open fields, came under the fire of the Union batteries along the turnpike and suffered heavy loss. The net result on the Union left was that the attack on Jackson was repulsed as well as Jackson's unintended counterattack. For the rest of the day little occurred on this front.

Four miles up the river, in front of the little town, Burnside made his next effort. It was more hopeless than the first. Marye's Heights, just back of the place, were crowned by artillery, and the sunken road at the foot of the heights was crammed with infantry. When the Unionists, leaving the shelter of the houses, advanced over the open fields, they came under a fire that was simply infernal and were cut to pieces. Yet so great was their gallantry that some of them almost reached a stone wall held by the Southern infantry.

French's division was in advance, followed by Hancock. Under the Confederate fire the various units became mixed. Couch says, "I had never before seen fighting like that, nothing approaching it in terrible uproar and destruction. There was no cheering on the part of the men, but a stubborn determination to obey orders and do their duty. I don't think there was much feeling of success."

At two o'clock, Hooker, commanding the Center Grand Division (Stoneman's and Butterfield's corps) came on the field. He was in command of the troops making the assault. Couch, meeting Hooker, told him that an attack in front could not succeed, that the only chance was on the right.

Hooker replied, "I will talk with Hancock." After a short conference with that officer, Hooker turned to Couch and said, "Well, Couch, things are in such a state I must go over and tell Burnside it is no use carrying this line." Going off, Hooker left Couch in command. After that Humphreys' division moved to the charge, most bravely, but met with no better success. Everything was confusion on the Union line. Some troops, lying on the ground to escape the Confederate fire, were stepped over by Humphreys' men going forward. At last, with the evening shadows coming on, the Union forces in front of Marye's Heights had become almost disorganized, little more than a mob. At nightfall the troops fell back into the town and bivouacked in the streets. Never before had the brave Army of the Potomac been in such low spirits as in that night of December 13-14, 1862. "The men, knowing that they had been unsuccessful, were in a nervous state, and officers suffered also from the reaction, the worst of it being that the mass of the army had lost confidence in its commander." [4]

Midday of December 14, Burnside held a council of war, at which it was decided to hold Fredericksburg. Burnside declared

[4] *Ibid.*, p. 117.

he would renew the assault with the Ninth Corps, placing himself at the head. Getty, hearing of it, begged Couch to dissuade him, as it could result in nothing but the slaughter of more men. At the council Hooker opposed retreat, believing the Union army could hold on. It is certain that Burnside wished to attack again, and even gave orders for that purpose, but he was overborne by his subordinates. Hooker, in especial, seems to have put pressure on him. At all events, in the night of December 15-16, 1862, the Army of the Potomac retreated across the river. A storm was raging, and the half-frozen Confederate pickets hugged the fires too closely to note the enemy's movements.

Jackson had urged Lee to counterattack, in spite of the Union guns on the northern heights, but Lee, who expected another assault, demurred. Thus he made no effort to follow up his success. Jackson had been proved right again.

Shortly after the battle Lee fell into a state of depression, at the very time that the South was celebrating another victory. He was too astute not to see that a great mistake had been made. The Union army, the moment it recrossed the Rappahannock, was safe, with its short supply line fully covered. There was no way for Lee to make a counterattack; he had repulsed the enemy, but that was all. How different would it have been if he had met and defeated Burnside on the North Anna? In that case the Union army would have been miles from its base, limited for supply to bottomless roads and suffering from exposure to arctic weather. A defeat at the Rappahannock was only a repulse; a defeat at the North Anna might have been a débâcle.

Lee should not have let himself be overborne by his government. Lincoln (or rather, Halleck) had presented the war to the South on a silver platter; Davis had, politely, handed it back. The war would go on now, with indecisive battles, to the exhaustion and downfall of the South.

This was not the end of the benefactions conferred by the Confederate government on the Union. That government was distracted by enemies everywhere, and especially by the nightmare of a naval raid up the James River from Newport News. There was small danger of this, but the authorities shivered over it. Lee paid the penalty of permitting the politicians in Richmond to interfere with his military plans. They began to manage things, much as the authorities had managed them for the Union, thereby handicapping McClellan fatally and frustrating his movement on Richmond.

The government induced Lee to send Longstreet with two of his divisions to ward off the threatened advance up the James River. Longstreet, departing from Lee, found himself made head of the Department of Southern Virginia and North Carolina, a foolish move on the part of the government, for Longstreet was still supposed to be Lee's subordinate and his troops a part of Lee's army. Unfortunately for the Confederate cause, Longstreet now began to indulge in visions of independent command.

The government, having succeeded in weakening Lee by taking away from him two of his best divisions, sought to subtract from him further. The cause was not doing well in Tennessee; Lee was asked to furnish troops for Bragg's army. There were suggestions that he might send detachments elsewhere. In fact, Lee was faced by the possible break-up of his army to supply other points, something that might well have happened if he had not at last lost patience and protested. Thus, it will be seen that the authorities in Richmond were fully as incompetent in military affairs as their rivals in Washington.

Meanwhile matters were not going well with the Army of the Potomac, which remained in position opposite Fredericksburg through the rest of the winter. Lincoln paid a visit, and a great review of troops was held at Falmouth. Halleck, soon after the battle of Fredericksburg, visited Burnside and consulted with him about future operations, not realizing that Burnside's day was over.

The officers, almost without exception, had lost all confidence in the army commander. Two of them, W. B. Franklin and William F. Smith, took the unprecedented course of sending Lincoln, on December 20, their ideas as to the proper conduct of the campaign.[5]

The want of confidence extended to the government. Burnside, longing to redeem himself, planned to cross the Rappa-

[5] *O.R.*, Ser. I, Vol. XXI, p. 870

hannock by the fords above Fredericksburg and attempt to turn Lee's left, a better idea than the assault on the almost impregnable heights of Fredericksburg. On December 30, Lincoln telegraphed him, "I have good reason for saying you must not make a general movement of the army without letting me know." Burnside replied that he had rescinded his orders and would see the President shortly. About this time Meigs wrote him, imploring him to cross the river again and defeat the enemy, as the country was being exhausted by the war and could not continue long to support it.

McClellan was not alone in being indiscreet. The unfortunate Burnside, as the magnitude of his failure at Fredericksburg became apparent, was now the victim of criticism more severe than McClellan had endured, and he poured out his heart to Lincoln in a New Year's letter.

It is interesting to note that he states his force, present for duty, at 120,000 men. At this moment Lee had less than 60,000, indeed only about 50,000, present for duty.

Burnside went on to say, "The Secretary of War has not the confidence of the officers and soldiers, and I feel sure that he has not the confidence of the country. In regard to the latter statement, you are probably better informed than I am. The same opinion applies with equal force in regard to General Halleck. It seems to be the universal opinion that the movements of the army have not been planned with a view to coöperation and mutual assistance." He had determined to make another movement against the enemy, "but I am not sustained in this by a single grand division commander in my command.... Doubtless this difference of opinion between the general officers and myself results from a lack of confidence in me. In this case it is highly necessary that this army should be commanded by some other officer, to whom I will most cheerfully give way." [6]

This letter is creditable; Burnside was a highly honorable man. It is a confession of inadequacy, almost a plea for relief. He had been struck to the heart by the want of faith in him of the higher officers, which they hardly took the trouble to conceal. He had never desired the command; he desired it still less after his un-

[6] *Ibid.*, p. 941.

PRESIDENTIAL COURTESIES 251

fortunate experience. It is strange that he should have expected to remain in place after writing such a letter, but he hoped to do something ere retiring that would put him in a better light before the country.

On January 5, Burnside wrote Lincoln that the general officers of the army were all opposed to the crossing of the river, but that he thought the passage should be attempted and had given orders to that effect. He enclosed his resignation as major general of volunteers in case the President did not approve of the movement. "I beg leave to say that my resignation is not sent in any spirit of insubordination, but, as I before said, simply to relieve you from any embarrassment in changing commanders, where lack of confidence may have rendered it necessary." [7] At the same time he wrote Halleck that he was going to make the movement on his own responsibility but would like instructions from the general in chief.

On January 7, Halleck wrote at length to Burnside. He stated he had always been in favor of a forward movement across the Rappahannock, and still favored it. Feints should be made at various points in order to deceive the enemy as to the true crossing. "It will not do to keep your large army inactive. As you yourself admit, it devolves on you to decide upon the time, place and character of the crossing which you may attempt. I can only advise that an attempt be made, and as early as possible." [8]

Lincoln endorsed this, stating, "I approve this letter. I deplore the want of concurrence with you in opinion by your general officers, but I do not see the remedy. Be cautious, and do not understand that the Government or country is driving you. I do not yet see how I could profit by changing the command of the Army of the Potomac, and if I did, I should not wish to do it by accepting the resignation of your commission."

McClellan's demands for hospital equipment were justified by the report of the medical inspector general, made on January 8, 1863. He says, "I do not believe I have ever seen greater misery from sickness than exists now in our Army of the Potomac. In some regiments, which have been long in the field . . . where

[7] Ibid., p. 945.
[8] Ibid., p. 954.

medical officers have acquired experience from long service in the field, the regimental hospitals are tolerably comfortable in their appointments.... The new regiments are suffering very much for everything that goes to make the condition of the sick and wounded men tolerable. Indeed, after the battle of Fredericksburg, for three or four days, some of the general depots for wounded men were without food except bad bread.... There were no stoves in any of the hospitals until Friday or Saturday, a week after the battle, although the weather was very cold.... I am assured that the diseases which now prevail in the army are the result of want of proper food for the troops, especially fresh vegetables and bread."

Burnside now attempted to put in motion the various corps toward the fords of the Rappahannock above Fredericksburg. But he was frustrated by lack of coöperation on the part of his subordinates, who had so low an opinion of the commander that they could with difficulty be got to do anything at all. The deciding factor, however, was the weather. Rain came in torrents, turning the dirt roads into bogs through which it became impossible to drag the pontoons. Mules stalled; men barely made their way through the deep mire; and the "Mud March," as it is called, came to an inglorious end without bringing about a collision with the Confederates. Poor Burnside found that nothing whatever could be done at that season of the year.

He wired Halleck, on January 22, urging him to visit the army. Halleck answered by suggesting that Burnside come to Washington. On the same day Hooker, now intensely hostile to Burnside, sent word to his chief that the road on which his troops were stationed would have to be corduroyed before even provisions could be brought up. On January 23, Burnside wired Lincoln, "I have prepared some very important orders, and I want to see you before issuing them. Can I see you alone if I am at the White House after midnight? I must be back by 8 o'clock to-morrow morning." [9]

The orders were as follows: "General Joseph Hooker, major general of volunteers and brigadier general U. S. Army, having been guilty of unjust and unnecessary criticisms of the actions

[9] *Ibid.*, p. 998.

of his superior officers, and of the authorities, and having, by the general tone of his conversation, endeavored to create distrust in the minds of officers who have associated with him, and having, by omissions and otherwise, made reports and statements which were calculated to create incorrect impressions, and for habitually speaking in disparaging terms of other officers, is hereby dismissed from the service of the United States as a man unfit to hold an important commission during a crisis like the present, when so much patience, charity, confidence, consideration, and patriotism are due from every soldier in the field."

W. T. H. Brooks, John Newton, John Cochrane, brigadier generals, were also recommended for dismissal. Major General W. B. Franklin, Major General W. F. Smith, Brigadier General Samuel D. Sturgis, Brigadier General Edward Ferraro, being of no service to the army, were to be relieved from duty with it.

Thus Burnside, tormented as few commanders have been by disloyal subordinates, threw down the gauntlet. The government was obliged to support him or accept his resignation. Stanton, as well as Lincoln, had long since lost faith in him. Put in command in order to eclipse McClellan, he had dismally failed and had been, in fact, fortunate not to lose his army. Lincoln seems to have held off from accepting his resignation out of a desire to spare his feelings, knowing that, while Burnside was incapable of command, he was nevertheless loyal and devoted.

Lincoln sent word to Halleck, on January 25, to meet Burnside at the White House that morning. The same day orders issued from the War Department relieving, at his own request, Burnside from command of the army. Sumner (old and sick) was relieved of duty. Franklin was too. Hooker was assigned to Burnside's place.

Disloyalty and intrigue have seldom been more signally rewarded than in the elevation of Hooker to the command of the army. He had long worked for this end, and without scruples. He had not been loyal to McClellan and had been openly untrue to Burnside. He had not stopped at criticizing his commanding officers; he had been actively hobnobbing with politicians to overthrow Burnside and get his place. It is said he promised not to be a candidate for president if successful as a general, and that it was this consideration that secured him the position. It is certain that Stanton, who had turned thumbs down on Burnside, favored him. He was now the genius who would defeat Lee and end the war.

The psychology of criticism is peculiar. It is human nature to agree with the critic, especially the ardent and fluent critic. And in listening to the recital of the mistakes of the person criticized, one naturally, almost inevitably, comes to believe the critic could do better himself. This was the case with Hooker. He had demonstrated Burnside's mistakes to the authorities so plausibly that he came to be looked on as the man of destiny.

It was a mediocre selection. Hooker's career had not been distinguished. He had done pretty well in the Seven Days, especially Glendale, but he had not accomplished much in the Second Manassas and had been a failure at Sharpsburg. At Fredericksburg, however, he seems to have served the Union by bullying Burnside into recalling the order for a second day's attack; perhaps this service had something to do with his appointment. Still it was hard for Burnside to endure seeing his chief enemy, instead of being punished as he deserved, rewarded with the command of the army. Burnside himself was given the Ninth Corps, with which he was much happier and better off than as the head of the army. Franklin was the only high officer punished. He was slated for castigation because of the denunciations of two commanders, Pope and Burnside. Actually, his main offense was that he was McClellan's friend and had not adjusted himself to the change created by Burnside's elevation. He went West and was not conspicuous again. Since he was a capable officer the army gained nothing by his removal.

The dismissal of Burnside brought on a furious controversy. He demonstrated before a committee the treacherous nature of Joseph Hooker. He also attacked Franklin, and Franklin, exasperated by the attack, published a pamphlet in which he stated that Burnside had suggested the removal of Stanton and Halleck when offering his own resignation. Halleck did not know of this, and he was moved. An attempt was made to prove Franklin a liar, but he had told the truth. Halleck wrote to Burnside, "As you could have no motives personal to yourself for giving this advice to the President, and as you were well aware that I was placed in my present position contrary to my own wishes, and that I had endeavored to be relieved from it, I am bound to believe that in my case you were actuated in giving the alleged advice to the President solely by a desire to confer a personal favor upon me." Heavy sarcasm, just what one would expect from old Halleck.

In the exchange of letters between Halleck and Franklin, the former made a statement that is important, if true. He declared that Lincoln appointed Hooker to command without consulting Stanton or himself. "The President announced his decision to relieve General Burnside and put General Hooker in command. He asked no opinion of or advice either from the Secretary or myself, and none whatever was offered by either of us." Nevertheless, it is probable, almost certain, that Lincoln and Stanton had often conferred on the subject of the army commander and that Stanton had favored letting Burnside go. In fact, there was nothing else to do in view of the sentiment of the army, officers and men alike. It was unfortunate, however, that Burnside should have been succeeded by his bitterest critic and leading enemy. Lincoln and Stanton could have made a better choice. Probably Stanton knew that Burnside had suggested his removal from the War Department and resented it. Perhaps Hooker's appointment was by way of punishing Burnside for freely expressed opinions. It is singular that Burnside, who was put in command by McClellan's enemies, should have encountered the same enmity from Stanton that McClellan had. It lends weight to the suspicion that Stanton and Hooker were plotting against him shortly after his appointment to command. Stanton was the type that lives in a spider's web of intrigue.

Once more the Washington authorities offered the war to the Confederates; once more the Confederates declined it.

The Southern authorities had learned nothing from the lessons of Fredericksburg. They still wished Lee to hold the line of the Rappahannock against the Army of the Potomac. The trouble with this position was that the communications of the Union army were safe, since they ran to the Potomac River, only a few miles away, and were perfectly covered. Consequently any victory on the Rappahannock was likely to take the Fredericksburg pattern—a repulse, without any chance of destroying the defeated army. And the Confederacy, now feeling severely the effects of the war, needed something more than a frustration of an advance on Richmond; it needed a decisive victory and needed it badly.

The opportunity for Lee was not as good in the spring of 1863 as it had been in December, 1862. For one thing, the weather would be better instead of worse, drying the roads. Again, Lee's army was much smaller than in the preceding winter, since Longstreet, with two divisions, was absent and disinclined to return. Indeed, the government, by making Longstreet the commander of a department, seemed to have taken him away from Lee, who wished his return but, as usual, failed to assert himself. Lee's good nature, his acquiescence in the measures of his government, however fatuous, was the weak element in the character of one of the greatest soldiers of modern times.

Lee knew he was facing a greater crisis than in the preceding December. Hooker lacked the qualities necessary in a successful general, especially a cool head in an emergency, but he was abler than Burnside and he had in a greater degree the confidence of his subordinates. He reorganized the army energetically, getting rid of Burnside's awkward Grand Divisions and consolidating the cavalry in a division. Unlike Burnside, he was able to project a definite plan of campaign, and a pretty good one. That plan he outlined to Lincoln in a letter of April 11, 1863. He intended to cross the Rappahannock by the fords above Fredericksburg, which movement, he thought, would force Lee to fall back toward Richmond. He expected to prevent this by launching his cavalry at Lee's rear, holding him until the army itself could come up and win a victory. The flaw in the plan was the extent to which the cavalry was depended on; the Union cavalry, while vastly improved, was not yet good enough to hold the Confederate infantry. This plan, Hooker maintained, would make it unnecessary for the government to push out a force from Washington to Warrenton to cover the capital. Once more the strategy of the Unionists was influenced by fear for the safety of Washington.

The Confederate authorities countered by a nervousness for the safety of Richmond. Longstreet, instead of being returned to Lee, was sent off on a wild-goose chase to Suffolk, near the lower James, which was held by a Union garrison. The reason assigned was the hope of securing supplies in eastern Virginia and North Carolina; the actual reason was fear of a naval raid up James River. Thus in mid-April, while Hooker was pushing his preparations to move, the Confederate government was sending a large portion of Lee's army on a futile movement where it would be out of touch with Lee. If McClellan had been hampered by his government, Lee was almost as fatally handicapped by his. The Richmond government desired Lee to hold the line of the Rappahannock, but with a greatly weakened army; in fact, it was playing tricks with him. If he had not at length protested he would have faced the Army of the Potomac, 120,000 strong, with about 40,000 men. As it was, he now had less than 60,000. Lee, aware that Hooker would soon move, wrote repeatedly to Longstreet to come back. Longstreet, who had no wish to be a subordinate again, did not return. Instead, he wrote Lee suggesting that he should fall back to the North Anna River.

This was good advice; it was what Lee had thought of doing in November, 1862. A victory on the North Anna would be worth two or three on the Rappahannock, for if Hooker should be defeated far from his base of supplies he might be destroyed, not merely driven back. More than ever the weakening Confederacy needed a crowning mercy, destruction of the enemy; once again it was to drive the Unionists back across the Rappahannock. Lee did not follow Longstreet's advice; he fought on the Rappahannock with his weakened army. However, when he made a strong protest to the government at Longstreet's absence, the reluctant one was ordered back to the main army. But Longstreet, who construed orders as he saw fit, moved with such deliberation that he did not reach Lee until the battle of Chancellorsville had been fought. Thus Hooker, with an army twice as large as Lee's, had an advantage that had been denied the unfortunate Burnside.

In the middle of April, Hooker launched Stoneman with the cavalry. The design was to cut the railroad behind Lee's lines; if Lee fell back, Hooker planned to cross the river and follow.

On April 15, he wired Lincoln that Stoneman's artillery was stalled in the mud and that Stoneman would proceed without it. Lincoln answered rather dispiritedly, "General S. is not moving rapidly enough to make the expedition come to anything. He has now been out three days, two of which were unusually fair weather, and all three without hinderance from the enemy, and yet he is not 25 miles from where he started. To reach his point he still has 60 to go, another river (the Rapidan) to cross, and will be hindered by the enemy. I do not know that any better can be done, but I greatly fear it is another failure." [10]

Hooker was now undergoing the same razzing for delay that McClellan had had to endure. Lincoln, a civilian though an exceptionally intelligent one, simply did not appreciate the difficulties attending army movements, especially over the bottomless roads of Virginia. Stoneman could not get his guns through the deep mud, and he did not wish to move without guns. Thus the expedition was foredoomed to failure. All the streams were in spring freshet; army movements for the time being were impossible. Bridges everywhere had been carried away; rivers were far past fording.

On April 21, Hooker wrote apologetically to Lincoln, "As I can only cross the river by stratagem without great loss, which I wish to avoid, it may be a few days before I make it. I must threaten several points, and be in readiness to spring when a suitable opportunity presents itself."

The government, eager to press the war, had driven poor Burnside on to defeat at Fredericksburg and was now attempting to force Hooker forward, despite adverse weather conditions. Hooker, wishing to advance but not to cross unfordable streams, found himself in the same situation in which McClellan had been. He, the critic, was now being criticized for slowness.

Lincoln waited for some days and then, on April 27, wired Hooker, "How does it look now?" The unfortunate Hooker, whose cavalry was still impeded by high water, answered, "I am not sufficiently advanced to give an opinion. We are busy. Will tell you all soon as I can, and have it satisfactory."

Pressed, Hooker was making rapid preparations to move. Pon-

[10] *O.R.*, Ser. I, Vol. XXV, Pt. 2, p. 214.

toon bridges were thrown across the Rappahannock; orders were sent to the various commands to cross. Rain was still falling, but the commander knew he could delay no longer, even for the best reasons.

Balloon observations were constantly being made. A sample may be interesting.

"BALLOON IN THE AIR,
April 29, 1863—2:45 p.m.

"MAJOR-GENERAL SEDGWICK,
Commanding Corps, Army of the Potomac:
General: About two regiments of the enemy's infantry have just moved forward from the heights and entered the rifle-pits opposite our lower crossing.

"Heavy smokes are visible about 6 miles up the river, on the opposite side, in the woods.

"Very respectfully, your obedient servant,
T. S. C. LOWE,
CHIEF OF AERONAUTS, ARMY OF THE POTOMAC."

At the end of the month Hooker moved. Stoneman crossed ahead; the infantry followed. The preparations had been well made. Before Lee could prevent the crossing if he desired to do so, a large part of the army was over the Rappahannock and Rapidan and converging at the crossroads known as Chancellorsville. Up to a certain point Hooker had been successful.

Then the unexpected happened. In the morning of May 1, Union forces pushed eastward from Chancellorsville toward Fredericksburg; but instead of finding Lee in retreat, as Hooker had anticipated, they discovered Confederate columns moving westward toward them. Lee had snatched up the gauntlet, quite ready to fight.

At that point Hooker lost his nerve and the campaign. He had taken the offensive against Lee. Now, instead of pushing it with vigor, he fell back to Chancellorsville and attempted to dig in. He would remain on the defensive and force Lee to attack him behind breastworks. That seemed the wise thing to do.

It was the unwise thing against such opponents as Lee and Jackson. Sitting on hardtack boxes over a camp fire, the two generals considered a report from Stuart that Hooker's right flank was in the air, and determined to strike there. The way was clear, for Stoneman was off on his part of the plan, to break the railroad in the Confederate rear. He broke the railroad and did some damage, but was lost for several critical days.

The next morning, May 2, Stonewall started off on the last and greatest of his ventures. Marching all day by woods roads, he found himself in the afternoon on Hooker's right flank, unsuspected and in an admirable position for attack. Pressing through the dense woods, preceded by stampeded deer and turkeys, the Confederate line struck the surprised Unionists with terrific force, rolling them up. Down the turnpike to Chancellorsville came a perfect rout of running, yelling men, followed by the gray line in rapid pursuit. The noise grew louder, until it became apparent to Hooker at his headquarters, the Chancellor house. He learned, to his utter dismay, that his right flank had been routed, and that the Confederates were approaching.

Only the oncoming of twilight saved him. The Confederates became somewhat disorganized in the dense forest. Jackson, with the usual recklessness of Confederate generals, decided to go ahead and reconnoiter in person. Advancing with some aides beyond his line of battle, he was fired on by the Unionists from the direction of Chancellorsville. When he rode back toward his line, that line suddenly rose up and blazed furiously at the shadowy horsemen. Several of Jackson's party were hit and he himself was badly hurt. Taken to the Richmond railroad the next day, he developed pneumonia and died just a week after his most famous exploit.

Lee, dazed by this terrible mischance, made the best disposition possible, putting Jackson's corps temporarily under Stuart. The next day the Confederates, pressing forward from several sides, stormed Hooker's lines at Chancellorsville. Hooker himself was stunned by the concussion of a cannon ball that struck a pillar of the house against which he happened to be leaning.

But a new danger confronted Lee. Sedgwick, left at Fredericksburg, had crossed the river and stormed Marye's Heights, so fatal to Burnside the year before. He was rapidly coming westward along the Chancellorsville turnpike, threatening to take Lee in the rear. The Confederate commander, forced to turn aside from his prey, came down on Sedgwick, defeating him and driving him back across the river. But when he returned to Chancellorsville, he found that Hooker had taken advantage of the respite and had hurriedly gained the north side of the Rappahannock. The campaign was over in less than a week. If Lee had won a great victory he could not follow it up. Hooker was safe on the north side of the river with his communications with the Potomac covered. Thus Lee, at heavy loss, had won an advantage, but not a decisive one. Once more the disadvantage of fighting on the Rappahannock had demonstrated itself. In fact, Lee had suffered far more than the Union, for in addition to thousands of his men he had lost one of the greatest soldiers of all time, Stonewall Jackson. Never again would the Confederacy have so potential a chance. The possibilities had been thrown away by holding the line of the Rappahannock and detaching a large part of Lee's army for useless operations elsewhere. The Union had offered the war; again the South had declined it.

Lincoln, however, was almost in despair when the news of Chancellorsville reached him. He was too intelligent to be deceived by covering up; he realized the magnitude of the disaster. How completely McClellan had been vindicated! Both of the men who had succeeded him had met with defeat. If the Southern government had made the most of the situation, either Burnside or Hooker would have been, in all probability, destroyed. But the gods fought on the side of the new mechanical civilization represented by the North. What happened had to happen.

CHAPTER SIXTEEN

HE SEEKS VINDICATION

McCLELLAN WENT TO Trenton, New Jersey, to which point he had been ordered by way of punishment. No doubt he hoped that he would be offered another command, but none ever came. He was too important to be given a small assignment and too potential politically for a large one; there was nothing the government could do but keep him cooling his heels—that is, nothing militarily.

The dismissal of McClellan was most unpopular with the army, affecting its morale. The Democratic party in the North, which had loyally supported a Republican administration in its war policy, regarded it as a slap in the face. There was widespread criticism of a course of action that so nearly resulted in a Confederate victory and the separation of the South from the North.

The government in its animosity (Stanton was now in the saddle and Halleck was a mere figurehead) was not satisfied with the humiliation of McClellan. It struck at his friends. Few things in American history are more shameful than the treatment accorded the brave and capable Fitz John Porter. Arraigned on the charge that he did not carry out Pope's absurd order of August 30, 1862, which would have brought him into the angle between Jackson and Longstreet, he was dismissed from the service. Not until years afterward was his case reopened. Then the evidence supplied by Longstreet resulted in a reversal of the verdict and Porter's reinstatement. But that did not make up for the lost years and the wholly unjust humiliation of as gallant and patriotic an officer as the United States army has ever contained.

Other changes followed. Franklin, as we have seen, went West. Sykes, to whose heroic stand the saving of the army at Second Manassas was due, was also ordered elsewhere. No one of McClellan's intimates remained in a conspicuous place. Stanton had his way in this proscription, which was intended to bring the officers of the Union army into full political accord with the government. Generals were watched with some suspicion; Grant occasioned quite a bit of anxiety in 1864 when the politicians attempted to get at him. John C. Frémont became a positive menace.

McClellan remained at Trenton for a time, being meanly refused permission to live in New York. Halleck took great pleasure in heaping humiliation on him, encouraged by the sardonic Stanton. But nobody ever had truer friends than McClellan; they raised a sum of money to buy him a house in New York, which afforded a part of his support.

Another ordeal awaited McClellan. The Congressional Committee on the Conduct of the War "investigated" him in February and March, 1863, asking all manner of offensive questions as to his operations. One might think, from the action of the government, executive and legislative alike, that McClellan was almost a criminal, not an officer who had rendered his country most distinguished services. And that verdict has been reflected in the writings of most historians to this day. Even recently McClellan's distinguished biographer, Dr. William Starr Myers, a notable scholar, exhausted his ingenuity in expatiating on McClellan's faults or alleged faults while making out something of a case for Stanton's attitude toward him. If McClellan resented the treatment accorded him both by the administration and Congress he cannot be blamed. Political differences are no justification for persecution. What McClellan and his friends suffered was that, and nothing less.

That his sufferings should color his own opinions and his political outlook was inevitable. The war made necessary a degree of arbitrary action unknown to Americans of that day and most unwelcome to them. Political arrests and the suspension of the habeas corpus aroused widespread indignation. In our time, of course, we understand that such things must be in war, that in war laws are indeed silent. But Americans of the mid-century enjoyed the incredible liberty that had been secured for them by Jefferson and his party; they could not understand that war must curtail that freedom.

McClellan was in a false position politically and did not know it. He was a states' rights Democrat who denied the right of secession. But this stand is inconsistent. If the states are indeed sovereign, as the states' righters claimed, they have the right to withdraw from any confederacy whatever. In other words, the Southerners, in asserting the right of secession, were merely drawing the logical conclusion. McClellan, in declaring for states' rights but denying the right of secession, held that the states were sovereign up to a certain point, but that there sovereignty ceased. But unless states are altogether sovereign, they are not sovereign at all. The denial of the right of secession resulted, as was inevitable, in the denial of other rights to the states; or, rather, in the assertion of new rights by the federal government, which comes to the same thing. The process has continued until the rights of states are now greatly reduced and will be much more so in the future. In fact, we may anticipate the disappearance of state government at some time or other.

McClellan's popularity with a large part of the country remained unabated throughout 1863; the contrast between his able methods and the blundering attempts of Burnside and Hooker was too apparent to be ignored. Just after the Union defeat at Chancellorsville, George Custer wrote him, "You will not be surprised when I inform you that the universal cry is 'Give us McClellan,' everyone is speaking of this and all are unanimous in saying that you alone can extricate the country from its present difficulties." Many other such messages came to him.

It would have been impossible, of course, for the government to restore McClellan to command. If it had done so it would have lost prestige in the country, because no government can afford to admit itself to be wrong in such a crisis. Yet the government could and should have done something to allay McClellan's just indignation at the treatment accorded him and his best friends.

It could have conferred on him the rank of lieutenant general, even if it gave him no definite assignment, or it could have sent him abroad in some honorable capacity. For historians to blame McClellan and his supporters for becoming hostile to a government that had acted as the Washington administration did is inconsistent. As a matter of fact, the United States still wore the appearance of being a constitutional state, even though it was engaged in war. If the Democrats were opposed to the Republican conduct of the war, what wrong was it to attempt to carry the election of 1864? The historians, in their partisanship, seem to regard any opposition to the Republican administration as in the nature of treason. This is nonsense. The Whigs in 1848, with the Mexican War hardly over, carried the country in opposition to the existing administration, and no one criticizes them for it.

The Union army continued to mourn McClellan. It greeted the appointment to command of the able George Gordon Meade with no particular enthusiasm; the depression resulting from Fredericksburg and Chancellorsville enabled Lee once more to take the offensive in June, 1863. But now the death of Stonewall Jackson told decisively against the Southern cause. The new corps organization of the Army of Northern Virginia was so defective that Lee, in spite of the magnificent machine he had built up—an army that for the quality of its men and the devotion that inspired it has no equal in American history—dashed himself to defeat against the bowlders of Gettysburg. Yet so great was the valor of the Southerners that, in spite of everything, they almost won.

As that tremendous battle echoed and reëchoed among the Pennsylvania hills, the Union troops did their duty grimly and effectively but without enthusiasm. When, however, the rumor ran down the line that McClellan had been restored to command, the men gave way to wild joy. It was partly the inspiration of that mighty memory that enabled them to hold off the Southern attacks and win the day. In all probability, if Meade had been defeated on that fateful field, McClellan would have been restored to command by a government forced to admit its mistake and battling for life.

So great was McClellan's popularity among rank and file that a movement got under way in the army to raise a fund for him by subscription. Meade took charge of it, not knowing that he was committing a wrong, that McClellan was a heretic, not a hero to be rewarded. When Meade went to Washington he was soundly scolded by Lincoln, Halleck, and Stanton. He then dropped the matter, and it came to nothing. This would appear to be another case of Stanton's petty malice. A gift to McClellan from the army could not have hurt the government.

The many testimonials made McClellan aware that a large part of the country sympathized with him. He came in contact with members of the Democratic party, with which he was generally in accord. This appreciation, writes Dr. Myers, "undoubtedly had the bad results of inclining McClellan gradually to listen more and more to the tempting words of the Democratic national leaders." Why shouldn't he have listened? A singular reward the Democrats received for supporting the Washington government—being considered traitors by historians! In other words, according to such historians, only Republicans were loyal. This is absurdity.

The Democratic party of the North occupied the same position as McClellan. It was strongly opposed to secession, but it looked with great disfavor on the encroachments of the federal government—including the income tax—on states' rights; it was also unenthusiastic over emancipation, which conservative business men thought savored too much of revolution. Democrats would have liked to bring the war to an end by concessions to the South, though few of them wished to end it at the price of Southern independence. Through the latter part of 1863 and the early months of 1864, this spirit of unrest, of dissatisfaction, deepened; it might possibly have resulted in a change of administration if events had been otherwise.

It was inevitable that there should be serious opposition to Lincoln after the defeats of Fredericksburg and Chancellorsville because these disasters reflected seriously on the conduct of the war. Moreover, the feeling was widespread in the country that the government was going too far in the direction of curtailing individual liberty, though its action nowadays would be considered conservative. Besides, numbers of people were weary of the war and desired that peace overtures be made to the South. As President Davis would have accepted nothing short of independence, such negotiations would have been foredoomed to failure, but the people did not know this. There was a feeling that peace might be possible, if only the government would strive for it, a common enough and natural enough sentiment in wartime.

McClellan received testimonials to his services from many sources. The most interesting of these were the resolutions passed by the Washington City aldermen in May, 1863. McClellan, in acknowledging this testimonial, said, "I receive this expression of confidence with unusual pride and satisfaction, for I must confess that the most anxious hours of my life, and my most unremitting labors, have been bestowed upon the safety of our Capital, which I once found entirely open and defenseless, and on another occasion threatened by a powerful and victorious army."[1]

Among the errors and misstatements of Nicolay and Hay (*Life of Lincoln*) is one to the effect that by the summer of 1863 McClellan was the acknowledged leader of the Democratic party in the North.[2] On the contrary, McClellan had been remarkably circumspect in his statements and had taken no political action whatever, though it was certain that he was by far the most important man the Democratic party contained at that juncture and was no doubt considered as a presidential possibility even before his retirement from the war. It really appears as if his chief concern in this period was that of making a living. He was still a major general and still drew his pay, but he was aware that his resignation might be demanded at any time. He showed good sense in refusing to address a war meeting, to be held in June, 1863, looking to the organization of a "Union" party that would embrace men of various political opinions.

He made a mistake, however, in lending support to the candidacy of Judge George W. Woodward, who was running for governor of Pennsylvania on the issue of opposition to the draft. Both in the North and the South the draft was regarded as un-

[1] Myers, *op. cit.*, p. 423.
[2] *Ibid.*, p. 425.

constitutional; Jefferson Davis's enemies attacked him bitterly over it. The fact that no general draft had been necessary before made men believe that it was wrong, even in the great crisis of the Civil War. But the South could hardly have continued the war without conscription, while the North by 1863 was also in need of it. At the present time it is a commonplace of war, though still extremely unpopular. The draft of 1917 aroused strong feeling.

It does not appear that McClellan was opposed to the draft (in fact he urged it), but that he was in accord with Woodward in a general way. His letter declared, "I understand him [Woodward] to agree with me in the opinion that the sole great objects of this war are the restoration of the unity of the nation, the preservation of the Constitution, and the supremacy of the laws of the country."[3] Apparently, even at this late day, McClellan was not in favor of Lincoln's emancipation policy.

By the end of 1863, McClellan was tending to consider the idea of becoming a presidential candidate. His principal motive was less ambition—for ambition with him was mainly military—than a desire for vindication and a very sincere belief that the Republican party was veering too much to the left. A section of that party, led by Thaddeus Stevens, not satisfied with emancipation, had begun to advocate confiscation of landed property in the Southern states and, practically, the overthrow of the Constitution. McClellan thought that Lincoln was too weak fully to combat the leftists successfully, that the individual liberties of American citizens as well as the rights of states were endangered. He was mistaken in thinking Lincoln unable to cope with the situation—or any other political situation—but he was quite right in dreading the leftists, who afterward brought about the nightmare of Reconstruction. It was with high motives, and reluctantly, that McClellan entered politics. Like most army officers, his knowledge of public life was limited; he felt at a disadvantage in a field so novel to him.

In regard to the continuance of the war McClellan never wavered. He was determined that it should be pushed until the South was willing to return to the United States and resume its

[3] *Ibid.*, p. 429.

place in a reunited country, but he differed from the Republicans in the means to the end. Probably McClellan would have advocated payment for the emancipated slaves if reunion could have been brought about on that basis; he was opposed to any violation of individual liberty not made necessary by the state of war.

The people of the United States in the early months of 1864 went through a period of war weariness that might have had important consequences if the politicians could have turned it to account. The South, after three years of resistance, still seemed strong and confident; the inner weakness of the Confederacy was only revealed by Sherman's march to the sea. While Lee had failed in Pennsylvania, and was now fighting along the line of the Rapidan River, his army appeared as far from being beaten as at any preceding period; many people thought it could not be beaten on its own soil. This defeatist sentiment was by no means confined to Democrats; Republicans shared it. In fact, a movement began early in 1864 to shelve Lincoln (regarded by a large section of the Republican party as a failure) and nominate another candidate. It led to a convention of irregulars that nominated John C. Frémont for president in opposition to Lincoln. If the Republicans divided, there might be a chance for the Democrats with a popular candidate, and McClellan was far and away the strongest man the Democrats could name.

The danger was adroitly avoided by Lincoln. Frémont was induced to withdraw in September, thus relieving the President of the threat. It appears that the consideration offered was the ousting of Montgomery Blair, Postmaster General, from the cabinet. At all events, Frémont gave up the fight and retired to innocuous desuetude. At one time, however, the radicals who backed him seem to have tried to hold out the hand to McClellan after he became the nominee of the Democrats. But an alliance of extreme leftists and extreme rightists was impossible.

It may be that Lincoln also had overtures made to McClellan to induce him not to become a candidate. The elder Blair (Francis P.) visited him and may or may not have offered him something; at all events nothing came of it. Blair went back to Washington and McClellan accepted the nomination.

The Republican convention met at Baltimore, on June 7-8, 1864, and nominated Abraham Lincoln and Andrew Johnson. Or, rather, the convention of the "Union party" met on those days and nominated the Republican Lincoln and the Democrat Johnson. People who afterward denounced Johnson failed to remember that he was elected as a "Union" man and not as a Republican. Many Republicans, prominent among them Horace Greeley, accepted Lincoln's nomination as a disagreeable necessity; they would have preferred another candidate. Enthusiasm was entirely lacking.

The Democratic convention met in Chicago on August 29, 1864. Governor Horatio Seymour, of New York, one of the most distinguished public men in the country, was chairman. The platform, adopted only after a bitter fight, was somewhat ambiguous. The first plank pledged allegiance to the Union under the Constitution. The second plank, designed to attract the peace people, has suffered obloquy at the hands of historians ever since.

"This convention does explicitly declare, as the sense of the American people, that after four years of failure to restore the Union by the experiment of war, during which, under the pretense of a military necessity, or war power higher than the Constitution, the Constitution itself has been disregarded in every part, and public liberty and private right alike trodden down, and the material prosperity of the country essentially impaired,—justice, humanity, liberty, and the public welfare demand that immediate efforts be made for a cessation of hostilities, with a view to an ultimate convention of the states, or other peaceful means, to the end that, at the earliest practicable moment, peace may be restored on the basis of the federal Union of the States."

Analysis shows that this celebrated article has been somewhat maligned. It was not a peace-at-any-price sentiment. It expressed a belief that if an armistice were declared and a convention of all the states (including the seceded states) called, a basis might be found for the restoration of the Union. In fact, if Sherman had failed at Atlanta, it is possible that some such measure would have been forced on the United States government by the pressure of public opinion. The people of the North were worn out by the slaughter of Grant's Wilderness Campaign, which had not brought the expected victory at all; to the outside Lee seemed almost as formidable as ever. If Sherman had likewise failed, the situation for the Union would have been desperate. It was Sherman's victory before Atlanta, not the intrinsic folly of the article, that made it futile. Indeed, it is a testimonial to the constitutional feeling of the American people of that period. The implications of the article have been exaggerated by historians to demonstrate the folly and disloyalty of the Democratic party. It simply brought out the fact that many Americans preferred a negotiated peace, with concessions to the South, to a peace imposed by force.

There followed an article containing the gist of the whole matter. "The aim of and object of the Democratic party is to preserve the federal Union and the rights of the states unimpaired; and they hereby declare that they consider that the administrative usurpation of extraordinary and dangerous powers not granted by the Constitution; the subversion of the civil by military law in states not in insurrection. . . ."

This was much the same attitude as that of the extreme constitutionalists in the South; both the Washington and Richmond governments were accused of violation of the Constitution (the same for both governments) and undoubtedly with truth. The Constitution was violated; otherwise, a great war could not have been maintained by either side.

It might be supposed that the Democrats would have been unanimously in favor of McClellan, since he was by far the most important man belonging to the party. An attempt to boom former President Franklin Pierce failed; McClellan was really the only candidate considered. And yet few candidates have ever been more bitterly denounced than he was on the floor of the convention by B. G. Harris, of Maryland, and Alexander Long, of Ohio. Indeed, to many extreme states' rights men, McClellan was little less obnoxious than Lincoln. The cause of the ill-feeling was his arrest of the Maryland legislature in 1861, an act that may have prevented Maryland from seceding. Long said, "Lincoln has been guilty of interfering with the freedom of speech, the freedom of elections and of arbitrary arrests . . . yet you propose to nominate a man who has gone even farther than Lincoln in perpetrating similar tyrannical measures upon the sacred privileges and rights of the people."

One can sympathize a little with the viewpoint of these men to whom individual liberty was the supreme benefit of existence. They simply could not be brought to understand that liberty cannot exist in wartime, that war exacts the sacrifice of freedom. Still we who see liberty perishing, and autocracy casting its shadow across the world as never before, know that any concession to arbitrary power is dangerous. Utterly misunderstood and censured in history ever since, these Democrats of the Old School were fighting—no doubt mistakenly—for a great principle. But they were confounded by the fact that an indissoluble Union and states' rights were not compatible. They wanted the Union but they also wanted full states' rights, and they could not have both.

The opposition to McClellan had no other effect than to make him a more acceptable candidate. He was nominated on the first ballot, receiving a vast majority of the votes. Thomas H. Seymour, of Connecticut, candidate of the extreme states' righters, and Horatio Seymour, of New York, received a few votes. On the motion of the well-known Clement L. Vallandigham, of Ohio, the nomination was made unanimous.

McClellan accepted the nomination, for which he has been so generally condemned by historians. Why? one may ask. If McClellan had been elected, the war would have gone on, and under a great military executive. Indeed, considering the fact that Lincoln lived for less than six weeks of his second term, it might have been better if McClellan had been elected. The Union would have been restored, but the Southern states would have been given some concessions and would not have been subjected to the humiliation and misery of the Reconstruction. (It may be interesting to note that Calhoun predicted the Reconstruction almost as it occurred.) Half a century of bitterness and sectional hate might have been spared the country. McClellan would have been the ideal man to heal the war wounds. Respected and admired both in the North and in the South, he would have held out the olive branch as no other man of that day in America could have done.

In accepting the nomination he stated his position. He declared, "The re-establishment of the Union in all its integrity is and must continue to be the indispensable condition in any settlement." There was no question of the recognition of secession.

The campaign was not inspiring, overshadowed as it was by the war news. The victories of Sherman in Georgia and Sheridan in the Valley of Virginia foretold the end; it was now evident to all discerning persons that the South was fast weakening and could not maintain resistance many months longer.

McClellan did not do much campaigning but what he did was good. A little speech he made at a serenade at Orange, New Jersey, on September 27, 1864, illustrates his style. "I am not here tonight to make a long speech but merely to acknowledge this most pleasing compliment. I trust this demonstration is the prescience of that great civil victory which we hope to win at the polls in favor of the Constitution and country. I hope the glorious victories won by the gallant and skillful Sherman, the heroic and dashing Sheridan and the intrepid Farragut are the forerunners of the great victory for the defense of the Constitution, which shall soon, I hope, be achieved." As might have been expected, McClellan was vigorously libeled by the Republican orators. His record was belittled and ridiculed; from the statements made on the stump one might have imagined that McClellan, instead of being a great soldier and a devoted patriot, was a traitor of the first water. But in that age the indecencies of politics were beyond belief; fortunately, we are better in that respect than in the past, in whatever other ways we may be worse.

McClellan had little or no chance of election. The Democratic statement about the war's being a failure (made at the very moment the war was won) had little real effect. A government in possession in wartime, and a government that is obviously successful in the war, is very difficult to displace; it controls all the vast patronage. Furthermore, every kind of pressure was used in behalf of the administration, and corrupt practices seem to have been employed.

E. H. Wright, one of McClellan's aides, stated years afterward that, on October 29, 1864, he met Allan Pinkerton who told him that Lincoln would be elected by any majorities that might be desired, that McClellan had absolutely no show. In some states the polls were watched by soldiers, and it appears that coercion was used. The army was voted for Lincoln, who received 116,887 votes to 33,748 for McClellan. A commentary on this result is the vote taken by the prisoners in Libby Prison, Richmond. A majority of the officers were for Lincoln but a large majority of the privates favored McClellan. The soldiers, generally, voted as they were desired by their officers to do.

Lincoln carried all the states except Delaware, Kentucky, and New Jersey, then all strongly Democratic. But McClellan lost New York, Connecticut, and several other states by a narrow margin and was not far behind in Indiana, Ohio, and Illinois. In fact, Lincoln's plurality was not very large. If Sherman had been defeated at Atlanta, in September, it is even possible, though not probable, that McClellan would have been successful. In that case he would have been elected by a wave of peace sentiment demanding some understanding with the Southern states to end the war. That McClellan would not have conceded independence to the Southern states is certain; from the beginning to the end he was strongly, even bitterly, opposed to any recognition of secession. If he had been elected the war would have ended in favor of the Union but not so much in disfavor of the South. A generation of misery for that section was the price of his defeat. If he had been a politician, he would never have accepted the nomination in 1864. He was a patriot—one who felt for the South as well as for the North—and he tried and failed. He should be commended, not censured.

CHAPTER SEVENTEEN

THE PLACID YEARS AND PEACE

The second half of McClellan's life was, in many respects, happier than the first. He was profitably engaged, building up a competence; he traveled much; he was popular and well received wherever he went, he enjoyed the companionship of devoted friends; his home life may be called ideal. Such things are the prime blessings of existence; and if a man can forget the strivings of ambition and cast off the remembrance of anguish over undeserved humiliation, he may well be called fortunate to be able to get out of living all that George B. McClellan did. But there is always the fiend at the elbow raking up the past, whispering of the greatness one might have had and barely missed, calling attention to the glory of those who stood in one's own shoes. As the Grant administration advanced from one degradation to another, McClellan must have reflected on the difference there would have been if he had sat in the presidential chair which Ulysses S. Grant occupied but could not fill, the worst anti-climax in the whole course of American history.

It was much of a relief to McClellan to be no longer in a position of terrible responsibility, exposed to the venomous hatred of a thousand enemies—that is, after the first sting of mortification passed. He had served an ungrateful country—well, republics were noted for being ungrateful. He had done his best and he would have won if let alone; he was always quite certain of that. Apparently he had no doubts as to the course he had pursued in his military career. That was well; no hell compares with those might-have-beens with which men who have fallen from high place usually torment themselves.

At the time of his presidential defeat McClellan was low in funds, having been unable to save anything while seeking to save the country. But he had many friends and enjoyed the reputation of being an able engineer. The friends came to his rescue by making him the recipient of a part of the proceeds of a stock investment. This money, together with the rent of his New York house, rendered it possible for him to take a trip abroad, as he had long desired to do.

The family sailed from New York in January, 1865. In London, the general experienced the first of the many heart-warming receptions that awaited him in Europe. He found that his reputation had preceded him, that he was looked on as one of the foremost soldiers and public men of the western republic. In London, his former staff officers, the Prince de Joinville and the Duc de Chartres, called. Through them he met Queen Amalia, Louis Phillipe's exiled consort. McClellan called on the Prince of Wales (Edward VII) at Marlborough House. He visited the great military school at Sandhurst, where he was cordially entertained by British officers.

The McClellan family went on to Paris; there they remained a few days, and then on to Rome. After spending the rest of the winter in the imperial city, the family proceeded to Naples; they were received by the king and queen. While McClellan was abroad the news came of the downfall of the Confederacy and the end of the war. McClellan showed the feeling that would have animated him if he had been President at the time: "I hope most sincerely that a spirit of Christian wisdom will prevail and that our people will have the magnanimity to act with the utmost generosity towards a conquered foe."[1]

The family spent some time in Switzerland, from which country McClellan himself went to Dresden, where he expected to spend the following winter. Mrs. Marcy and a daughter came over to be with Mrs. McClellan; the general journeyed to Hamburg to meet them. In November, 1866, Mrs. McClellan gave birth to a son who was named for his father and was destined

[1] Myers, *op. cit.*, p. 472.

to be a mayor of New York and a professor at Princeton. Nellie McClellan had a long illness following her confinement, a circumstance that led her husband to decide to remain in Europe indefinitely. The family spent the winter of 1867 in Nice, the following summer in Switzerland, mostly at St. Moritz. A trip through England and Scotland preceded another tour of the Continent in the winter of 1868.

The sojourn in Europe did McClellan a world of good, taking his mind off his troubles, opening to him the treasures of Old World civilization at its best, that cultured world that has passed away, probably never to return. The travelers who saw Europe prior to 1870 enjoyed a privilege not open to later generations.

McClellan, still a young man with long years ahead of him, at length grew restless and tired of sightseeing. It was then that he turned to business. Robert L. Stevens had designed an armored warship, known as the "Stevens battery." McClellan accepted a commission to sell this invention to some European power, thinking that his military prominence would aid him. He offered the battery to the governments of Prussia and Russia, both of which declined it. The venture came to nothing. About the same time President Johnson sent McClellan's appointment as minister to England to the Senate in February, 1868. Apparently the Senate did not act on it; at all events the appointment was withdrawn.

McClellan now longed to return home but did not care to do so until after the Democratic nominating convention of 1868; he seems to have thought the nomination might be offered him again. The family finally sailed in September, 1868. Although he did not desire it, a great demonstration was staged in New York in his honor, in which many soldiers took part.

And now he found himself in the midst of varied activities. He opened offices as a consulting engineer in Hoboken. The board of the University of California offered him the presidency of that promising institution, which he declined; he also refused the presidency of Union College, in New York state. However, he accepted the place of chief engineer of the Department of Docks, New York City, holding it until 1873.

He visited Grant in the White House, which he pronounced

to be somewhat less uncouth in atmosphere than under Lincoln. Long experience in the best society of Europe had made him critical of conditions at home.

McClellan was prospering. In 1869 his income was $7,500; in 1870 it rose to $18,800 and to $21,000 in 1871. At that time this was the income of a man of wealth. He was able to indulge all reasonable tastes; he built a house in Orange, New Jersey, which became his permanent home.

His prominence made him the recipient of political offers, none of which he accepted. Tammany wished to use him in covering its shameless regime in New York City; Mayor A. Oakey Hall tendered him the position of city comptroller, which he at once declined.

His growing income made him independent. He took trips abroad while his family spent summers at fashionable resorts. He and his wife went much in society in New York, Philadelphia, Baltimore, and Washington.

McClellan became president of the Atlantic and Great Western Railway. In 1873, he established a firm of consulting engineers and accountants that had in view the making of contacts with European investors in American railroads. In the winter of 1874-75, he traveled in Egypt, spending the succeeding summer in France. The family lived for a time in Baltimore on its return to the United States and went much in Washington society.

By this time McClellan's own presidential campaign was so far in the background that he felt he could enter politics again in a limited way. Disgusted with the graft and incompetence of the Grant administration, he took the stump for Samuel J. Tilden in 1876, speaking in Indiana, Ohio, New York, Pennsylvania, New Jersey and elsewhere. What he stressed was the necessity of leaving the South to the control of the Southern people; he wished to do away with the last vestiges of the Reconstruction. He sought the appointment of superintendent of public works of New York state, but a Republican state senate refused to confirm his nomination.

In 1877 McClellan made his last essay in public life. At that time the Democratic party in New Jersey was divided in two bitterly antagonistic factions. When a deadlock occurred in the convention for nominating a candidate for governor, it was broken by somebody's proposing the name of McClellan. A stampede followed; he was nominated by acclamation. He carried the state in November by a majority of nearly 13,000, a good figure for those days of smaller populations.

The inauguration took place at Trenton on January 15, 1878. As governor, McClellan made a fine record. He lowered state taxes; he advanced technical education; he reorganized the militia of New Jersey, making it second to none in the United States. In the autumn of 1879 he suffered a severe illness but was soon well again. In the presidential campaign of 1880, McClellan took the stump for one of his former subordinates, the gallant and admirable Winfield Scott Hancock.

After the expiration of his term as governor, McClellan became somewhat of a wanderer, living in New York and then spending the winter of 1882-83 in Washington. Here his young daughter, May, a charming girl, was prominent socially. Always occupied, he became a director or president of a number of commercial companies, among them the Grand Belt Copper Company of New York and the Rosario Mining Company. He was also the president of a company designed to build a subway in New York City, a premature movement in an idea destined to succeed many years later. In the presidential campaign of 1884, McClellan spoke for Cleveland in a number of cities. He was seriously considered for the office of secretary of war by the Democratic president, but his appointment was blocked by his political foes in New Jersey. Offered the place of minister to Russia, he declined. He was just about to be made a member of the Civil Service Commission at the time of his death.

McClellan spent much of the time in his last days in writing his memoirs, published after his death under the title of *McClellan's Own Story*. It contains a full survey of his military career.

No man ever mellowed more gracefully than McClellan did in his final years. Always a man of high reputation, about whom there were no compromising rumors, no tales of lapses and irregularities, he became more and more religious as time passed. An elder in the Presbyterian Church, he held family prayers each day and took much interest in church matters. He seems to have been a Christian of a rather fundamentalist type, though essentially tolerant and charitable to other faiths. Rather unconsciously he describes himself in his book. In May, 1862, McClellan had been in St. Peter's Church, New Kent, "where he [Washington] was married. It is an old brick church with a rather pretentious tower. . . . As I happened to be there alone for a few moments, I could not help kneeling at the chancel and praying that I might serve my country as truly as he did."[2]

McClellan was a strong and healthy man through the greater part of his life, but nobody could pass through such excitements and such sufferings as had been his without physical injury. In the autumn of 1885, after an extended trip through the West, he began to suffer attacks of what appears to have been angina pectoris. The seriousness of his condition does not seem to have been recognized. He himself was not alarmed. He hoped for recovery.

In the evening of October 28, 1885, he was seized with a severe attack of pain, which continued until early the following morning. He then expressed himself as feeling better and, almost immediately, expired.

The funeral took place in the Madison Square Presbyterian Church, New York. His opponent in the Peninsula, Joseph E. Johnston, was among the mourners present. The Confederate general later wrote, "This death has been to me like the loss of my last brother." McClellan was buried in Riverview Cemetery, Trenton, where a monument stands to his memory. His wife, many years later, was buried beside him.

As a military leader George B. McClellan has suffered from his own time down to the present day from political associations. Since he was a Democrat, and American history has been written by historians sympathetic to the Republican tradition, it is natural that he should not receive justice at the hands of the Muse. But all that is in the past; other times have come; it is silly to continue to look at our history through the spectacles of 1865. Beyond doubt, an impartial study of McClellan's career must lead to a juster appraisement of his life and deeds. He will

---

[2] *McClellan's Own Story*, p. 358.

THE PLACID YEARS 281

remain in history, when partisanship shall have passed away, as one of the most scientific and able of American soldiers. He saved the Union from defeat in the early stages of the conflict. There is little doubt that the war would have been shortened if he had remained in command.

One of the best appraisals of McClellan was made by a cultured and gifted staff officer in Meade's army, Colonel Theodore Lyman, of Massachusetts. Colonel Lyman saw the later phases of the war, from 1863 to the end. He wrote on June 2, 1864:

"You know I was never an enthusiast or fanatic for any of our generals. I liked McClellan, but was not 'daft' about him; and was indeed somewhat shaken by the great cry and stories against him. But now, after seeing this country and this campaign, I wish to say, in all coolness, that I believe he was, both as a military man and as a manager of the country under military occupation, the greatest general this war has produced. You hear how slow he was; how he hesitated at small natural obstacles. Not so. He hesitated at an obstacle that our ultra people steadily ignore, the Rebel Army of Northern Virginia; and anyone that has seen that army fight and march would, were he wise, proceed therewith with caution and wariness, well knowing that defeat by such an enemy might mean destruction. When I consider how much better soldiers, as soldiers, our men now are than in his day; how admirably they have been handled in this campaign; and how heroically they have worked, marched, and fought, and *yet*, how we still see the enemy in our front, weakened and maimed, but undaunted as ever, I am forced to the conclusion that McClellan (who did not have his own way as we have) managed with admirable skill. I say he was our best.... McClellan had over 20,000 men taken from him at the very crisis of the campaign. Suppose at the culmination of our work, a telegram from the President should come: 'Send General Wright and 25,000 men at once to Winchester.' How would that do?" [3]

But the best testimonial to McClellan comes from his great foe. Cazenove Lee, a cousin of Robert E. Lee, wrote, "I asked him

---

[3] Meade's Headquarters, 1863-65, *Letters of Colonel Theodore Lyman from the Wilderness to Appomattox* (Boston, 1922), p. 141.

which of the Federal generals he considered the greatest and he answered most emphatically, 'McClellan by all odds.'"[4] Who would know better than Lee, who faced them all?

The character of McClellan is not complex, not difficult to analyze. He had a powerful mind, clear and penetrating. Indeed, some of his troubles arose from his superior mentality, for he lost patience with those slower minds that could not grasp what he saw so easily. He was positive in opinion, not given to compromise, and far too outspoken for his own good. He was one of the cultured men of his day, highly educated and polished. Again, one might say that his social traits militated against him, for Lincoln's crudities left him blind to Lincoln's great qualities. As a man of honor McClellan has no superior in American history. He was one about whom there were no sexual or financial scandals. He earned money, it is true, but when he left the army in 1864 he was a poor man; it was in later civil years that he prospered. The tragedy of McClellan's life arose from the fact that he was a thorough conservative engaged on the radical side. The Confederates were the conservative party in the great American conflict; the Democrats of the North, who had so much in common with them, were also conservatives. But the Republicans, who controlled the United States government, were radicals engaged in establishing a new political and economic order in America. In our own time the parties have reversed positions: the Democrats are the radicals today, and the Republicans are now fighting to save the order they created in those distant years of 1861-65. McClellan, opposed to them and their principles, could not be entrusted to win the war, which he would probably have done. That was the hardship he had to bear. There is no reason whatever that, after so many decades, historians should judge him, as they do, by the politics of the Civil War period. He was a great American, and a singularly pure and honorable one, and he should be recognized as such.

[4] Captain Robert E. Lee, *Recollections and Letters of General Lee* (New York, 1904, 1924) p. 416.

INDEX

INDEX

Abolitionists, McClellan on, 45, 123-124; See also Emancipation Proclamation

Amalia, Queen, McClellan meets, 276

Anderson, Gen. Joseph R., and McDowell, 58; driven from Ashland, 62

Andrew, Gov. John Albion, 33

Antietam. See Sharpsburg

Army, Confederate. See Confederates

Army, Union, supply system of, 220 ff.; McClellan's concern for welfare of, 28, 229, 251-252; attachment towards McClellan, 158, 166-167, 172-173, 265; equipment of at Mechanicsville, 82-83

Army, American, in Mexico, 4-9

Aspinwall, William Henry, advises McClellan, 215

Atlantic and Great Western Railroad, McClellan becomes president of, 278

Averell, William Woods, at Yorktown, 51; pursues Imboden, 216-217; pursues Stuart, 217, 218

Baker, Col. Edward D., and Ball's Bluff Affair, 33-34

Balloons, observation, 51, 78, 259

Ball's Bluff Affair, 33-34

Banks, Maj. Gen. N. P., retreat of, 64; at Rockville, 175; in command at Washington, 175

Barnard, Gen. John G., and siege of Yorktown, 48, 50; sent to confer with McClellan, 142; selects place for Porter's stand, 90

Bates, Att. Gen. Edward, and petition against McClellan, 158; and opposition to McClellan, 170, 171

Bayard, Cavalryman, reports on Longstreet, 214

Beauregard, Gen. P. G. T., in Mexico, 6; commended by Totten, 8; considers invasion of Maryland, 30

Berdan, Hiram, near Hanover Courthouse, 62; Malvern Hill, 112

Blair, Francis P., and election of 1864, 269

Blair, Montgomery, McClellan confers at home of, 36; and petition against McClellan, 159, 160, 171; ousted from cabinet, 269

Blenker, Louis, division of, detached from army, 45

"Bloody Lane," 198

Bragg, Maj. Gen. Braxton, Lee asked to furnish troops for, 249

Brewerton, Captain Henry, and tilts with McClellan at West Point, 10

Brick House Landing, battle of, 55

Brinton, Elizabeth S., 2

Brooks, W. T. H., at Yorktown, 52; at Savage's Station, 104; dismissal sought, 253

Buchanan, James, 14

Buckner, Simon B., insists on Kentucky's neutrality, 22

Burgess, John W., on the web of intrigue about McClellan, 46-47

Burns, Wm. W., at Savage's Station, 103

Burnside, Ambrose E., succeeds Porter, 28; denounces Stanton, 42; and attempt to take Richmond, 121; as McClellan's possible successor, 124, 129, 136; assigned to Pope, 125-126; visits McClellan at Fort Monroe, 128; McClellan's desire for forces of, 127-128, 128-129, 130, 133; at Aquia Creek, 135; Pope waits for arrival of, 136; at Falmouth, 136-137; McClellan sees,

286 INDEX

Burnside (Cont'd)
138; McClellan's army transferred to, 139; McClellan writes, 139; inquires concerning Pope's location, 140; Porter reports to, 141; Pope prepares to join, 148; Chase recommends, 161; and intrigue against McClellan, 170; reports to McClellan, 172; on condition of troops, 175; at Rockville, 175; ordered toward Westminster, 175; moves westward, 176; near Fredericksburg, 177; at South Mountain, 184-185; at Sharpsburg, 189-210; McClellan turns over command of army to, 234-235; and failure to destroy Lee, 236; record of, 239-240; and loyalty to McClellan, 240; assumes command, 241; at Fredericksburg, 242 ff.; seeks to redeem himself, 249-250; criticism of, 250-251; sends in resignation, 251; officers fail to co-operate with, 252; asked to meet Halleck, 253; relieved of command, 253; Stanton's opposition to, 254; controversy following dismissal of, 254-255; Hooker compared with, 256; lacks ability, 142, 238, 264

Butterfield, Daniel, at Hanover Courthouse, 62; at Fredericksburg, 247

Byron, George Gordon, 1

California, McClellan desires to visit, 11

California, University of, offers McClellan presidency, 277

Cameron, Simon, supports McClellan, 29; Scott complains to, 35; replaced by Stanton, 38

Casey, Silas, succeeds Porter, 28; at Fort Magruder, 54; at Fair Oaks, 59, 65, 66, 67, 68; at the White House, 79

Chancellorsville, 257 ff.

Chandler, Zachariah, McClellan confers with, 36; and animosity toward McClellan, 170-171

Chapultepec, McClellan in action of, 8

Chartres, Duc de, McClellan meets in London, 276

Chase, Salmon P., and conspiracy against McClellan, 64, 125, 154, 158-159, 161-162, 167-171; denounces McClellan's report, 158-162

Chickahominy, at flood level, 65, 66, 75

Churubusco, McClellan in action of, 8

Cochrane, John, dismissal sought, 253

Colquitt, Alfred H., at South Mountain, 184

Confederates, McClellan exaggerates number of, 74-75; equipment at Mechanicsville, 82-83; officers of, 83; quality of underestimated, 83-84; supply system of, 220-221

Conscription, 267-268

Contreras, battle of, 8

Couch, Gen. Darius N., at Fort Magruder, 54; near Seven Pines, 59; at Fair Oaks, 66, 67, 68; at Malvern Hill, 112, 114; at Rockville, 175; McClellan visits, 227; informed that McClellan has been relieved of his command, 235; at Fredericksburg, 245, 247, 248

Cox, Jacob D., at South Mountain, 184-187; on McClellan, 189-190; at Sharpsburg, 189-210; at Mountain House, 183

Crampton's Gap, 183-184

Crook, Maj. Gen. George, at Sharpsburg, 201

Curtin, Gov. A. G., dispatch from, 173; fears attack, 175, 177, 178; reports on Longstreet, 180

Custer, George, defends McClellan, 235; informs McClellan of his popularity, 264; helps map terrain, 61

Davis, Jefferson, grandfather of, 2; sends McClellan to San Domingo, 13; and the transcontinental railroad, 12; refuses to reinforce Beauregard and Johnston, 30; assigns command of army to Lee, 71; his confidence in Lee, 73; caution of, 75, 129; out-blunders Washington, 134-135; character of, 243-244; interferes with Lee, 244; and battle at Fredericksburg, 243-244; loses opportunity for victory, 248; and peace overtures, 267; and draft, 268

Delafield, Major Richard, chosen to observe Crimean War, 13-14

Democratic Party, McClellan as member of, 11; and McClellan's dis-

INDEX
287

missal, 262; and opposition to war, 265; policies of, 266; McClellan as leader of, 267; defeatism of, 269; convention of, 270-274; conservatism of, 282

Demoralization, after First Manassas, 26-27; after Second Manassas, 153

Dix, Gen. John A., halted by Stanton, 126; Stanton wires, 128

Doubleday, Abner, at Sharpsburg, 194, 195

Douglas, Stephen A., and the transcontinental railroad, 12

Early, Lieut. Gen. Jubal A., at Sharpsburg, 195 ff.

Eltham Landing. *See* Brick House Landing

Emancipation Proclamation, McClellan's view of, 132, 214-215, 216, 222, 238, 268

Engineers, Military, McClellan becomes member of, 4

Eugenie, McClellan views, 14

Europe, McClellan's stay in, 4, 13-15, 276 ff.

Ewell, Lieut. Gen. R. S., at Gordonsville, 129; at Sharpsburg, 193; wounding of, 149

Fair Oaks, 65-71. *See also* Seven Pines

Ferraro, Edward, dismissal sought, 253

Foote, Andrew Hull, on Pope, 169

Franklin, W. B., loads transports, 54-55; at Brick House Landing, 55; McClellan accused of partiality to, 56; on the Chickahominy, 61; at Gaines's Mill, 92; at Savage's Station, 103-104; at Glendale, 107; at Yorktown, 139; ordered to report to Pope, 141, 145; condition of corps of, 143; stopped by McClellan at Annandale, 144; and Second Manassas, 144, 145, 148, 149; accused by Pope's friends, 160; blamed by Pope, 162; relieved from duty, 164; vindicated, 168; at Rockville, 175; at Crampton's Gap, 183; at Sharpsburg, 199 ff.; at Fredericksburg, 242 ff.; loses confidence in Burnside, 249; dismissal sought, 253; relieved of command, 253; punishment of, 254; and controversy over Burnside's dismissal, 254-255; Burnside attacks character of, 254-255; goes west, 263

Fredericksburg, 241 ff.

Frémont, John C., and Jackson, 73; as political menace, 263; nominated, 269

French, William H., at Fair Oaks, 67; at Gaines's Mill, 93; at Sharpsburg, 196 ff.; at Fredericksburg, 245, 247

Gaines's Mill, 90-97; preservation of battlefield at, 91

Garland, Brig. Gen. Samuel, at South Mountain, 184

Garnett, Gen. Robert S., opposes McClellan, 23-24; death of, 24

Germans, and McClellan's talent for organization, 100, 215

Getty, G. W., at Fredericksburg, 248

Gettysburg, 147, 219, 265

Glendale, 104-111

Grand Belt Copper Co., 279

Granger, Gordon, 21

Grant, Ulysses S., visits McClellan's headquarters, 19; and siege of Richmond, 99; and defeat of Lee, 100; and attempt to take Richmond, 121; narrow escape of, 129; adopts McClellan's idea, 131; reticence of, 132; and siege of Richmond, 134; and Vicksburg, 235; and failure to destroy Lee, 236; and politicians, 263; and Wilderness Campaign, 271; degradation of administration of, 275; McClellan visits, 277-278; mentioned, 1, 124

Greeley, Horace, 122, 270

Greene, Colton, at Sharpsburg, 194 ff.

Griffin, Charles, at Sharpsburg, 204

Hall, Mayor A. Oakey, 278

Halleck, Maj. Gen. H. W., Scott on, 35; incompetence of, 36, 163; McClellan's letter to, 45; considered for post of commander in chief, 124; made general in chief, 126-127; visits McClellan on the James, 130-131; deprecates McClellan's plan, 130-131; alludes to rumors about McClellan, 131-132; McClellan expresses views on slavery to, 132; and McClellan's evacuation of Harrison's Landing, 133-138; attitude toward McClellan changes,

Halleck (*Cont'd*)
139-140; reassures Pope, 141; turns to McClellan for help, 142-143; and Second Manassas, 141-147; asks McClellan's aid in crisis, 153; orders McClellan to take charge of Washington defenses, 155; demoralization of, 157; and conspiracy against McClellan, 160, 167, 169-170, 228; Welles on, 161; Pope recommends, 162; relieves Pope of command, 164-165; refuses to evacuate Harper's Ferry, 165; Foote on, 169; and McClellan's reorganization of the army, 172 ff.; and battle of South Mountain, 186, 189; and Sharpsburg, 198, 205, 208; and problem of stragglers, 212-213; and McClellan's request for troops, 213-214; orders McClellan to cross Potomac, 216; and rebel raid in Pennsylvania, 217; impatient at McClellan's delay, 222; and fear of Stuart, 224; and supplies for army, 222 ff.; and protection of upper Potomac, 232-233; and Burnside, 241-242, 249, 250, 251, 252, 253, 254-255; as figurehead, 262; humiliates McClellan, 263; scolds Meade, 266; mentioned, 75, 166, 211

Hamilton, Schuyler, dismissal of, 28; Lincoln on, 56, 58

Hancock, Winfield Scott, at Fort Magruder, 54; sent out from Harper's Ferry, 227; at Fredericksburg, 245; McClellan takes stump for, 279

Hanover Courthouse, action near, 62

Harris, B. G., and the democratic convention, 271

Harrison, William Henry, 122

Haupt, H., and repair of railroad, 223

Heintzelman, Maj. Gen. S. P., made corps commander, 40; embarks at Alexandria, 45; accompanies Lowe, 51; Lincoln accuses McClellan of ignoring, 55; McClellan's attitude toward, 56; at Fair Oaks, 65 ff.; and Malvern Hill, 112; at Savage's Station, 101-104; at Glendale, 105-108; at Yorktown, 139; and Second Manassas, 149; placed under Banks, 175; mentioned, 116

Henderson, G. F. R., vindicates McClellan, 37

Hill, A. P., at Fort Magruder, 54; at Mechanicsville, 85, 86; at Gaines's Mill, 90-91; at Savage's Station, 101; at Glendale, 106-111; and Malvern Hill, 113, 118; size of forces exaggerated, 173; left at Harper's Ferry, 190; at Sharpsburg, 202

Hill, D. H., at Mechanicsville, 86; at Gaines's Mill, 89, 91-92; on Jackson, 106; at Malvern Hill, 113; and "Lost Dispatch," 179; at Frederick, 176; at Turner's Gap, 183-184; at South Mountain, 182, 183, 186; at Sharpsburg, 193-210

Holmes, Theophilus, at Glendale, 108

Hood, John B., at Gaines's Mill, 92; at Sharpsburg, 193-210

Hooker, Joseph, at Yorktown, 51; at Williamsburg, 52; at Fort Magruder, 54; at White Oak Swamp, 59; at Fair Oaks, 66, 68, 70; and Glendale, 107-110; and Malvern Hill, 112; and attempt to take Richmond, 121; and Second Manassas, 149; Chase recommends, 161; moves westward, 176; protests against losing Reynolds, 177-178; at South Mountain, 184-186; at Sharpsburg, 190-210; and failure to destroy Lee, 236; angles for high command, 239; and Burnside, 242, 252-254, 257; at Fredericksburg, 242 ff.; record of, 254; intrigue and disloyalty of, 253-254; at Chancellorsville, 257 ff.; blunders of, 264

Huger, Benjamin, with McClellan in Mexico, 6; at Savage's Station, 102-104; at Glendale, 108-110

Humphreys, A. A., at Fredericksburg, 247

Hunt, Henry J., at Malvern Hill, 112; at Fredericksburg, 245-246

Hunter, Maj. Gen. David, McClellan seeks troops of, 130; arrives at Fort Monroe, 128

Imboden, Geo. W., captures Pennsylvania troops, 216

Ingalls, Rufus, on McClellan's skill in transferring troops, 140; wires about supply depot, 213; asks for repair of railroad, 223; wires for clothing, 223; and supplies for the army, 230

INDEX

Jackson, Gen. Thos. J., "Stonewall," as classmate of McClellan, 4; at V.M.I., 11; humility of, 37; his feats in the Shenandoah, 47, 63-64, 73, 78; threatens Washington, 62; reported as coming to Richmond, 79; at Mechanicsville, 81 ff.; meets Lee at Walnut Grove Church, 89-90; at Gaines's Mill, 90-92; and battle at Savage's Station, 102; at Glendale, 104-111; at Malvern Hill, 113 ff.; Pope assigned to dispose of, 125; sent to oppose Pope, 129; at Cedar Mountain, 137; crosses Rappahannock, 141; at Second Manassas, 147-151; and Pope, 154, 155; transforms character of war, 166; Pope elects to attack, 168; his superiority to Pope, 172-173; at Frederick, 174-175, 176; captures garrison at Harper's Ferry, 177, 180; and "Lost Dispatch," 179; consents to plan to take Harper's Ferry, 182; Lee seeks union with, 187; at Harper's Ferry, 184, 188, 214; at Sharpsburg, 190-210; ability of, 240; at Fredericksburg, 242 ff.; at Chancellorsville, 259 ff.; illness and death of, 260; mentioned, 213, 219, 239, 241

Jefferson, Thomas, 264

Jefferson Medical College, McClellan's father at, 2

Johnson, Andrew, nominated, 270; appoints McClellan minister to England, 277

Johnston, Joseph E., reveals inefficiency of Patterson, 5; seeks reinforcement, 30; McClellan urged to move against, 34; evacuates fortifications at Manassas, 41; McClellan follows, 42; as obstacle to Union advance, 49; at Yorktown, 50; withdraws from Yorktown, 51-52; at Williamsburg, 52, 54; his wagon trains threatened, 55; wariness of, 58, 60; eager for advance near Seven Pines, 59; McClellan unaware of the impending attack of, 65; at Fair Oaks, 66, 68; his plans upset, 70; wounded at Fair Oaks, 71; and Davis, 73; on death of McClellan, 280

Joinville, Prince de, joins McClellan's staff, 32; meets McClellan in London, 276

Jones, D. R., and Sharpsburg, 200, 202

Jones, J. R., and Sharpsburg, 193

Kearny, Philip, at Yorktown, 51; at Fort Magruder, 54; at Savage's Station, 59; at Fair Oaks, 65, 66; at Glendale, 107-110; at Malvern Hill, 112; and Second Manassas, 150

Kelley, Benj. F., at Cumberland, 217

Kelton, John C., 157

Keyes, Maj. Gen. E. D., made corps commander, 40; on Confederate strength at Yorktown, 48; McClellan accused of ignoring, 55-56; at Fair Oaks, 65, 66, 67; at Savage's Station, 101; at Glendale, 105; at Malvern Hill, 112; writes Lincoln, 126; his prediction of degeneration of army proves wrong, 128; denounces McClellan, 130

King, Gen. Rufus, and Second Manassas, 149, 151

King's Schoolhouse, action at, 79

Lee, Cazenove, on McClellan, 281-282

Lee, Gen. R. E., commended by Totten, 8; with McClellan in Mexico, 6; crosses Pedregal, 8; and Jefferson Davis, 63; and Jackson's march down the Shenandoah, 63-64, 73; at Seven Pines, 70; size of his army at Richmond, 75; quality of, 76; sends cavalry to reconnoiter, 77; prepares to send Jackson against McClellan, 78; at King's Schoolhouse, 79; tactics and strategy of, 80; at Mechanicsville, 81 ff.; meets Jackson at Walnut Grove Church, 89-90; at Gaines's Mill, 90-96; cause of his defeat, 100; at Savage's Station, 101-104; at Glendale, 104-111; at Malvern Hill, 113-121, 122; and Pope, 128 ff.; at Second Manassas, 147-150; superiority over Pope, 155; Washington fears attack by, 163; transforms character of war, 166; desertion from army of, 169; generalship of, 172; McClellan sends flag of truce to, 172; reported to be threatening Washington, 173; and failure of Maryland Campaign, 173;

INDEX

Lee, Gen. R. E. (Cont'd)
McClellan blamed for not moving against, 174; at Frederick, 176; and "Lost Dispatch," 178, 179; and plan to invade Pennsylvania, 179; in peril, 180-181; determines to take Harper's Ferry, 182; retires from Frederick, 182-183; at South Mountain, 182 ff.; and Harper's Ferry, 188; at Sharpsburg, 190-210; contrasted with Jackson, 209; and aftermath of Sharpsburg, 211; Washington loses fear of, 213; harmed by Stuart's raid, 219; recovers from Maryland campaign, 221; and rumors about McClellan, 236; his toughness as foe, 240; his opinion of Burnside, 240; on McClellan's removal, 240-241; at Culpeper, 242; and Fredericksburg, 242 ff.; his need for a decisive victory, 255-256; and Hooker's plan, 256; handicapped by government, 257; at Chancellorsville, 257 ff.; and death of Jackson, 260, 265; and seeming invincibility, 269, 271; on McClellan, 281-282; mentioned, 1, 168, 225, 226, 227, 232, 234, 239, 241, 255

Lincoln, Abraham, McClellan undervalues, 30-31; appoints McClellan commander of the army, 36; prejudiced against McClellan by Scott, 36; impatient with McClellan's delay in attacking Johnston, 39; orders McClellan to open the Baltimore and Ohio Railroad, 39; orders advance on Manassas, 41; prejudiced against McClellan by Stanton, 42; his respect for Stanton, 42; consents to plan of attack on Richmond, 44; surrounded by ruthless persons, 46-47; pained by McClellan's complaints, 49; urges attack on Yorktown, 49; fails to appreciate McClellan's difficulties at Yorktown, 50; criticizes McClellan for favoritism, 55-56; promises McClellan control of McDowell's corps, 57-58, 61; his dispute with McClellan over Hamilton, 58; sets date for McDowell's march, 61; fears for safety of Washington, 44, 62; thanks McDowell, 63; informs McClellan of Jackson's invasion, 64; telegraphs McDowell of fight at Hanover Courthouse, 64; seeks news of main army, 65; thanks McClellan for victory at Seven Pines, 72; desire for McClellan's success, 73; on Jackson's reinforcements, 78; fears attack on Washington, 80; grateful to McClellan for battle of Malvern Hill, 123; and McClellan's attitude toward abolition, 123-124; and McClellan's lack of deference, 124; fears for Washington, 124-125; unites forces in Northern Virginia, 125; visits McClellan at Harrison's Landing, 125; appoints Halleck general in chief, 126-127; asks McClellan to account for reduced size of army, 127; undecided about Burnside's joining McClellan, 128; McClellan informs him of Jackson's movements, 129; shocked by McClellan's message to Halleck, 132; seeks news of front from McClellan, 143; confers with McClellan at Halleck's house, 155-156; instructs McClellan to reorganize army, 156-157; places McClellan in command at Washington, 157; halts McClellan from taking command of army, 158; unaware of Stanton's treachery, 159; and conspiracy against McClellan, 159-160; unwilling to dismiss McClellan, 160; consults Winfield Scott, 162; reappoints McClellan commander of troops around Washington, 166; and rebellion of cabinet, 171; explains appointment of McClellan, 172; checkmates Lee, 173; telegraphs McClellan at Rockville, 173-174, 176; restrains Curtin, 175; authorizes calling out of Pennsylvania militia, 177; notified of occupation of Frederick, 177; refuses to send troops to Curtin, 178; McClellan sends wire from Frederick to, 178; and battle at South Mountain, 188; issues Emancipation Proclamation, 214; visits McClellan on Potomac, 215-216; on Stuart's raid, 218-219; urges McClellan to take the field, 228; influenced against McClellan by Halleck, 227; and supplies for army,

230; orders McClellan to turn over command of army to Burnside, 234-235; and rumors about McClellan, 236; policy of, 237; and political consequences of a victorious McClellan, 238; comments on Burnsides' plan, 241-242; interferes with Burnside, 244; loses opportunity for victory, 248; visits Army of Potomac, 249; Burnside writes, 250-251; approves Halleck's letter, 251; Burnside seeks interview with, 252; and loss of faith in Burnside, 253; and controversy following dismissal of Burnside, 255; Hooker submits plan to, 256; and Chancellorsville, 258 ff.; scolds Meade, 266; opposition to, 266-267; McClellan's belief in weakness of, 268; and Emancipation Proclamation, 268; and Frémont, 269; movement to shelve, 269; and McClellan as presidential candidate, 269; nominated, 270; Long on, 271-272; and election of 1864, 274; McClellan's attitude toward, 282; mentioned, 227, 271

Lincoln, Mary, Pope related to, 124; McClellan sends respects to, 178

Long, Alexander, and democratic convention, 271; on Lincoln, 271-272

Longstreet, James, at Fort Magruder, 54; at Seven Pines, 70; at Gaines's Mill, 91-92; at Savage's Station, 102; at Glendale, 106-111; and Malvern Hill, 113, 114, 136; at Evlington Heights, 119; joins Lee in march against Pope, 137; and Second Manassas, 148, 150, 151; reported near Frederick, 175; and "Lost Dispatch," 178, 179, 182; reaches Hagerstown, 180, 181; opposes Lee's plan to take Harper's Ferry, 182; urges Lee to evacuate Hagerstown, 183; and battle of South Mountain, 184, 185-186; and Sharpsburg, 188, 190-210; reported to be nearing Leesburg, 214; on McClellan's development, 234; near Culpeper, 241, 242; made head of the Dept. of Southern Virginia, 249; taken from Lee, 256; sent to Suffolk, 257; advises Lee to fall back to North Anna River, 257; ordered to join Lee, 257

Lowe, Prof. Thaddeus, "chief of aeronauts," and the observation balloon, 51, 259

Lyman, Col. Theodore, on McClellan, 281

McCall, George A., McClellan waits for on the Chickahominy, 74; Stanton promises arrival of, 75; and McDowell, 77; at Gaines's Mill, 91, 92; at Savage's Station, 101; at Glendale, 107-110; at Malvern Hill, 112

McClellan, George, father of McClellan, 2; death of, 9

McClellan, George B., birth and ancestry, 2; education, 2 ff.; and Mexican War, 4 ff.; dissatisfied at West Point, 10-11; applies at V.M.I., 11; as engineer on exploring expeditions, 11-13; and Ellen Marcy, 12; sent to observe Crimean War, 13-15; enters civil life, 15-16; courtship and marriage, 16-17; appointed major general of Ohio Volunteers, 18; appointed to command of Department of the Ohio, 19; antagonism toward Scott, 19, 21, 35-36, 29-30; and conquest of Western Virginia, 20 ff.; and Army of Potomac, 27 ff.; arrests Maryland legislature, 30; considers Lincoln incompetent, 31-32; and Ball's Bluff affair, 32-34; appointed to supreme command, 36; humility of, 36-37; stricken with typhoid, 37; criticized for delay in attacking Johnston at Manassas, 37 ff.; relieved of chief command of armies, 42; McDowell's army corps detached from, 46 ff., 62 ff.; at Yorktown, 50 ff.; at Fort Magruder, 52-54; at Brick-House Landing, 55; and action at Hanover Courthouse, 62; at Fair Oaks, 65-71; and preparations for attack on Richmond, 72 ff.; at Mechanicsville, 85 ff.; at Gaines's Mill, 89-99; writes Lincoln after battle of Gaines's Mill, 97-98; at Savage's Station, 102-105; at Glendale, 107-111; at Malvern Hill, 112-120; and appointment of Halleck as commander in chief, 127; and evacuation of troops from Harrison's

McClellan (Cont'd)
　Landing, 133 ff.; partially reinstated to command, 142-143; conspiracy against, 153-154, 158 ff., 168 ff.; eager to join Pope at Manassas, 145-146; called on to combat demoralization after Second Manassas, 153; placed in command of defense of Washington, 157 ff.; restored to command, 173; at Rockville, 175 ff.; and "Lost Dispatch," 178-179; at Sharpsburg, 188-210; and demoralization of army after Sharpsburg, 211-212; and Emancipation Proclamation, 214; Lincoln visits, 215-216; and Stuart's raid, 217-219; and problem of supply, 220 ff.; relieved of command of Army of Potomac, 234-235; and Lincoln's political prestige, 237 ff.; goes to Trenton, 262; investigated, 263-264; popularity of, 264-267; supports Woodward, 267-268; runs for president, 268 ff.; and democratic convention in Chicago, 270 ff.; his campaign speech, 273; in Europe, 276 ff.; enters business, 277; opens office as consulting engineer, 277; visits Grant, 277-278; income of, 278; becomes governor of New Jersey, 278-279; and *McClellan's Own Story*, 279; religion, 279-280; death of, 280; Lyman on, 281; Lee on, 281-282

McClellan, Mrs. George, McClellan meets, 12; courtship and marriage, 16-17; McClellan writes, 31, 155; birth of daughter, 37; birth of son, 276-277; illness of, 277

McClellan, George B., Jr., 276-277
McClellan, John, 9
McClellan, Mary, 37
McClellan, May, 279
McDowell, Irvin, made corps commander, 40; his army corps detached from McClellan, 46, 47; at Fredericksburg, 58, 64; Lincoln visits, 58; ordered to march against Jackson, 62-63; needed by McClellan at Seven Pines, 72; McClellan promised help of, 73, 74; division from his corps joins McClellan, 76; McClellan seeks leadership over, 77; and Mechanicsville, 87; and Gaines's Mill, 92; fails McClellan at Malvern Hill, 120; and attempt to take Richmond, 121; and Second Manassas, 150; McClellan meets, 158; and failure to destroy Lee, 236; mentioned, 38, 241

McLaws, Gen. Lafayette, at Sharpsburg, 196 ff.
McQuade, James, 62
Magruder, John B., at Contreras, 8; and works at Yorktown, 48-49; and art of camouflage, 49; at Gaines's Mill, 93; at Savage's Station, 102-104; at Glendale, 108
Magruder, Fort, 54
Malvern Hill, 112-121
Manassas, Confederates evacuate, 40-41; battle of, 147-152
Mansfield, J. K. F., at Sharpsburg, 193-210
Maps, McClellan's reliance on, 46, 61, 81-82
Marcy, Ellen. See McClellan, Mrs. George B.
Marcy, Captain Randolph B., expedition to Red River, 11-12; directs operations during McClellan's illness, 37; replies to Lincoln's inquiries, 65; and Malvern Hill, 117; and Lincoln, 126; Reynolds writes to, 225; notifies Porter of supplies sent, 226
Martindale, John H., 62, 86
Maryland Legislature, arrest of, 30, 271
Maury, Gen. Dabney H., on McClellan, 3-4
Meade, Gen. George G., at Mechanicsville, 86; and attempt to take Richmond, 121; and Sharpsburg, 195 ff.; and demoralization of the Union army, 212; and failure to defeat Lee, 213, 236; considered as possible successor to McClellan, 239; appointment to command, 265; at Gettysburg, 265; and fund for McClellan, 266; mentioned, 281
Meagher, Patrick, 93, 116
Mechanicsville, 81-88
Meigs, Montgomery, Keyes writes, 130; report of, 175; and army supplies, 213, 223, 224, 226, 250
Merrimac, destruction of, 56
Mexican War, 4 ff.; 265

Monitor, 56
Monroe, Fort, 45, 46
Mordecai, Major Alfred, and the Crimean War, 13-14
Morell, G. W., and action near Hanover Courthouse, 61, 62; and Mechanicsville, 86; at Gaines's Mill, 91; at Savage's Station, 101; at Malvern Hill, 112, 114, 116; at Falmouth, 140
Myers, Dr. William Starr, on McClellan, 3, 37, 263, 266

Naglee, H. M., at Seven Pines, 58; at Fair Oaks, 66, 67
Napoleon, 74
Newton, John, 253
Nicolay, John G., 155, 267
Nine Mile Road, 58-59

Old Church, skirmish near, 76-77

Paris, McClellan in, 14, 276
Paris, Comte de, joins McClellan's staff, 32
Patterson, Robert M., 5, 19
Peck, John J., 66
Pegram, Gen. John, 24
Peninsular Campaign, 44 ff.; McClellan's failure in, 120-121
Pennsylvania, University of, 2
"Philippi Races," 22
Phillipe, Louis, 276
Pickett, George E., 4, 54
Pierce, Franklin, 271
Pillow, Gideon J., 4
Pinkerton, Allan, 74, 80, 274
Pleasanton, Alfred, reports on Confederates, 176; at Sharpsburg, 208; at Knoxville, 217; and pursuit of Stuart, 218, 230, 231; cavalry of, 231; crosses Potomac, 233; drives Confederate cavalry out of Upperville, 234
Polk, Leonidas, 15
Pope, John, and attempt to take Richmond, 121; suggests Halleck as commander, 124; record of, 124; given command of Army of Virginia, 125; bombast of, 128; considered as McClellan's successor, 129; McClellan requests forces of, 133; McClellan urged to reinforce, 135; suspects that McClellan will be relieved of his command, 136; McClellan foresees defeat of, 137, n. 14; at Cedar Mountain, 137; escapes Lee's trap, 137-138; McClellan's co-operation with, 138, 168; and prelude to Second Manassas, 141-147; announces defeat of Jackson, 146; and Second Manassas, 147-151; and aftermath of Second Manassas, 153; McClellan meets at Upton Hill, 158; attempts to vindicate himself, 162; and plot against McClellan, 162, 165, 167 ff.; relieved of command, 164-165; opposition of military men to, 167; generalship of, 172; officers lost in campaign of, 226; Halleck's mismanagement of campaign of, 227; and failure to destroy Lee, 236; Franklin's denunciation of, 254; mentioned, 139, 140, 154, 220, 238, 241
Porter, Fitz John, given command, 28; embarks from Alexandria, 45; McClellan's confidence in, 56; at the Chickahominy, 61; at Hanover Courthouse, 62; and McDowell, 64; and Mechanicsville, 79 ff.; Lee's eagerness to destroy, 90; at Gaines's Mill, 91-96; and Savage's Station, 101; and Glendale, 105, 111; and Malvern Hill, 112, 114, 116; at Fort Monroe, 139; reports to Burnside, 141; at Aquia, 140; and Second Manassas, 149, 150, 168; court-martialed, 150; and Pope, 151, 156; Pope blames, 162; relieved from duty, 164; McClellan on, 165; at Arlington, 175; at Sharpsburg, 196 ff.; disgraced by Pope, 239; shameful treatment accorded him, 262-263; mentioned, 160, 173, 175, 226
Porterfield, Col. G. A., 22

Quitman, John A., at Victoria, 5

Reading, McClellan's, 11
Reconstruction, McClellan's attitude toward, 278
Religion, McClellan's, 36-37, 279-280
Reno, Jesse L., applies at V.M.I., 11; and Second Manassas, 150; at South Mountain, 184-185, 186

Republicans, and Buckner affair, 22; attitude toward McClellan, 45; and dismissal of McClellan, 262, 266, 282; and election of 1864, 265; defeatism of, 269; convention of, 270

Reynolds, Brig. Gen. John, and Mechanicsville, 86; and Second Manassas, 151; relieved from duty, 164; sought for defense of Philadelphia, 176, 177; and demoralization of Union Army, 211-212; writes Marcy, 225; as possible successor to McClellan, 239

Richardson, I. B., at Fair Oaks, 67, 69; at Savage's Station, 103; at Sharpsburg, 196 ff.

Richmond, McClellan's delay in attacking, 76; siege of, 121; fear for safety of, 257

Ricketts, J. F., and Sharpsburg, 194

Rodman, Isaac P., and Sharpsburg, 202

Rosario Mining Company, 279

Rosecrans, W. S., applies at V.M.I., 11

Royall, Captain, W. B., 76

Russia, McClellan offered post as minister to, 279

Santa Anna, 7, 8

Savage's Station, 101-104

Scammon, E. P., and Sharpsburg, 202

Schenk, R. C., and battle of Second Manassas, 150

Scott, Gen. Winfield, at Lobos, 5; in Mexico, 6, 7-8; detains McClellan, 26; and McClellan's tactlessness, 30; hostility toward McClellan, 19, 21, 29-30, 35-36; retirement of, 36; Lincoln consults, 162; and conspiracy against McClellan, 168

Sea Power, Union, 41

Sedgwick, John, at Fair Oaks, 67, 68, 69; and Savage's Station, 103-105; and Sharpsburg, 196 ff.; and Chancellorsville, 259 ff.

Seven Days' Battles, 72 ff.

Seven Pines, 58, 65-71, 72, 74, 76

Seward, William H., supports McClellan, 29, 56-57; his opposition to Stanton, 57; uneasy about Harper's Ferry, 165; and conspiracy against McClellan, 159, 171

Seymour, Truman, and Mechanicsville, 86

Seymour, Gov. Horatio, 270, 272

Sharpsburg, 2, 189-210

Shelley, Percy Bysshe, 1

Shepherd, "Boss," 161

Sheridan, Gen. Philip H., 273

Sherman, Gen. William T., 269, 271, 272, 273, 274

Sickles, D. E., 116

Sigel, F., 150, 151, 175

Smith, Caleb, and conspiracy against McClellan, 154, 158-159, 171

Smith, Gen. Gustavus W., at West Point, 3; succeeds Swift, 5; in Mexico, 6; commended by Totten, 8; applies for place at V.M.I., 11; occupies Mechanicsville, 61; at Williamsburg, 52; at Fort Magruder, 54; at Fair Oaks, 70; at Savage's Station, 104

Smith, Gen. Percifer, McClellan joins, 12

Smith, William F., loses confidence in Burnside, 249; dismissal of sought by officers, 253

Sprague, William, 126, 136, 238

Stanton, Edwin M., orders arrest of Gen. C. P. Stone, 33; meets McClellan, 38-39; replaces Cameron, 38; reassures McClellan, 39; characterized, 42; attempts to turn Lincoln against McClellan, 35-36, 42, 44-45, 55; and Thomas, 45; and detachment of McDowell's corps from McClellan, 46, 47, 48, 62, 74; Burgess on, 47; estimates number of McClellan's men, 49, 50; McClellan writes of Johnston's forces to, 52; spies of, 56; opposition to Seward, 57; his alliance with Chase against McClellan, 64; fears for safety of Washington, 64, 65, 124-125; gets report of battle at Seven Pines, 72; his desire to have McClellan removed, 73; and McClellan's request for troops from the West, 75-76; McClellan reports on Jackson to, 78, 80; McClellan reports on Gaines's Mill to, 97-98; his dislike of McClellan, 99; his suspicion of McClellan, 123; McClellan's lack of deference toward, 124; halts Dix, 126; and effort to remove McClellan, 126-127; determines to keep Burnside from Mc-

INDEX

Clellan, 128; Burnside asks interview with, 128; wires Dix, 128; Wool denounces McClellan and Grant to, 129; pleased by Keyes' letter, 130; Welles on, 133; and McClellan's transfer from Harrison's Landing, 135; Halleck prejudiced by, 139, 140; protests against reinstatement of McClellan, 143; Halleck answers his query regarding McClellan's movement of troops, 144-145; denounces McClellan at War Department, 154; and conspiracy against McClellan, 154, 155, 158-162, 167-172; and responsibility for defeat at Second Manassas, 161; Welles' sketch of, 172; restrains Curtin, 175; Influence on Lincoln, 215; and Stuart's raid, 222; and supplies for army, 229, 223, 231; and loss of faith in Burnside, 253; favors Hooker, 254; and controversy following dismissal of Burnside, 254-255; and dismissal of McClellan, 262; and humiliation of McClellan, 263; and suspicion towards generals, 263; scolds Meade, 266; mentioned, 227, 254
Stevens, Thaddeus, 268
Stevens, Robert L., 277
Stevens battery, 277
Stone, Gen. Charles P., arrested, 33-34
Stoneman, George, at Williamsburg, 52; and demoralization of Union army, 212; and Chancellorsville, 257 ff.; and Fredericksburg, 247; mentioned, 61, 224
Stuart, Col. J. E. B., raids Union army, 76-77, 79; and Savage's Station, 101; raids Pope's forces, 142, 148; at Urbanna, 175; and Pleasanton, 176; holds back Union cavalry, 181; and Crampton's Gap, 183; at Catoctin Ridge, 183; and Sharpsburg, 195 ff.; raids Union forces, 217; takes Chambersburg, 218; ruins his cavalry, 219; effect of raids, 222; fear of, 224; and Chancellorsville, 259, 260; and Union cavalry, 231; mentioned, 119, 216, 224, 230
Sturgis, Samuel D., 171, 253
Sumner, Col. E. V., McClellan enters regiment of, 13; made corps commander, 40; at Williamsburg, 52; at Fort Magruder, 54; McClellan's faith in, 56; at Fair Oaks, 66-67; and Savage's Station, 101-104; and Glendale, 108; and Malvern Hill, 112; Chase recommends, 161; at Williamsburg, 139; Halleck orders to reach Pope, 145; at Rockville, 175; near Urbanna, 177; and Sharpsburg, 193-210; and Burnside's reorganization, 242; and Fredericksburg, 242 ff.; relieved of command, 253; and Jackson's Valley campaign, 141, 142, 143, 144, 146; mentioned, 55, 70, 71, 116
Sykes, George, and Mechanicsville, 86; at Gaines's Mill, 91; and Savage's Station, 101; and Malvern Hill, 112; and Second Manassas, 151; saves Pope's army, 151; at Sharpsburg, 204

Taliaferro, Brig. Gen. W. B., wounding of, 149
Tammany, 278
Taylor, Gen. Zachary, 5
Thomas, Gen. Lorenzo, and Stanton, 45; and McClellan, 46; on McClellan's co-operation with Pope, 138
Tilden, Samuel J., McClellan takes stump for, 278
Toombs, Senator Robert, and Sharpsburg, 200-201
Totten, Joseph E., 5, 8
Trumbull, Senator Lyman, 36

Union College, 277
Union Party, 270

Vallandigham, Clement L., 272
Van Buren, Martin, 122
Vera Cruz, surrender of, 5
Virginia Military Institute, 11

Wade, Senator B. F., 36
Walker, J. G., and Sharpsburg, 196 ff.
Warren, G. K., 61
Washington, George, 1
Washington, rides into Naglee's pickets, 66
Washington, and fear of invasion, 40, 44, 64, 78, 120, 121, 124-125, 134, 156, 210, 239, 256; growth of, 161
Welles, Gideon, and withdrawal of

Welles, Gideon (*Cont'd*)
   army from Washington, 133; his loyalty to Lincoln, 171; and conspiracy against McClellan, 154, 158-160, 162, 166 ff.; meets McClellan, 168-169
West Point, McClellan at, 2-4, 10-11
Whiting, W. H. C., at Gaines's Mill, 92
Wilcox, Cadmus M., and Sharpsburg, 202; at Fort Magruder, 54
Williams, A. S., and requisitions for clothing, 226
Williams, Alpheus S., and Sharpsburg, 194, 195
Williams, Seth, 21
Williamsburg, battle near, 52-54

Willis Church, 105
Woodward, George W., McClellan supports, 267-268
Wool, Maj. Gen., John E., excepted from McClellan's command, 36; friction with McClellan, 45; condemns McClellan and Grant, 129; left in charge of garrison at Baltimore, 173, 174; and Gov. Curtin, 175; informs McClellan of Lee's position, 176; mentioned, 177
Wright, E. H., 274

Yale, George McClellan, Sr., at, 2
Yorktown, 48-49, 51-52

www.ingramcontent.com/pod-product-compliance
Lightning Source LLC
Chambersburg PA
CBHW021119300426
44113CB00006B/211